CREATIVE

WOODEN BOXES

from the SCROLL SAW

CREATIVE

WOODEN BOXES

from the SCROLL SAW

28 Useful & Surprisingly Easy-to-Make Projects

Carole Rothman

Fox Chapel Publishing

Published and distributed in North America by Fox Chapel Publishing Company, Inc., East Petersburg, PA.

ISBN 978-1-56523-541-0

Library of Congress Cataloging-in-Publication Data

Rothman, Carole.

Creative wooden boxes from the scroll saw : 28 useful & surprisingly easy-to-make projects / Carole Rothman.

p. cm.

Includes index.

ISBN 978-1-56523-541-0 (pbk.)

1. Wooden boxes. 2. Woodwork. 3. Jig saws. I. Title.

TT190.6.R68 2012

684'.08--dc23

2011031460

To learn more about the other great books from Fox Chapel Publishing, or to find a retailer near you, call toll free 800-457-9112 or visit us at www.FoxChapelPublishing.com.

Note to Authors: We are always looking for talented authors to write new books in our area of woodworking, design, and related crafts. Please send a brief letter describing your idea to Acquisition Editor, 1970 Broad Street, East Petersburg, PA 17520.

Printed in China
First printing

About the Author

Carole Rothman, a psychologist, retired college professor, and author of *Wooden Bowls from the Scroll Saw*, has been a craftsperson for most of her life. In this new book, she continues to give her work a distinctive look by integrating concepts from many crafts, applying them in unexpected ways, then sharing her discoveries with the woodworking and scrolling communities. As a cake decorator for many years, she specialized in cake sculptures, and in creating objects, such as bows, books, and miniature furniture, from sugar paste and other edible materials. Many of the projects in this book were created by combining these techniques with those from traditional woodworking. The result is a variety of innovative and attractive projects that are fun to make and well within the capabilities of the typical woodworker.

Almost all the equipment Carole uses for her projects fits within a two-foot wide strip along the wall of a one-car garage. (A large freezer took priority over a drum sander.) A wall-mounted heater provides the warmth required to make this space useable year-round. The nearby kitchen allows for much-needed coffee breaks, and it's not unusual to find bread rising as the scroll saw hums away. Projects emerge on their own timetable, "announcing themselves" when ready to be created. Most are quickly claimed by appreciative family and friends.

Dedication

This book could not have happened without the support and critical guidance of Joe Ilardo, my best friend and partner, and Kerri Landis, my talented and creative editor. I would be remiss, however, if I failed to acknowledge the suggestions, encouragement, and feedback provided by the many members of Fox Chapel's scroll saw forum. These are the people I kept in mind as I designed my projects, and it is to them that this book is dedicated. Thanks, guys!

Contents

Introduction

This book is neither a traditional box book nor, strictly speaking, a scroll saw book. Rather, it is a book of original and creative crafts projects organized around the theme of boxes that can be made with the scroll saw. I selected projects that were attractive, fun to make, and unusual. None use conventional box joinery. The ideas for many projects came from techniques I've used as a professional cake decorator, adapted for use with the scroll saw.

Some projects are quick and easy, others more demanding and complex, but all are within the capabilities of the typical scroller. Small amounts of specialty woods, veneers, and resins enhance eye appeal with little additional work or cost, making these boxes ideal choices for crafts fairs and gifts.

Projects are marked with ratings so you can tell, before you jump in, the level of skill required to create each box. The scroll saw blade icon relates to the cutting difficulty, while the sanding disc corresponds with the sanding difficulty. One icon signifies the easiest level, while three-icon projects require more skill.

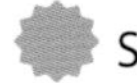 Sanding disc  Scroll saw blade

Scroll a beautiful bow-topped box (page 22).

Cook up a creative food-inspired box (page 50).

Use your scrap wood to make unique jewelry boxes (page 86).

Craft elegant boxes fit for an art gallery (page 152).

Build miniature furniture boxes complete with tiny details (page 110).

Handsome pivot lid boxes make fantastic gifts (page 138).

I suggest you start out by reading Chapter 1 (page 10) to find out everything you need to know. From there, the book's your oyster. Feeling silly? Perhaps you'd enjoy cooking up a project from the chapter full of food-inspired boxes (page 50). If you're looking to impress someone with a mind-bending box, try on one of the bow boxes for size (page 22). You'll soon have people marveling over the wooden bows and asking, "How did you do that?!" If you'd like to make a special-occasion ring box, page through Chapter 4 (page 86)—it's full of unique alternatives to the black velvet store-bought box. There's also a suite of realistic-looking miniature furniture—complete with accessories—and each project is a fully functional box (page 110). The pivot lid boxes (page 138) are handsome and have a bit of puzzle-box flair to them—but don't worry, it won't take all day to get the lids open. And finally, if you're feeling artistic, take a crack at the more complex gallery-quality boxes in Chapter 7 (page 152). No matter which project you select, you'll be creating handsome and creative boxes in no time!

Chapter 1

Things You Need to Know

This chapter uses a question-and-answer format to provide general information about the book, and the wood, materials, tools, and techniques used. Every effort has been made to anticipate your questions, and to give you the knowledge needed to approach the projects with confidence, and with a reasonable expectation of success. More specific information is given at the "point of use"—the projects themselves. Additional information and tips appear throughout the book to guide your creation of boxes that make people smile.

How is this book organized?

Arrangement: The projects in this book are arranged by type, such as "boxes with bows," or by themes, such as "fun with food."

Complexity: Projects vary in complexity within each chapter. To differentiate between simpler and more demanding projects, a two-part rating system is used. A cutting icon (a scroll saw blade) and a sanding icon (a sanding disc) appear at the start of each project. A single icon means the project is easy with regard to that skill; two, that moderate skills are required; and three, that the project is challenging. For example, the Cupcake Box (page 63) is easy to cut and to sand, and is given a rating of one scroll saw and one sanding disc. The Linzer Tart Box (page 75) requires moderate cutting skills, but is challenging to sand because of all the flutes. It is given a rating of two scroll saws and three sanding discs. The Bookcase Box (page 133) is moderately difficult to cut because of the thick wood used, but not difficult to sand. It rates two scroll saws, but only one sanding disc. For many projects, you can reduce the level of difficulty by using a softer wood.

Step-by-step lead projects: Each chapter begins with a lead project in step-by-step format, chosen to illustrate procedures and techniques common to other projects in that chapter. While you need not start with that project, you'll find it helpful to familiarize yourself with its explicit instructions. For projects not in step-by-step format, photos are provided as needed for clarity.

Sidebars and cross-references: These are used where projects share common techniques or features. Although inconvenient at times, this space-saving strategy avoids redundancy and increases the number of projects that can be included in the book.

Amount of wood: When patterns are provided for a project, the amount of wood specified allows for a small margin around the pattern. The same holds true for patterns that are drawn by the reader while making a project, such as the back for a box. For some pieces, however, such as shelves or box tops, the dimensions are designated as "actual size needed." This means the size listed is the size to be used for the project and must be cut precisely.

Changing size. Tweaking a project's size is usually OK, but make sure the wood thickness stays proportional or the results could look strange.

Small pieces. Save your scraps for projects that feature many small pieces, such as the Bookcase Box.

Can I change the size of a project?

Stacked ring method: Patterns for projects based on stacked rings, such as the Laminated Oval Box (page 154), should not be enlarged or reduced, because the resulting change in ring width will affect the cutting angle.

Other projects: Changing the size of other types of projects is usually not a problem, especially if the changes are small. If a substantial change in size is considered, however, the wood used may need to be thicker or thinner than in the original plans to keep the proportions attractive. For example, enlarging the Chest of Drawers Box without using thicker wood may result in the box appearing too shallow for its height and width.

Multi-color wood. Wood with multiple colors, such as pieces containing both sapwood and heartwood, make very convincing cupcake "icing."

What kinds of wood can I use?

Almost every type of wood has its place somewhere in this book; use common sense, personal preference, and availability as your guides. Here are some considerations that may help.

Wood hardness: Wood varies in hardness or density, even within the same variety. Generally, varieties that are difficult to cut should be avoided for projects requiring wood thicker than 1" (25mm). Those that are dense will be tedious to sand, making them demanding choices for projects based on stacked rings. In general, the softer hardwoods, such as mahogany, walnut, or poplar, are easier to use than cherry and maple. If you're not sure about a particular piece of wood, test it out by cutting and sanding a sample piece.

Less-than-perfect wood: Attractive wood makes attractive boxes, but even wood that is less than prime has its place. Surface blemishes can be hidden by laminations. Knots or unusual grain configurations can be featured on a lid. Off-colors can be placed where they'll be less visible. Multi-colored pieces, containing both heartwood and sapwood, make great cupcake "icing."

Small pieces: Projects like the Bookcase Box are a perfect use for small pieces of colorful wood.

Color combinations: To preview the finished color when considering combinations for laminations and glue-ups, moisten the unfinished wood with mineral spirits.

Strongly colored wood: Padauk, bloodwood, and dyed veneers should be used with care. When combined with lighter colored wood, their sawdust can migrate into the pores of the lighter colored wood, or bleed into it during finishing. To minimize the likelihood of problems, vacuum the raw wood frequently during sanding to remove colored dust, and apply the finish in thin coats.

Dyed veneer. Dyed veneer is a great way to get color into your projects, but be careful with it or you could get color where you don't want it.

What if I can't get the recommended wood for a project?

If you want the same look as the original project, choose wood that is similar in color. If you want wood that will handle the same, look for an equivalent hardness.

Mahogany and sapele are similar in color, and the somewhat greater hardness of sapele is not significant for most projects.

Heartwood cherry and Honduras mahogany have a similar reddish cast, although cherry is significantly harder to cut and sand.

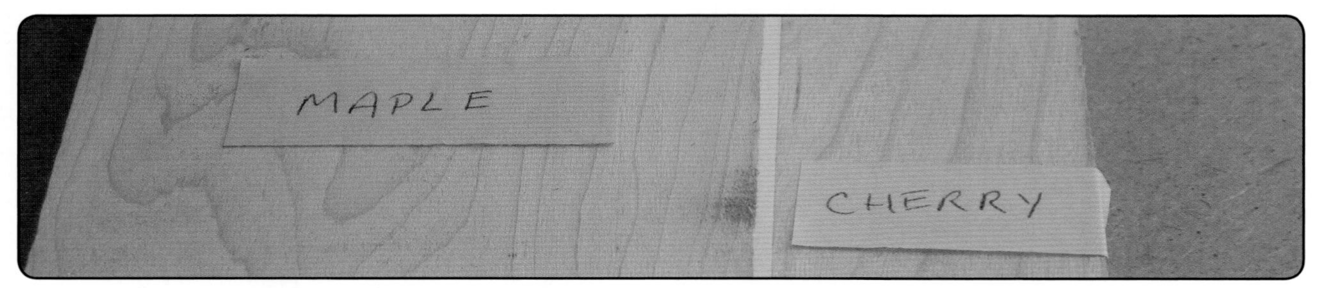

Sapwood cherry and maple are similar in grain, color, and hardness.

The Striped Pivot Lid Box (page 146) shows tasteful (and economical) use of veneers and exotic woods.

How can I avoid spending a fortune on specialty wood?

Scraps: For maximum impact at minimum cost, use narrow strips of exotic wood in glue-ups, and scraps for small parts, such as handles.

Veneer: When purchased in bulk, veneer is not expensive, and adds interest and elegance at relatively little additional cost. When you plan to use veneers primarily for color contrast, buy common woods in light, medium, and dark shades.

Exotic wood. Strips and scraps of exotic wood provide contrast and are an economical way to use expensive wood.

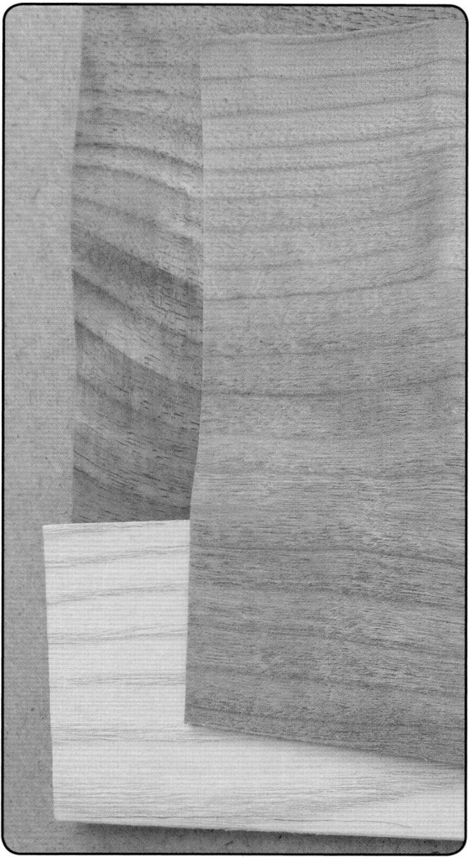

Veneer. Veneer can add the same effect as thin sheets of contrasting wood, but at far less cost.

Where can I get thin wood?

Re-sawing: Thin pieces of wood, with thicknesses varying from 1⁄16" to 1⁄4" (2 to 6mm), are used throughout the book. If you have access to a band saw, re-sawing is the most economical way to obtain this wood. In addition, for projects requiring both thick and thin wood of the same type, wood cut from the same board will give the best match in color and grain. If re-sawing is not an option, a variety of thin wood is readily available through the Internet.

How can I control warping of thin wood and veneer?

Clamp: Thin wood tends to curl when glue is applied to its surface. To keep the finished piece flat, apply glue evenly, rub adjacent surfaces together to eliminate air pockets, and clamp the piece securely until thoroughly dry.

Press: The use of a press, either square or round, which exerts even pressure, is preferable to conventional clamps when thin wood is glued to another surface.

Rescuing warped wood: Thin wood that has warped slightly may flatten out if glued to thicker stock. If you cannot flatten it, choose another piece and use the warped piece for strips. Veneer that is wavy can be flattened by moistening both sides and weighing it down, using paper to absorb the moisture.

Gluing up thin pieces of wood. When gluing up thin pieces of wood, use a clamp to ensure good adhesion and prevent curling.

Press. Use a press to exert even pressure when gluing.

When do I need to consider the direction of the wood grain?

Throughout a project: In general, keeping the grain running in the same direction for all components of a project—box body, bottom, and lid—will give the most attractive results.

When gluing: When a component, such as the bottom, is glued to the body of the box, keeping the grain running in the same direction will minimize separation or splitting caused by seasonal wood movement.

When cutting delicate parts: When a component is delicate, such as the "steam" of the Coffee Cup Box (page 60), cutting it with the grain reduces the likelihood of breakage.

When doing angled cutting for projects using stacked rings, why is the table tilted one way rather than the other?

Cutting wood at a steep angle may seem daunting, but is not very different from making cuts with the saw table level. Cutting clockwise with the table tilted in one direction will give the same results as cutting counterclockwise with the table tilted in the other direction. For simplicity and uniformity, all projects in this book use the saw table tilted left side down.

What is the best way to clamp projects for gluing?

Press: The easiest way to clamp most projects is with a shop-made press that exerts strong, even pressure, making it unlikely that pieces will shift out of position. It works well for laminations, and is invaluable for gluing up stacked rings. Instructions for making a press are given in the Appendix (page 173).

Standard clamps: These can be more cumbersome to use, but also give satisfactory results.

Spring clamps: These inexpensive clamps are useful when spot pressure is important, or when you need visibility to check for slippage, as when gluing on lid liners.

Press. Make this press following the instructions on page 173.

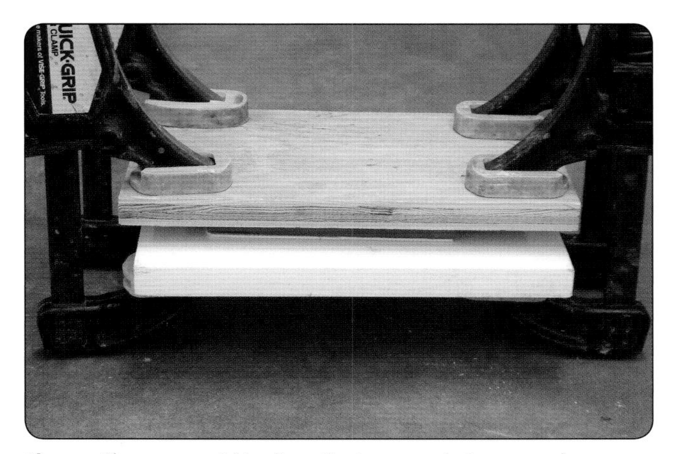

Clamps. Clamps are a viable alternative to a press, but more cumbersome.

What types of adhesives should I use?

For attaching patterns to wood: Repositionable spray adhesive is a good choice for attaching patterns, especially if they will be removed and re-attached.

For most projects: Although a good woodworker's glue, such as Titebond II, can always be used, other adhesives may be recommended for certain projects. When this occurs, the recommendation will be specified in the Materials list for that project.

When gluing up rings: Weldbond—a catalyzed PVA glue that dries clear, has a quick "grab," and is weather-resistant—helps minimize the likelihood of ring creep for projects based on stacked rings. It is also appropriate where clamping is not feasible, as when gluing up small or angled pieces. For those situations, rubbing the parts together until tacky usually provides an acceptable bond. If Weldbond is the adhesive of choice for a particular project, it will be specified in the Materials list.

When using brass parts: Epoxy is the best adhesive to use with brass components, such as barrel hinges and rods used for pivots.

What does cut "in a clockwise direction" mean?

Cutting in a clockwise direction means that the wood is fed in a counterclockwise direction, creating the illusion that the blade is moving clockwise. When combined with the saw table tilted left side down, this creates a cut that is wider at the top of the wood than the bottom. Nearly all the angled cuts in this book are made in a clockwise direction. The few exceptions are clearly indicated.

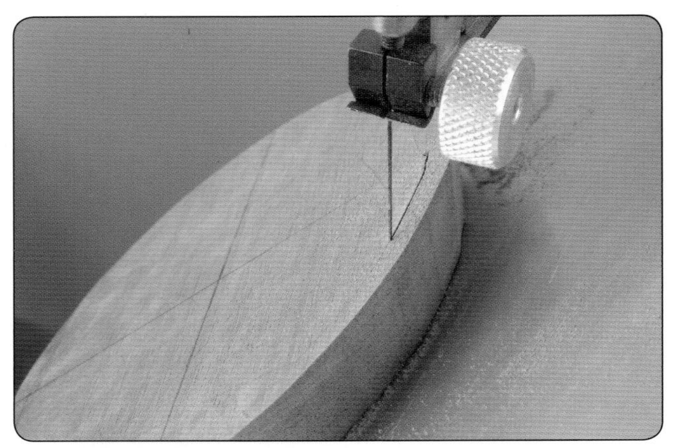

Cutting clockwise with the saw table tilted left side down creates a cut that is wider at the top of the wood than the bottom.

How do I drill an angled entry hole?

Angles: Entry holes for cuts made at a particular angle must be drilled at that angle. A drill press with a tilting table can be used to obtain the correct angle. More commonly, an angle guide, consisting of a piece of wood cut at the desired angle, is used to guide the hole. (See Sidebar: Making an Angle Guide, below.)

Drill bit size: Every project made from concentric rings cut at an angle will have drill marks that must be sanded out when the rings are glued together. To facilitate sanding, use the smallest size drill bit that can accommodate the saw blade.

Location: Angled entry holes are always drilled toward the center of the blank. This allows the blank to sit flat on the saw table when the blade is inserted, and prevents the wood from jumping at the start of the cut.

If the wood does not lay flat on the table when the blade is inserted, the entry hole has not been drilled at the correct angle, or was not drilled toward the center of the blank. The best way to handle this situation is to start and stop the saw briefly, holding the wood firmly as it jumps. You should then be able to continue the cut.

Making an Angle Guide

To make a guide for any drilling angle, cut one edge of a small block of hardwood at the needed angle. Sand the cut face smooth, and write the angle clearly on the top of the guide.

How important is the cutting angle?

Correct angle: For every wood thickness and ring width, there is a particular cutting angle that will produce concentric rings that can be stacked in near-perfect alignment. Cutting at this angle is critical for projects of this type. If wood thickness or ring width is changed, the angle must also be changed or the rings will not align properly.

Special effects: For creating a special effect, such as the fluted crust of the Apple Tart Box (page 52) or the rippled edge of the Cupcake Stand (page 67), the ring must be cut at several different angles to rough out the desired shape.

Stacked rings. This type of project requires cutting at a precise angle in order to produce sides that can be sanded smooth.

Special effects. Ripples and flutes require several cutting angles.

Why must I sometimes draw my own cutting lines?

Most projects contain complete sets of patterns. However, sometimes the exact size of a piece cannot be predicted because of variations in cutting and shaping. In those instances, to size the piece correctly, instructions are given for drawing a cutting line directly on the wood. Lid liners, for example, should fit snugly into the opening of the box, but the size of this opening varies with the amount of sanding that has been done.

What equipment do I need for sanding?

Sanding preferences tend to be highly personal. They also depend on the tools available. However, certain types of sanders are required, or strongly recommended, for some projects.

All-purpose sanders: Mechanical sanders, such as belt, disc, and random orbit, are not listed under Tools or Materials. It is assumed that these tools are available.

"Sanders of choice": When this designation appears in the Tools list for a project, it means no special equipment is required, and choice is a matter of personal preference.

Specific sanders: When certain sanders are essential or strongly recommended for a project, they will be listed under Tools for that project.

Which projects require specific types of sanders?

Inflatable round sander: This unique tool is invaluable for sanding the inside of glued-up rings, and for sanding flutes on both inner and outer box surfaces.

Hook-and-loop pad sander: This specialty sander, in the 2" (50mm) size, is useful for sanding the outside of curved surfaces, especially those with lobes.

Small drum sander: This little tool is invaluable for sanding straight flutes or tight corners.

Vertical belt sander: In addition to making quick work of smoothing box exteriors, its tilting table makes it easy to create or smooth beveled edges.

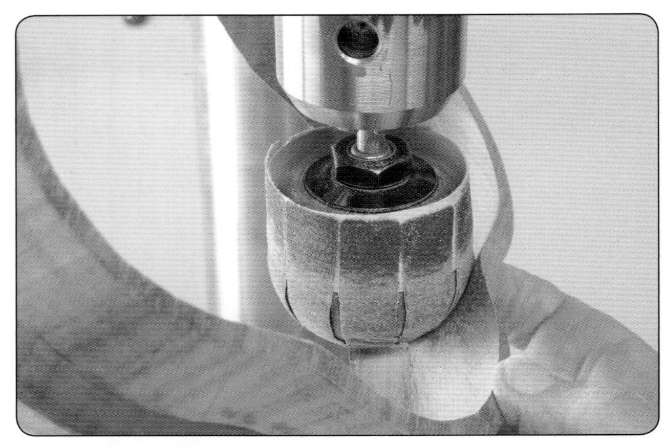

Inflatable round sanders are necessary to sand the inside of rings, flutes, and other concave surfaces.

What grits of sandpaper do I need?

60–80 grit: When sanding involves shaping and wood removal, grits of 60 or 80 will remove wood effectively.

150–320 grit: Use grits between 150 and 320 for smoothing and finishing, working your way from coarser to finer grits. Be sure to remove all sanding marks made by the coarser grits.

Final sanding: All projects should be given a final sanding by hand. Feel the wood with your eyes closed to detect small dents and ridges, and sand them out before applying the finish. A foam-backed sanding pad is especially effective for this purpose.

Hook-and-loop pad sanders are useful to sand convex surfaces.

Foam-backed sanding pads are very effective for removing small ridges.

Small drum sanders are great for straight flutes like these.

What type of finish should I use?

The projects in this book rely on gloss or semi-gloss finishes to highlight the natural colors of the wood. The following method is easy and works well:

1. Apply shellac: Apply a thin coat of shellac, brushed or sprayed on, after you sand the project smooth and remove all sanding dust by vacuuming, tacking, or both. The shellac seals the wood and reveals any glue spots. Mark the glue spots with chalk so they will be visible when the shellac has dried.

2. Sand off glue spots: Sand off glue spots with the finest grit that will do the job. If a glue spot is stubborn and requires a coarse grit for removal, re-sand that area, working your way through the grits to the finest one used previously. Then, apply a little shellac to re-seal the wood.

3. Smooth the surface: Rub down the project with 0000 steel wool to smooth the surface for the final coats of finish. Then, vacuum the project thoroughly to remove any particles that could mar the finish, and tack off with a tack rag or damp paper towel.

4. Apply final coats of finish: Apply several coats of shellac or clear spray lacquer. Rub down each coat with 0000 steel wool as needed, until the desired luster is obtained.

What else should I know about finishing?

Enclosed spaces: Apply a thin coat of shellac to the inside of boxes and drawers to seal the wood and give a finished look. Unlike oils and other finishes, its odor dissipates quickly. The wood should be sanded lightly when the shellac has dried.

Food safety: Shellac is the least toxic clear finish for objects that will be in contact with food.

Application methods: Brushed or wiped-on clear finishes can be used as an alternative to sprays.

Oil finishes are not recommended, as they do not produce the luster that is optimal for the projects in this book. If you choose to use them, never apply them to the inside of drawers or other enclosed spaces, because the odor will never fully disappear.

As you move on to the projects themselves, use the information contained in this chapter as any other tool for the creation of your own beautiful boxes.

Spray shellac and lacquer are appropriate for finishing the projects in this book.

Boxes with Bows

Everyone loves a bow box, and here are four versions, each topped with a colorful, loopy bow. Although the boxes vary in size, shape, and construction, and each bow is different in some way, they are all attractive, unique, and impressive projects that are sure to please.

Bow-Making Basics

To make the bow for your box, follow the steps below, using the wood, patterns, and drill bit specified in the project instructions.

Keep in mind that the thickness of the blank for loops and tails is determined by the lamination used, and will match the face side of the pattern.

Attaching the loop patterns. Fold the loop patterns along the dotted lines and attach to the wood with repositionable adhesive. Attach the drilled side of the pattern to the plain (non-striped) side of the strip. The face side of the pattern is always attached to the striped side of the strip.

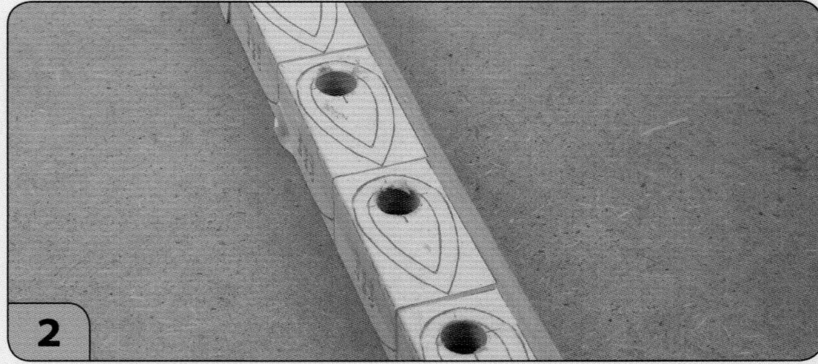

Drilling the inside of the loops. To keep the pattern from shredding when holes are drilled, cover the drilled side with clear packing tape. Drill the holes where indicated on the pattern, using the drill bit specified for that project.

Cutting the inside of the loops. Cut out the inside of the loops. Remove the waste.

Cutting the outside of the loops. Cut along the outer line of the loops. If you are using a strip, start at the bottom. When all loops are cut, tape them back securely into their original position.

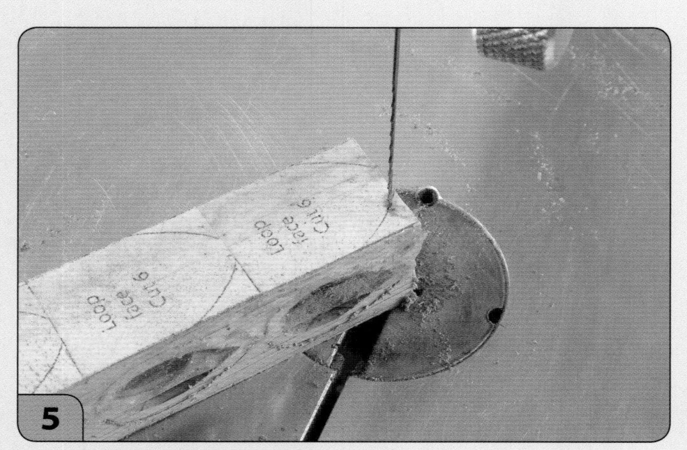

Cutting the face of the loops. Turn the wood so that the pattern side marked "face" is up. Cut along the side of each loop. If you are using a strip, start at the bottom, remove the loop when cut, and remove the waste before cutting the next loop.

Sanding the loops. Sand the loops inside and out to remove irregularities and blade marks. Soften and thin the outer edges as desired.

Attaching the tails pattern. Using repositionable adhesive, attach the tails pattern to the prepared strip of wood. The face of the tails is always attached to the striped side of the wood.

Cutting the sides of the tails. Cut along the curved sides of each tail, keeping them in order after cutting. Tape the tails and waste back together securely with clear tape.

Speedy Loops

If you have a vertical belt sander, it's much faster to cut only the drilled side of the loop, then shape the sides of the face by sanding. Here's how to do it:

Remove each loop after the first side is cut. Mark the loop about ½" (13mm) from the bottom edge. Extend the mark slightly onto the side of the loop.

Sand the outside of the loop smooth.

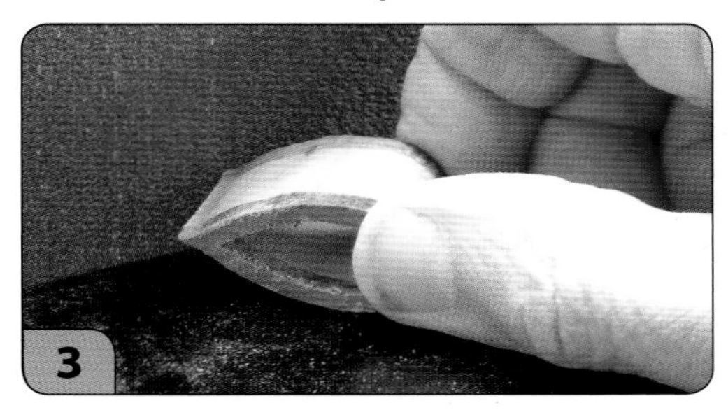

Shape the sides of the loop, using your marks as guides.

Cutting the face of the tails. Place the strip face side up and cut along the lines to complete the tails.

Sanding the tails. Sand the pieces smooth and thin the edges as desired.

Oval Bow Box: A Step-by-Step Guide

Difficulty Rating:

This festive box features multi-colored loops and tails, and ribbons that appear to bend around the curved ends of the box. The block lamination, made from seven layers of wood, is cut into strips to create the decorative components. Its generous size allows extra strips, if needed, and a cutting guide is provided to locate the parts. The lid and box fit snugly, creating the effect of a continuous ribbon. Should the lid bind, however, just sand the box slightly to ease the fit.

Materials and Tools

Wood

For the box:

- (1) 6½" x 3½" x 1⅛" (165 x 90 x 30mm) cherry for box body
- (3) 6½" x 3½" x ¼" (165 x 90 x 6mm) cherry for box bottom and lid

For the bow and ribbons:

- (1) 7" x 3" x ½" (180 x 75 x 13mm) purpleheart
- (2) 7" x 3" x ⅛" (180 x 75 x 3mm) oak
- (2) 7" x 3" (180 x 75mm) red veneer
- (2) 7" x 3" (180 x 75mm) yellow veneer

Materials

- Repositionable adhesive
- Glue (Weldbond recommended)
- Clear packing tape
- Blue painter's tape
- Sandpaper for sanders of choice, assorted grits
- Sandpaper for hand sanding, assorted grits
- Acrylic paint and matching fibers for flocking (optional)
- Shellac
- Clear spray lacquer

Tools

- #9 scroll saw blade for thick wood
- #3 scroll saw blade for thin wood
- #12 scroll saw blade for cutting the curved side ribbons
- ⅛" (3mm) drill bit for entry holes
- ⅜" (10mm) brad point bit for loops
- Clamps for gluing
- Sanders of choice
- Craft or X-Acto knife for cutting veneer
- Brush for acrylic paint (optional)

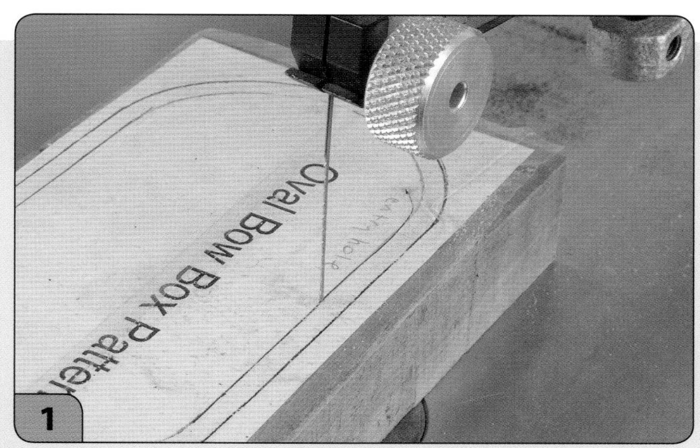

Cutting the box interior. Cover the piece of 1⅛" (30mm) cherry with clear packing tape to prevent burning. Attach the pattern for the box, using repositionable adhesive. Drill an entry hole where indicated. Insert the saw blade and cut along this line to create the box interior.

Sanding the box interior. Sand the inside of the box smooth.

Gluing on the base. Glue the box to one of the ¼" (6mm) pieces of cherry. Clamp, wait five minutes, then remove the clamps and clean away any glue squeeze-out. Re-clamp and let dry.

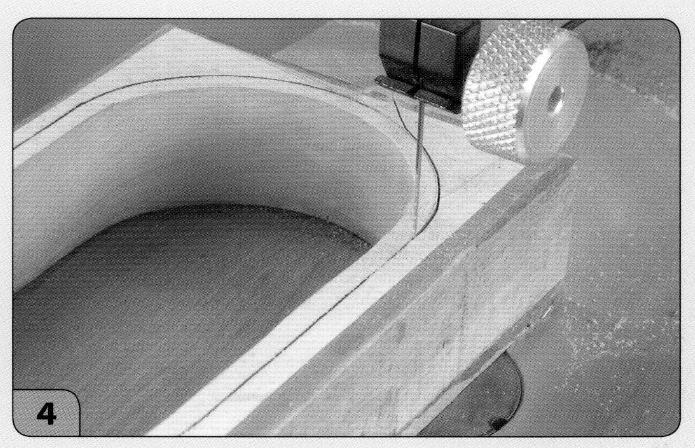

Cutting the box exterior. Cut along the outer line to complete the box body. Sand the outside of the box smooth.

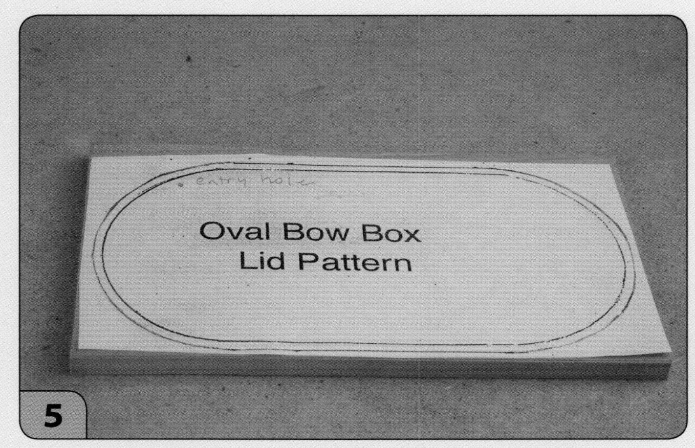

Cutting the lid. Attach a copy of the lid pattern to the second piece of ¼" (6mm) cherry, using repositionable adhesive. Drill an entry hole where indicated on the pattern. Insert the blade and cut along this line. Sand the inside smooth.

Gluing the lid. Glue the lid to the remaining ¼" (6mm) piece of cherry. Clamp, clean out any glue squeeze-out, and let dry.

Completing the lid. Cut along the outer line of the lid pattern to complete the lid. Sand the sides of the lid until smooth.

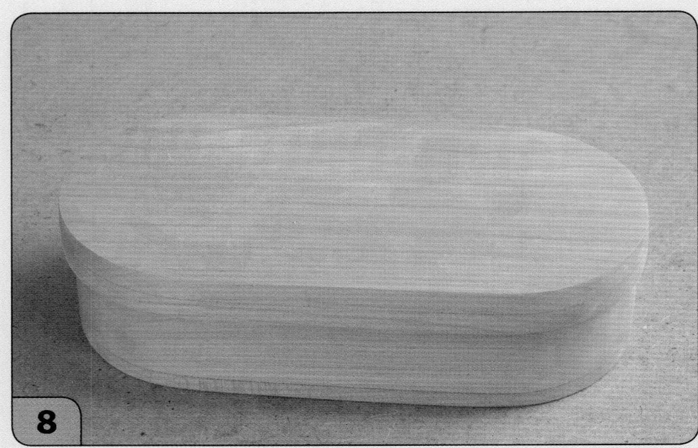

Preparing the box for the ribbons. Place the lid on the box. Sand the box if needed, until the lid fits on easily. Sand to soften all edges slightly.

Making the lamination. Glue together the remaining wood in this order: oak, red veneer, yellow veneer, purpleheart, yellow veneer, red veneer, oak. Clamp and let dry. Sand the edges of the blank smooth. The blank should be about $\frac{7}{8}$" (22mm) thick. If yours is different, adjust the width of the patterns for the faces of the loops and tails to keep them centered on the lamination.

Cutting the ribbons. Place the blank flat. Draw a line $\frac{1}{16}$" (2mm) from the long edge. Cut along this line to make a strip that measures 7" x $\frac{7}{8}$" x $\frac{1}{16}$" (180 x 22 x 2mm). Sand the cut edge of the blank smooth. Cut a second strip the same way. These are the flat ribbons for the box.

Gluing the long top ribbon. Glue one of the ribbons down the center of the lid, keeping the overhang even at both ends. Clamp and let dry.

Gluing the short top ribbons. Cut the second strip in half. Butt each half against the long ribbon at its center. Glue the pieces into place and let them dry.

Trimming the short ribbons. Place the lid upside down and mark a line on each short ribbon 1⁄16" (2mm) beyond the edge of the lid. Cut to the outside of each line. Save the cutoffs for Step 15.

Trimming the long ribbon. Repeat Step 13 for both ends of the long ribbon, marking a curve instead of a straight line.

Gluing the side ribbons on the lid. Use the cutoff from each short ribbon to cut a piece for the side of the lid. Each piece should extend just beyond the bottom of the lid; it will be sanded flush in Step 21. Glue each piece into place. Save the remainders of the strips for the next step.

Gluing the side ribbons on the box. Place the lid on the box. Use the remainder of each strip to cut a piece that meets the bottom of the lid and extends just past the bottom of the box. Glue each piece into place.

Drawing the first cutting line for the curved ribbons for the lid. Cut a 1¼" x 1¼" (32 x 32mm) piece from the laminated blank. The stripes of the block should be aligned with the stripes of the top ribbon. Trace the curve of the lid onto the block, about ¼" (6mm) back from the end of the block.

Drawing the second cutting line for the curved ribbons for the lid. Draw a second line toward the outside edge of the block that is about 3⁄32" (2mm) away from the first line, and parallel to it. These two lines are your cutting lines for the curved ribbons for the lid.

19

Cutting the curved ribbons for the lid. Using the #12 blade, cut along the outermost curved line, then the inner curve. This gives you one curved piece large enough for both ends of the lid. Mark and cut the pieces the same way as for the straight lid sides. Glue and clamp.

20

Making the curved side ribbons for the box. Using the remainder of the wood from the previous step, cut two pieces for the curved ends of the box. Mark and cut them in the same way as the curved pieces for the lid, using the bottom of the box as the guide for the first curved line.

21

Preparing the box for the loops and tails. Sand the ribbon faces smooth and their ends flush with the box edges. Round over the ribbons at the top edge of the lid. Using blue painter's tape, mask the area where the bow will be glued. Seal all surfaces with shellac. Sand away glue spots. Remove the tape and sand the box smooth.

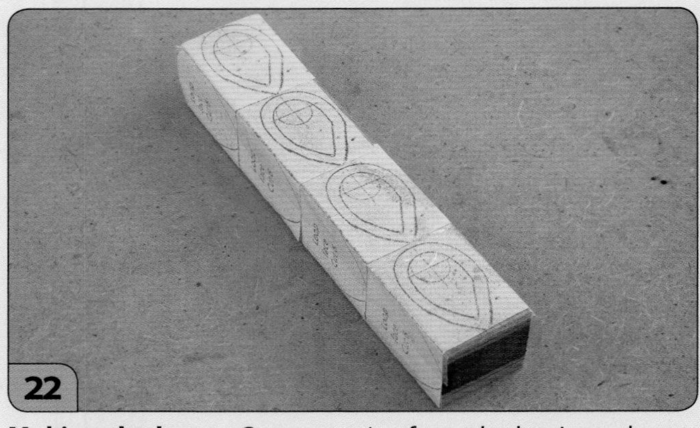
22

Making the loops. Cut two strips from the laminated blank, one 1" x 3" (25 x 75mm) and the other 1" x 6" (25 x 150mm). Attach two loop patterns to the shorter strip and four to the longer strip. Follow the instructions on page 24 to cut and sand six loops. Use a ⅜" (10mm) brad point bit to drill the centers.

23

Making the tails. Cut a strip 2" (50mm) long and 1" (25mm) wide from the laminated blank. Attach the tails pattern with repositionable adhesive so that the face of the tails is on the striped side. Follow the instructions given on page 25 to cut and sand the tails.

24

Gluing the tails into place. Place the point of each tail where the two ribbons cross and glue it into place. Support the ends, if needed, to hold the tails in place until the glue sets. Remove excess glue before it dries.

Gluing on the loops. Glue five of the loops on top of the ribbons, spacing them evenly. Sand down the pointed end of the sixth loop to increase the gluing surface and glue it into place in the middle of the bow. Let the loops dry thoroughly. Apply several coats of spray lacquer to the outside of the box. Finish the inside with flocking, if desired. See Fearless Flocking, page 130.

25

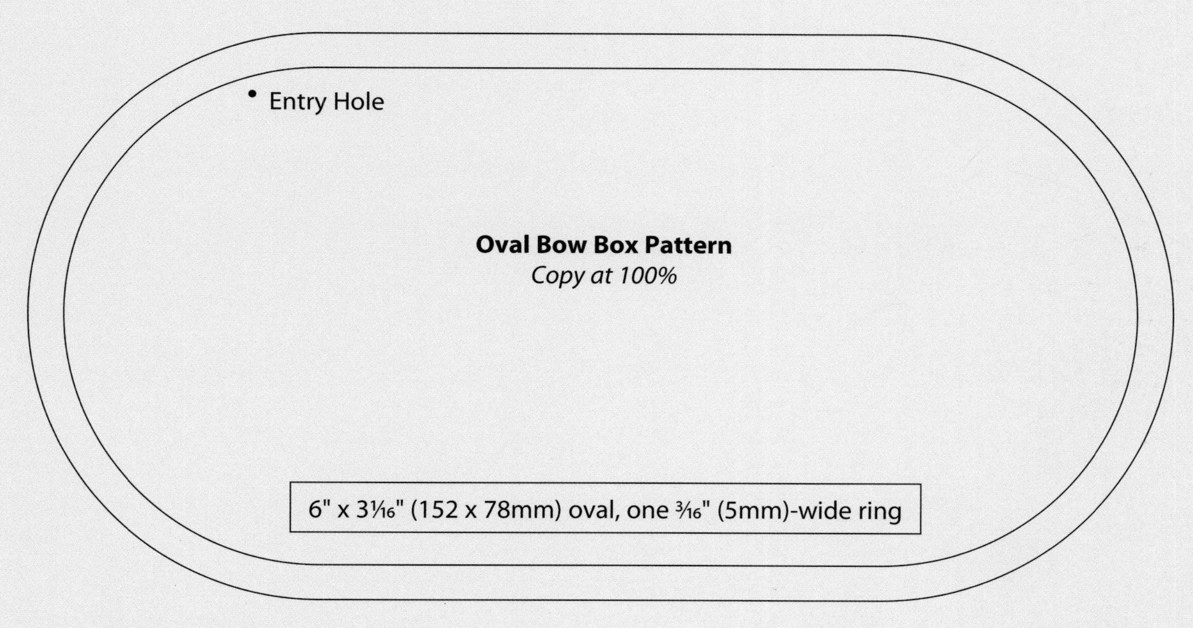

Loop Pattern
Copy at 100%

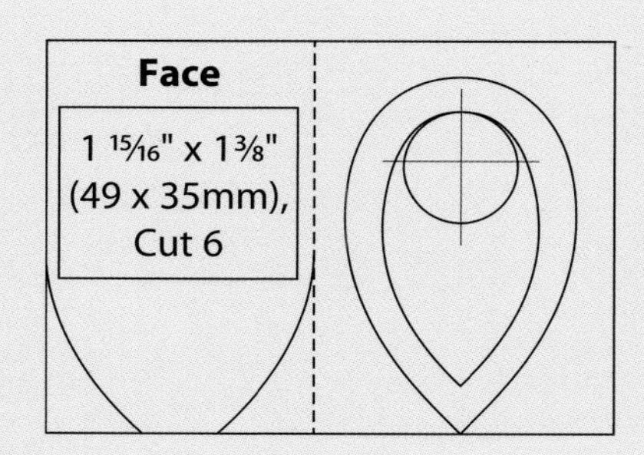

Tail Pattern
Copy at 100%

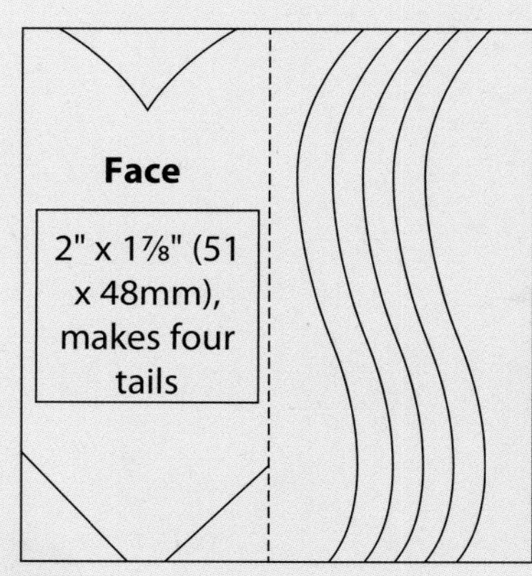

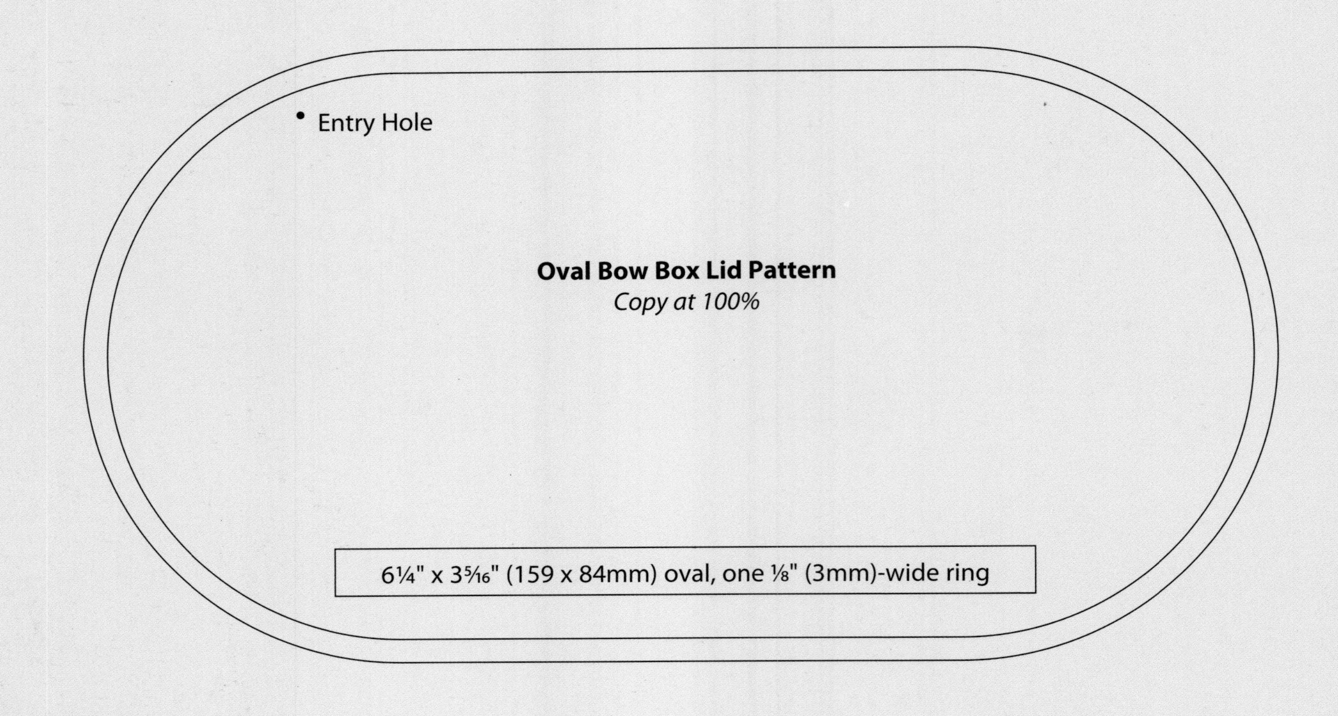

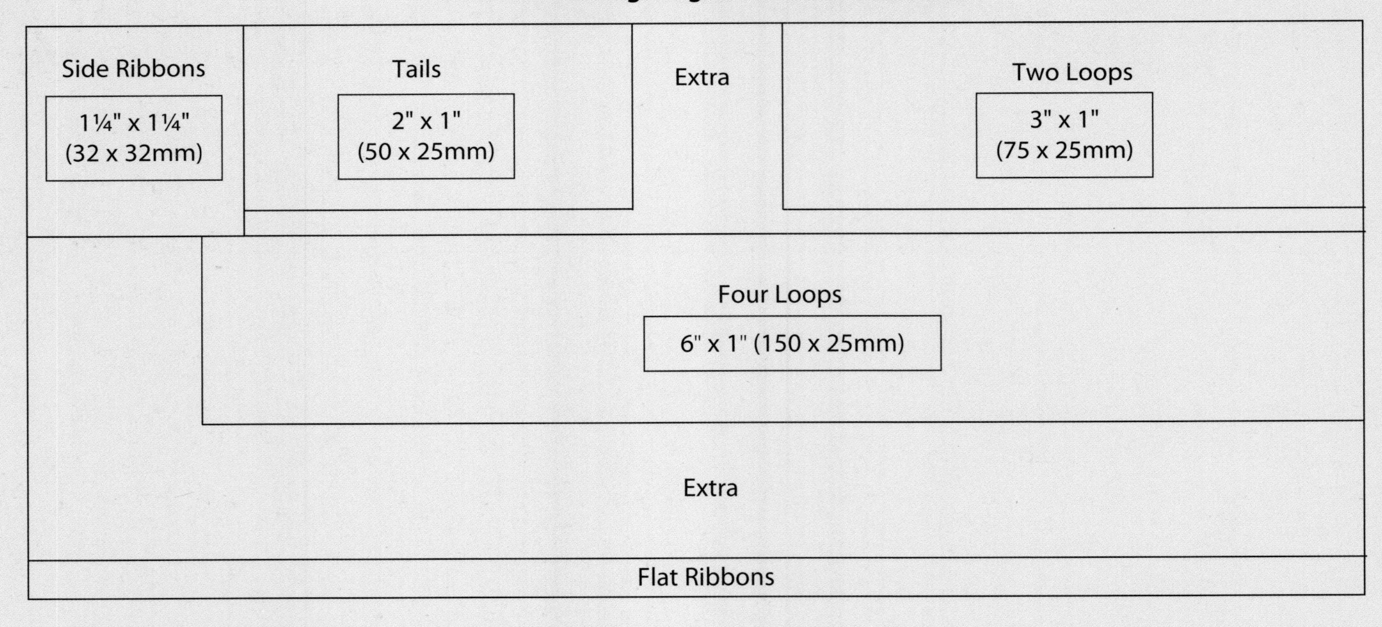

Note: This diagram is a cutting guide, but is not meant to be used as a pattern. Cut the pieces as directed in the steps. Drawing is not to scale.

Diagonal Bow Box

Difficulty Rating:

This box, with elongated loops and diagonal ribbons, contrasts nicely with the more typical bow and tails design. The easy-to-make flat lid enhances the illusion of a continuous side ribbon, and can be used as an alternate lid style for most boxes.

Placement of the diagonal top ribbons and cutting of the angled side ribbons takes some time and care, but is not difficult, and the unusual effect is worth it. The wrap-around side ribbons add a realistic touch.

Materials and Tools

Wood

For the box:

- (1) 6¼" x 4½" x ¾" (160 x 115 x 19mm) walnut for box body
- (2) 6¼" x 4½" x ¼" (160 x 115 x 6mm) walnut for bottom and lid
- (1) 6" x 4" x ⅛" (150 x 100 x 2mm) mahogany for lid liner

For the bow and ribbons:

- (3) 9" x ¾" x ¼" (230 x 20 x 6mm) maple for loops (actual size needed)
- (4) 9" x ¾" (230 x 20mm) dyed red veneer for loops (actual size needed)
- (3) 6" x ¾" x ¼" (150 x 20 x 6mm) maple for ribbons (actual size needed)
- (4) 6" x ¾" (150 x 20mm) dyed red veneer for ribbons (actual size needed)

Materials

- Repositionable adhesive
- Glue (Weldbond recommended)
- Clear packing tape
- Sandpaper for sanders of choice, assorted grits
- Sandpaper for hand sanding, assorted grits
- Acrylic paint and matching fibers for flocking (optional)
- Shellac
- Clear spray lacquer

Tools

- #9 scroll saw blade for thicker wood
- #3 scroll saw blade for thinner wood
- #2/0 scroll saw blade for ribbon strips
- ⅛" (3mm) drill bit for entry holes
- ¼" (6mm) brad point bit for loops
- Ruler
- Clamps for gluing
- Sanders of choice
- Brush for acrylic paint (if flocking is used)

1. To make the box, attach the box pattern to the ¾" (20mm)-thick piece of walnut. Drill an entry hole where indicated and cut out the interior. Sand the inside smooth. Glue the box to one piece of ¼" (6mm)-thick walnut, clamp, and let dry. Cut along the outer line to complete the box body. Sand the outside smooth.

2. Attach a copy of the box pattern to the remaining piece of ¼" (6mm) walnut. Cut along the outside line to form the lid. Remove the pattern, but do not discard it.

3. Attach the pattern removed in Step 2 to the ⅛" (3mm) piece of mahogany. Cut along the inner line to form the lid liner.

4. Place the lid liner on the lid. Invert the box body on the lid to position the liner properly. Mark the position with light pencil marks to ensure it does not slip out of place. Glue the lid liner to the lid. Clamp and let dry.

5. Place the completed lid on the box and sand the sides until the box and lid match perfectly. Sand the box and lid until smooth and soften the edges slightly.

6. Glue together the two sets of maple and red veneer in the order illustrated—red, maple, red, maple, red, maple, red. Clamp and let dry. Sand the striped faces smooth.

7. With the veneer side facing up, draw a line along one long edge of the 6" (150mm) strip that is 1⁄16" (2mm) from that edge. Cut along this line to make the first ribbon. Sand the cut edge smooth. Cut four more strips in the same manner. Set the strips aside until Step 10.

8. Follow the instructions on page 24 to cut and sand five loops. Use the 9" (230mm) laminated strip and a ¼" (6mm) brad point bit. This box uses straight-sided loops. They are not shaped on the face side, and will look like the loop shown in Speedy Loops, Step 2, page 25.

9. Using a ruler, mark the center of each side of the lid. Transfer the marks to the edges.

Attaching the lid liner.

Gluing the strips.

Marking the lid.

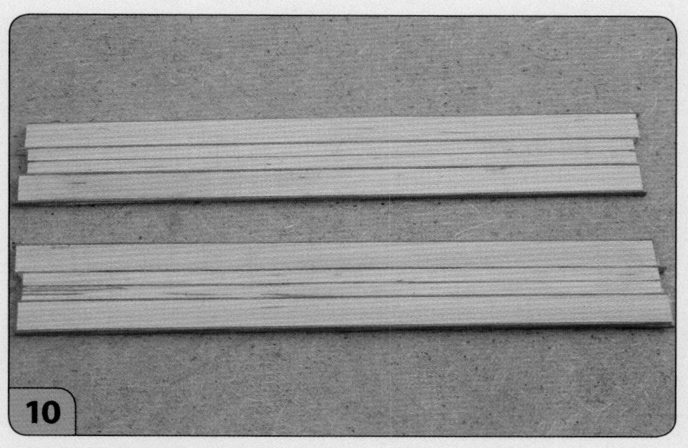
Marking the top strips.

10. Draw a line down the center of the sanded side of two of the 6" (150mm) strips cut in Step 7. This is the side that will be glued to the lid.

11. Invert the lid on the two marked strips, and position the strips diagonally so that the centers of the strips are aligned with the marks on the edges of the lid. Clamp the strips into place.

12. Turn the lid right side up and mark the sides of the strips with a light pencil mark to help you place them properly when gluing them to the lid. (The clamps have been removed in the photo for clarity.)

13. Glue the strips to the top of the lid. Be sure to leave equal amounts of wood overhanging on each side.

14. Place the lid with the ribbon side down and draw a line on the ends of each strip 1/16" (2mm) from the edge of the lid. Using the 2/0 blade, cut along these lines. Save each cutoff to use for the ribbon strips on the sides of the lid.

Positioning the top strips.

Marking the location of the strips.

Trimming the top strips.

15. Butt each cutoff piece against the underside of its matching edge. Mark the bottom edge of the side strip on its underside, using the edge of the lid as a guide. Cut each side strip a little longer than the marked line.

16. Glue each side strip into place, matching the stripes with the top strip. Clamp and let dry.

17. Sand the surface of the strips until smooth. Sand the lower edge flush. Round over the edges where the top and side strips meet.

18. Place the lid on the box. Starting at one of the short sides of the box, hold a straight edge against each side of the ribbon and extend the lines down the side of the box.

19. Align the top of the third laminated strip with the lines drawn in Step 18. Mark the top and bottom cutting lines on the underside, using the top and bottom edges of the box as guides.

20. Cut the marked piece slightly long and glue it into place. Sand the overhang flush. Repeat Steps 18-20 for the second short side, using the rest of the strip.

21. Place the lid on the box. Hold a straight edge against each side of the ribbon on one of the long sides of the box, and extend the lines as in Step 18. Hold the fourth strip in place and mark the top and bottom edges, and the side of the box.

22. Cut along the three marked lines. Save the piece cut off from the lower edge for Step 24.

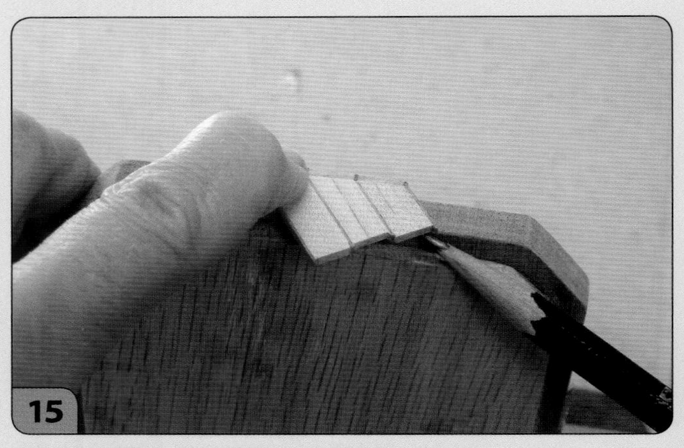
15

Marking the side piece for the lid.

18

Marking the angle of the strip for the short side of the box.

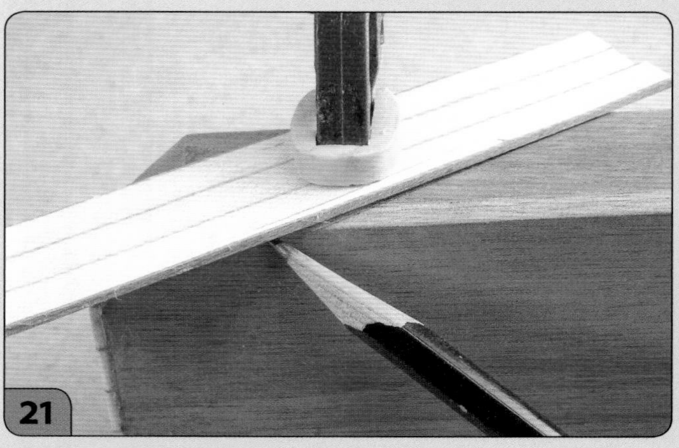
21

Marking the strip for the long side.

Gluing the strip for the long side.

Marking the wrap-around piece.

Finishing the box.

23. Glue the trimmed strip into position on the side of the box. Clamp and let dry. Sand a bevel into the corner edge of the ribbon that is continuous with the diagonal corner of the box. The bevel will be covered up in the next step.

24. Position the reserved cut-off piece on the diagonal corner of the box so that the piece extends over the beveled edge of the side ribbon, and the stripes are aligned. Mark the lower edge of the box on this piece and cut off the excess.

25. Glue the small piece into place. Sand the bottom edges of the ribbon flush with the box, and sand the joint between the two pieces into a smooth curve. Repeat Steps 21-25 for the other side of the box, using the last strip.

26. Glue the five loops into place on top of one of the diagonal ribbons. Remove any excess glue and let dry. Apply a coat of shellac to the box to seal the wood and reveal glue spots. Sand away any glue spots, then apply several coats of spray lacquer. Apply flocking fibers to the inside of the box, if desired (see Fearless Flocking, page 130).

Lid and Box Outside

• Entry Hole

Box Inside

Diagonal Bow Box Pattern
Make 2 copies at 100%

5¾" x 3¾" (146 x 95mm), one 3/16" (5mm)-thick wall

Narrow Loop Pattern
Copy at 100%

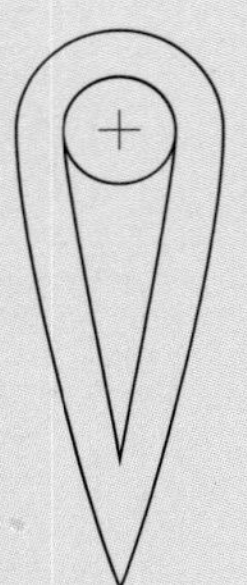
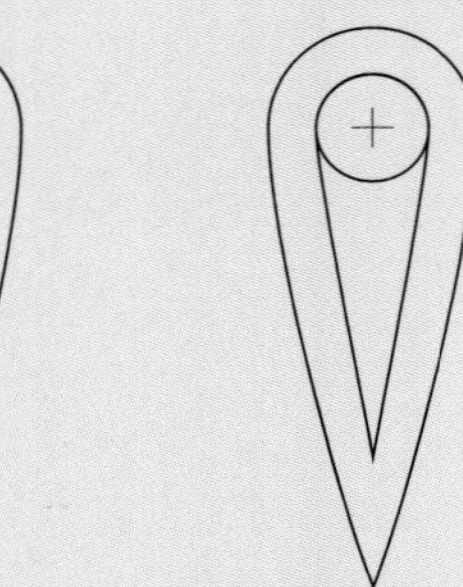
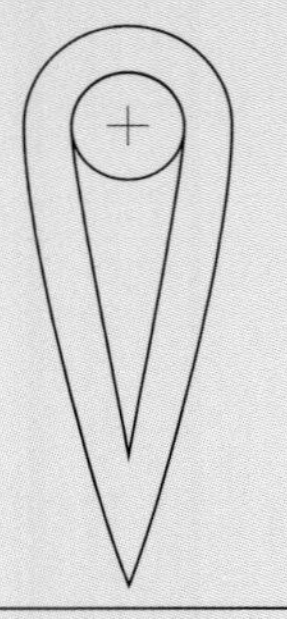
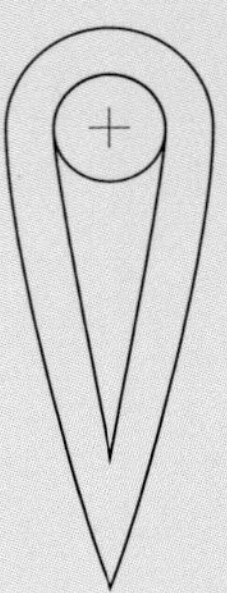

Five loops, 1⅝" x ¾" (41 x 19mm)

Bow Top Ring Box

Difficulty Rating:

This little box is an unusual variation of the traditional ring box, complete with barrel hinges and a velvet-covered insert. Its glued-in strips replace glued-on ribbons, and it is topped with a matching loopy bow. After much deliberation, I decided to group it with bow boxes, rather than ring boxes, and use cross-references to supply instructions for barrel hinge insertion and ring insert construction. Regardless of how it is categorized, it's a special box for a special occasion. Note that this ring box, as well as all others in this book, is sized for a standard ring or band. If you wish to create this box for a larger ring, you can increase the thickness of the primary wood up to 1" (25mm) and resize the width of the ribbons to match.

Materials and Tools

Wood

For the box:

- (1) 5" x 2½" x 13⁄16" (130 x 65 x 21mm) shedua or hardwood of choice
- (2) 5" x ⅞" x ⅛" (130 x 22 x 3mm) bloodwood
- (1) 5" x ⅞" x ¼" (130 x 22 x 6mm) cherry
- (4) 3" x ⅞" x ⅛" (75 x 22 x 3mm) bloodwood
- (2) 3" x ⅞" x ¼" (75 x 22 x 6mm) cherry
- (1) 2" piece of ⅛" (50 x 2mm) dowel, marked 7.5mm (19⁄64") from one end

For the bow:

- (1) 8" x ¾" x ½" (205 x 20 x 13mm) cherry (actual size needed)
- (2) 8" x ¾" x ⅛" (205 x 20 x 3mm) bloodwood (actual size needed)

Materials

- Repositionable adhesive
- Epoxy
- Glue (Weldbond recommended)
- Clear packing tape
- Sandpaper for sanders of choice, assorted grits
- Sandpaper for hand sanding, assorted grits
- 0000 steel wool
- (2) 5mm barrel hinges
- (1) 3½" x 2½" (90 x 65mm) piece of adhesive-backed velvet for ring insert
- (1) 2" (50mm) square of adhesive-backed velvet for top recess
- (1) 2½" x 1¾" x ½" (65 x 45 x 13mm) foam core for ring insert
- Shellac
- Clear spray lacquer

Tools

- #9 scroll saw blade
- #2/0 scroll saw blade for foam core
- 1½" (40mm) Forstner bit
- 5⁄16" (8mm) brad point bit
- 5mm brad point bit
- Awl
- Clamps
- Sanders of choice
- Toothpick or #3 cake decorating tip for epoxy
- X-Acto knife for thinning the insert

Gluing in the first strip.

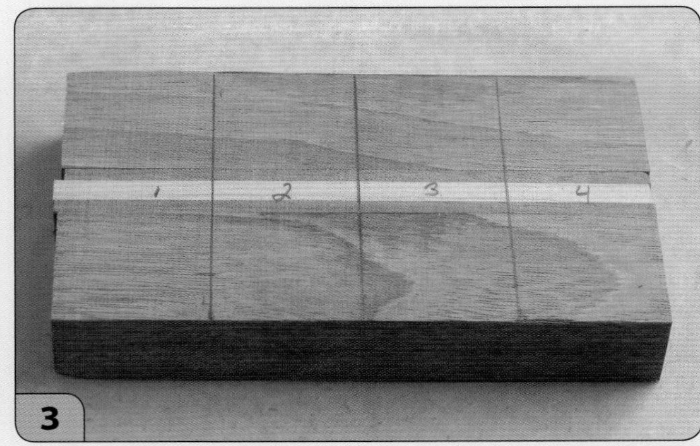
Dividing the strip.

Gluing in the cross strips.

Preparing the blanks for drilling and cutting.

1. Draw a line 1¼" (30mm) from the long edge of the shedua. Cut the piece in half lengthwise along this line. Sand the cut edges smooth, if needed, to be sure they are square with the top and bottom faces.

2. Glue up the two pieces of shedua cut in Step 1 with the 5" (130mm) long pieces of cherry and bloodwood in this order: shedua, bloodwood, cherry, bloodwood, shedua. Clamp the pieces, making sure that all of them are flush on the underside. The bloodwood and cherry will protrude slightly on the top face of the blank. They will be sanded flush in Step 6.

3. Draw three lines across the strip, 1¼" (30mm) apart, to divide the strip into four pieces, each 1¼" (30mm) wide. Number the pieces from one to four and cut along the lines.

4. If needed, sand the cut edges between pieces one and two, and between pieces three and four so that the edges are smooth and square to the faces of the wood.

5. Glue two 3" (75mm) pieces of bloodwood and one 3" (75mm) piece of cherry between pieces one and two of shedua, using the same order as in Step 2 (shedua, bloodwood, cherry, bloodwood, shedua). Clamp and let dry. Repeat with pieces three and four of the shedua, using the remaining pieces of bloodwood and cherry.

6. Sand both faces of each piece until they are completely flat. For each piece, select one face to be the inside of the box. Draw intersecting guidelines down the centers of the strips on that face.

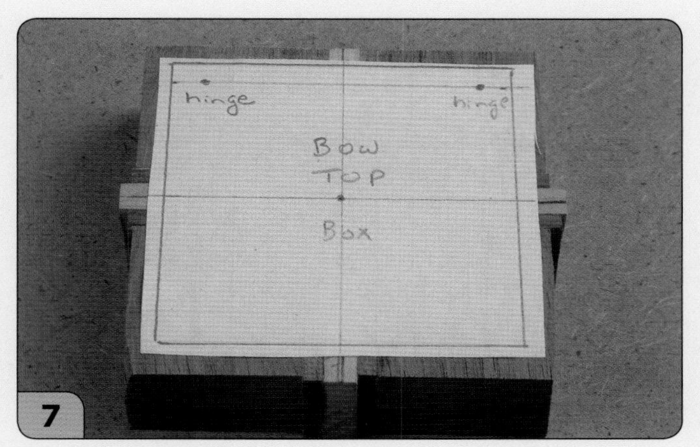

Marking the wood.

Gluing on the loops.

7. Using repositionable adhesive, attach the pattern to the marked face of each piece. Use the awl at the center point to align the guidelines on the pattern with those on the wood. Use the awl to mark the drill points for the center and the hinge holes.

8. Cut along the outline of each piece. Remove the patterns and discard.

9. Drill a ½" (13mm) or slightly deeper hole at the center point with the Forstner bit. Be sure the point of the Forstner bit does not come through the wood.

10. To insert the barrel hinges, follow the Steps 3–10 of Barrel Hinge Basics, page 88, using the 5mm brad point bit. Apply a coat of shellac to the drilled-out center spaces for a finished look.

11. Sand all sides of the box until they are even with each other. Sand with increasingly finer grits until the box is smooth. Soften all edges.

12. Glue together the 8" (205mm) bloodwood and cherry strips, sandwiching the cherry between the pieces of bloodwood. Sand the striped faces smooth.

13. To make the loops, use the strip glued up in Step 12 and the 5⁄16" (8mm) brad point bit. Follow the instructions on page 24 (Bow-Making Basics), Steps 1–6, to cut and sand six loops.

14. Place five of the loops in a circle on top of the box, best sides facing up. Sand the point of the sixth loop to increase its gluing surface and place it in the center of the circle. Glue the loops into place. Clean up any excess glue before it dries.

15. Finish the box with several coats of shellac or clear lacquer, rubbing down as needed with 0000 steel wool between coats.

16. Make a ring insert, using the 2½" x 1¾" x ½" (65 x 45 x 13mm) piece of foam core and the 1½" (40mm) insert pattern. Follow the instructions on page 93. The increased width of the foam core does not affect the instructions for the location of the slot. Place the insert into the recess in the bottom of the box, slot facing toward the back edge.

17. Use the insert pattern to cut a piece of velvet from the 2" (50mm) square of adhesive-backed velvet. Attach the circle to the recess in the box lid.

Bow Top Ring Box Pattern
Make 2 Copies at 100%

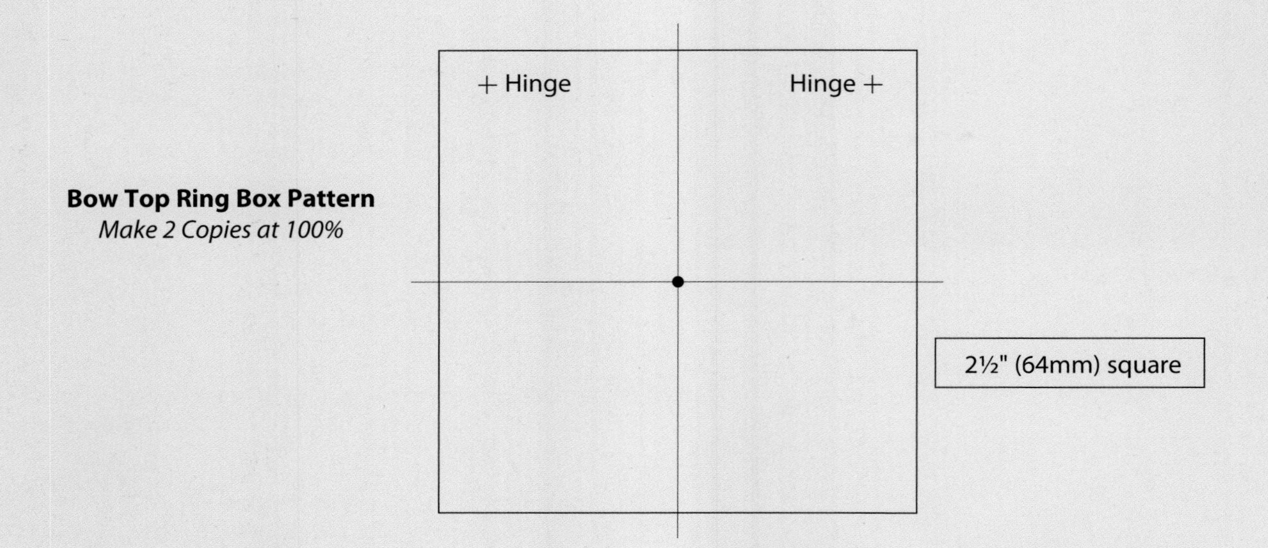

Foamcore Insert Pattern
Copy at 100%

Loop Pattern
Copy at 100%

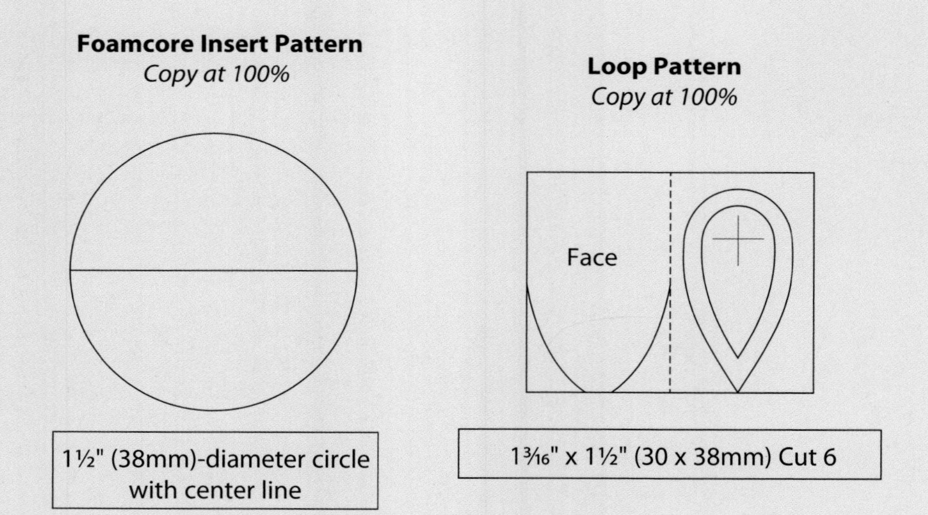

New Ribbons and Bows Box

The original Ribbons and Bows Box, my first published project, appeared in the Fall 2008 issue of *Scroll Saw Woodworking & Crafts*. For this book, I decided to give the box a new look with inlaid ribbons and stacked ring construction. If you are not familiar with the stacked ring technique, be sure to read Chapter One, and the step-by-step instructions for the Laminated Oval Box, pages 154–160 in Chapter Seven.

The project is fairly demanding, but sufficiently striking to justify the effort. Several points should be noted: First, when gluing up the blanks, be sure the strips form a continuous line and cross at right angles in the center. This will allow a near-perfect alignment of the rings, and create the illusion of a continuous ribbon. Second, when attaching the patterns to the blanks, make sure they are aligned precisely with the glued-in strips. And third, for reasons of access, rings are given a preliminary sanding on their inner faces before glue-up, rather than after.

Difficulty Rating:

Materials and Tools

Wood

- (2) 6½" x 6½" x ⅝" (165 x 165 x 16mm) cherry, preferably cut from a continuous piece of wood
- (1) 9⅝" x 4" x ½" (245 x 100 x 13mm) purpleheart
- (2) 9⅝" x 4" (245 x 102mm) light-colored veneer, such as ash or maple
- (1) 4" x 4" x ¼" (100 x 100 x 6mm) cherry for lid liner

Materials

- Repositionable adhesive
- Glue (Weldbond recommended)
- Blue painter's tape
- Sanding sleeves for inflatable round sander, assorted grits from 80 to 320
- Sanding discs for 2" (50mm) hook-and-loop pad sander, assorted grits from 60 to 320
- Sandpaper for hand sanding, assorted grits
- 0000 steel wool
- Shellac
- Clear spray lacquer

Tools

- #9 scroll saw blade
- 1⁄16" (2mm) or #54 drill bit for entry holes
- ⅜" (10mm) brad point drill bit for loops
- Awl
- Ruler
- 28° shop-made angle guide (page 18)
- 35° shop-made angle guide
- 40° shop-made angle guide
- Clamps for gluing up the blank and attaching the lid liner
- Press or clamps for gluing up the lamination and rings
- Inflatable round sander and pump
- 2" (50mm) hook-and-loop pad sander
- ¾" (19mm) sanding drum for drill press (optional)

1. Glue one piece of veneer to each side of the purpleheart. Clamp and let dry. Following the cutting diagram (page 49), cut four strips measuring 6½" x 11/16" (165 x 17mm). The remainder will be used for the loops and tails.

2. Mark the top edges of each piece of 6½" (165mm) cherry. Label one piece "top set" and the other "bottom set." Cut each piece in half, lengthwise, marking the wood clearly so you can reassemble the pieces in the same order. Sand each cut edge until smooth and square.

3. Glue one laminated strip, purpleheart side up, between the two halves of each piece. Clamp and let dry.

4. Cut each blank in half, crosswise. Sand the cut edges smooth. Glue a second strip between the two halves of each piece, keeping the pieces of the first strip aligned. Clamp and let dry.

5. Sand each blank smooth. The final thickness should be 5/8" (16mm).

6. Using repositionable adhesive, attach one copy of the pattern to each glued-up blank. Use the awl to center the pattern on the strips. Be sure the cross lines on the pattern are aligned with the centers of the strips.

7. Tilt the saw table to 28°, left side down. Using the blank for the top set, cut along the perimeter of the pattern in a clockwise direction.

8. Mark the entry hole with an awl where indicated on the pattern. Using an angle guide or drill press with a tilting table, drill a hole at a 35° angle, drilling toward the center of the blank. Tilt the saw table to 35°, left side down. Insert the blade into the entry hole and cut along the line, clockwise, to complete the first ring of the top set. Remove the pattern.

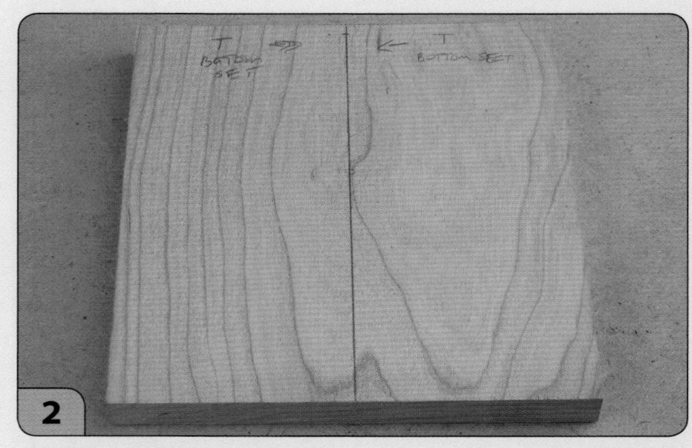
2

Making the first cut.

4

Gluing in the second strip.

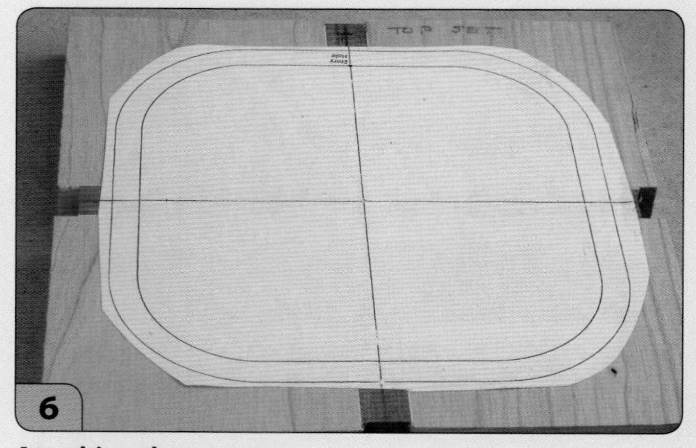
6

Attaching the pattern.

Variation

This variation was cut out of walnut. The darker wood really sets off the colors in the ribbon and bow.

12
Re-cutting the blank.

14
Cutting the bottom of the box.

15
Sanding the first rings.

9. Place the ring on the remainder of the blank, keeping the tops aligned, and trace the inner edge of the ring to form the cutting line for the second ring.

10. Drill a 40° entry hole on the cutting line, toward the center of the blank. Tilt the saw table to 40°, left side down. Insert the blade and cut along the line, cutting clockwise. This completes the second ring of the top set. The remaining piece will be used for the lid in Step 23.

11. Repeat Step 7 with the blank for the bottom set. Drill a 28° entry hole where indicated on the pattern, insert the blade, and cut on the inner line with the saw table tilted to a 28° angle, left side down. This completes the first ring of the bottom set. Remove the pattern. Place the ring on the blank, aligning the tops, and trace the inner edge to form the cutting line for the second ring of the bottom set.

12. Tilt the saw table to 35°, left side down. Using the top edge of the blank as a guide, re-cut the perimeter of the blank at a 35° angle, cutting clockwise.

13. To cut the second ring of the bottom set, drill a 35° entry hole on the cutting line, drilling toward the center of the blank. Insert the blade into the entry hole and cut along the line at 35°, cutting clockwise.

14. Place the second ring of the bottom set on the remainder of the blank and trace the outside of the ring on the blank. Tilt the saw table to 40°, left side down, and cut along this line. This piece is the bottom of the box.

15. Sand the inner faces of the first ring from each set to remove blade and drill marks. Be careful not to remove too much wood from the gluing surfaces.

16. Glue the two rings together at their top surfaces, making sure the strips on all four sides match where they meet. Clamp the rings and let them dry. Sand off dried glue from the inside of the rings.

17. Sand the inside of the second ring of the bottom set to remove blade and drill marks. Glue it to the first ring of the bottom set, keeping the strips matched on all four sides. Clamp and let dry.

18. Sand the inside of the first and second bottom rings where they join to remove irregularities and dried glue. Be sure the lower edge of the second ring is smooth on the inner face, since it cannot be sanded after it is glued to the base. Be sure not to remove too much wood from the gluing surface.

19. Sand the inside of the second ring from the top set until smooth. Sand the smaller edge with the ¾" (20mm) drum to soften the edge. This is the opening of the box. If you do not have a small drum, you can use the inflatable round sander and increase the curve at the corners slightly, or you can sand by hand.

20. Place the second ring of the top set, smaller opening down, on the ¼" (6mm) piece of cherry. Trace the inside edge. Cut along this line with the saw table level. This is the lid liner. Set it aside until Step 25.

21. Glue the second ring of the top set to the first ring of the top set, keeping strips matched on all four sides. Clamp and let dry. Sand the inside of the second top ring smooth where it joins the first top ring.

22. Glue the base to the second bottom ring, keeping the strips matched. When dry, sand and shape the outside of the box, rounding the seam where the two blanks join. Leave a flat area around the opening to support the lid.

Sanding the glued-up rings.

Shaping the second top ring.

Gluing on the base and sanding the outside of the box.

Thinning the lid.

Completing the bow.

23. Take the remainder of the blank saved from Step 10 and draw a line around this piece that is 1⁄16" (2mm) from the smaller face. Sand to this line to thin the piece. This will give a better proportion for the lid.

24. Contour the sides of the lid, shaping it to fit on the box. Keep the top flat for gluing on the tails and loops.

25. Place the lid liner on the underside of the lid. Invert the box on the lid to position the liner properly. Glue the liner to the lid, clamp, and let dry.

26. Mask the area of the lid where the loops and tails will be glued. Apply shellac to all box surfaces to seal the wood and reveal glue spots. Sand away glue spots. Apply several coats of clear lacquer, rubbing with 0000 steel wool between coats as needed. Remove the blue tape.

27. Cut a strip 2¼" x 1" (60 x 25mm) from the laminated piece, as indicated on the cutting diagram. Follow Steps 7–10 of Bow-Making Basics, page 25, to make the tails.

28. Cut two strips from the laminated piece, one 9" x ⅞" (230 x 22mm) and the other 3" x ⅞" (75 x 22mm), as indicated on the cutting diagram. Follow Steps 1–6 of Bow-Making Basics, page 24, using the ⅜" (10mm) brad point bit, to cut and sand eight loops.

29. Place the tails at the intersection of the ribbon (see Step 24, page 30). To adjust their angle, sand the underside at the tip end of the tail. Flatten the top of the tips, if needed, for ease in placing the loops. Glue the tails in place, supporting the ends until the glue dries, if necessary.

30. Glue one loop between each set of tails. Glue the remaining four loops into place, spacing them evenly and supporting them as needed. Clean off excess glue. When dry, spray the loops and tails with several coats of clear lacquer.

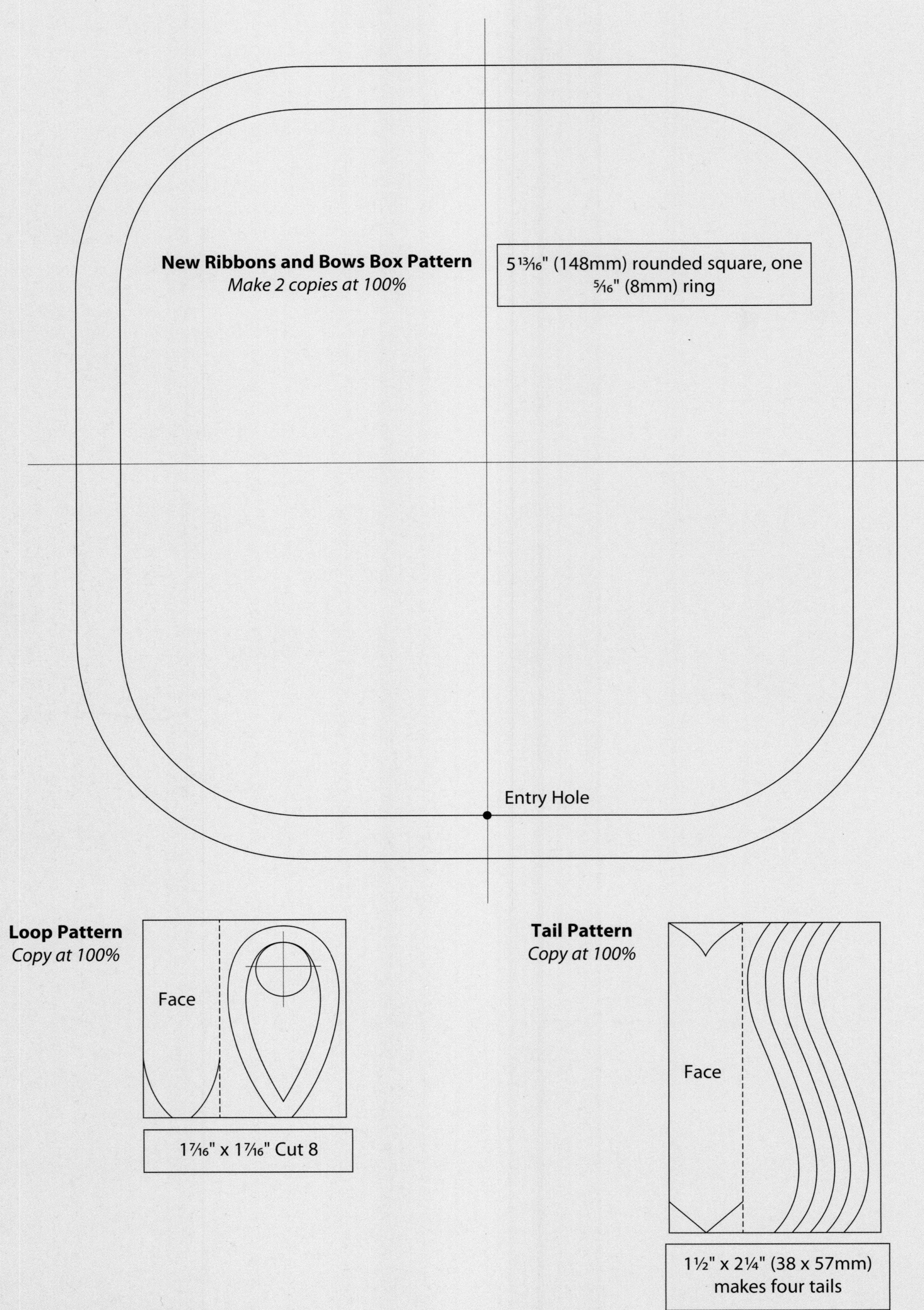
New Ribbons and Bows Box Pattern
Make 2 copies at 100%
5 13⁄16" (148mm) rounded square, one 5⁄16" (8mm) ring
Entry Hole
Loop Pattern
Copy at 100%
Face
1 7⁄16" x 1 7⁄16" Cut 8
Tail Pattern
Copy at 100%
Face
1½" x 2¼" (38 x 57mm) makes four tails

Ribbon Cutting Diagram

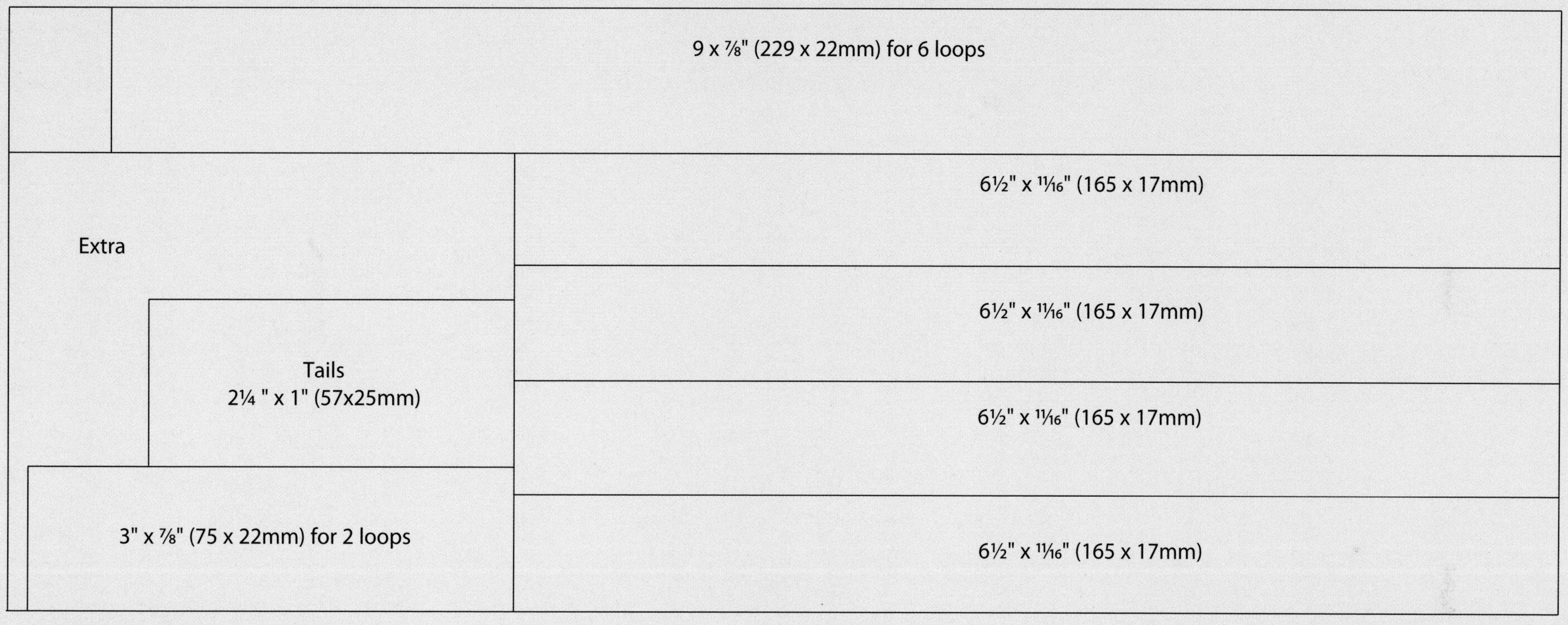

9 x ⅞" (229 x 22mm) for 6 loops

Extra

6½" x 1⅟₁₆" (165 x 17mm)

6½" x 1⅟₁₆" (165 x 17mm)

Tails
2¼ " x 1" (57x25mm)

6½" x 1⅟₁₆" (165 x 17mm)

3" x ⅞" (75 x 22mm) for 2 loops

6½" x 1⅟₁₆" (165 x 17mm)

Note: This diagram is a cutting guide, but is not meant to be used as a pattern. Cut the pieces as directed in the steps.

Fun with Food

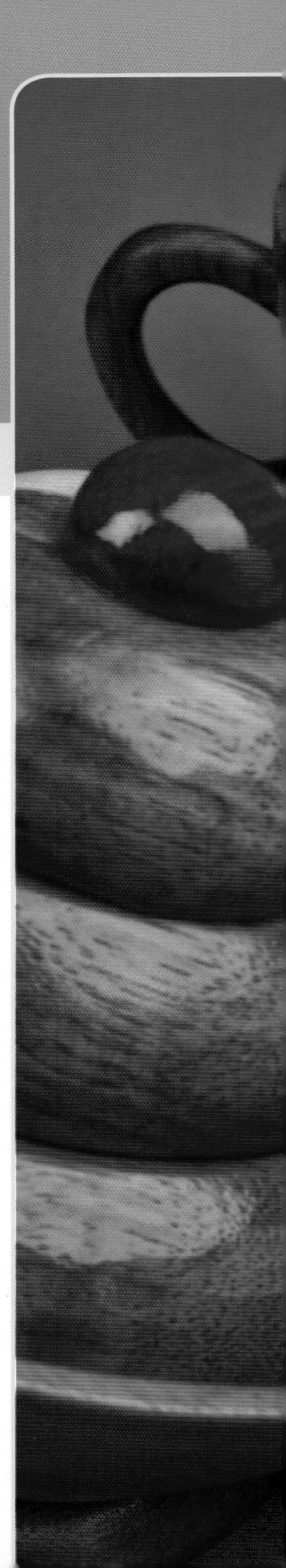

This chapter gives new meaning to "playing with your food." Challenged by my editor to create a box that looked like a cupcake, I designed one that could pass for the real thing, right down to the sprinkles. One cupcake looked lonely, so I added two more in different "flavors" and gave them a footed stand. That stand, with its "pie crust" edging, inspired the Apple Tart Box; each project, in turn, gave rise to the next, until I had a chapter full of boxes that looked good enough to eat.

Apple Tart Box: A Step-by-Step Guide

Difficulty Rating:

Cherry and aspen were the "ingredients" for this apple tart box. The "crust," made from a fluted rim and six-segment base, looks realistic and provides support for the decorative lid. Once your crust is "baked," top it with "apples" and slices of real cinnamon bark for a project that smells as good as it looks.

Materials and Tools

Wood

- (1) 8½" x 8½" x ¾" (215 x 215 x 19mm) cherry for ripple edge
- (1) 7" x 7" x ⅞" (180 x 180 x 22mm) cherry for box body
- (1) 6½" x 6½" x ¼" (165 x 165 x 6mm) cherry for box bottom
- (1) 7" x 7" x ¼" (180 x 180 x 6mm) plywood for lid
- (4) 9" x 1¼" x ½" (230 x 30 x 13mm) aspen for "apple slices"
- (1) Cinnamon stick, about 3" (75mm) long, with an attractive pattern on its end

Materials

- Repositionable adhesive
- Glue (Weldbond recommended)
- Clear packing tape (optional)
- Sleeves for inflatable round sander, various grits from 80 to 320
- Discs for 2" (50mm) hook-and-loop pad sander, various grits from 60 to 320
- Sandpaper for hand sanding, assorted grits
- 0000 steel wool
- 3" (75mm) square of thin cardboard for "apple slices" pattern
- Spray shellac
- Clear spray lacquer

Tools

- #9 scroll saw blade for thick wood
- #3 scroll saw blade for thin wood
- ¹⁄₁₆" (2mm) drill bit for ripple edge entry hole
- ⅛" (3mm) or larger drill bit for box body entry hole
- Awl
- Compass
- 25° shop-made angle guide (see page 18)
- Press or clamps for gluing
- Clamps and blocks for cutting "apple slices" (optional)
- Inflatable round sander and pump
- 2" (50mm) hook-and-loop pad sander

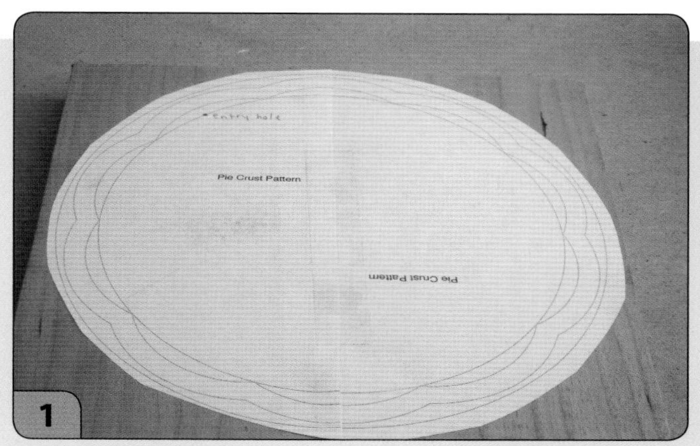

Attaching the pattern. Make two copies of the crust pattern and tape them together to form a circle. Using repositionable adhesive, attach the taped pattern to the 8½" (216mm) piece of cherry. Cover with clear packing tape, if desired, to prevent the wood from burning.

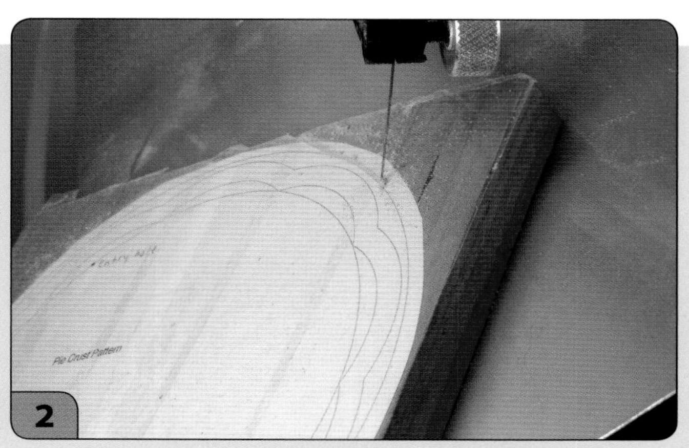

Cutting the outer circle. Tilt the saw table to 40°, left side down. Cut along the outer circle, in a clockwise direction.

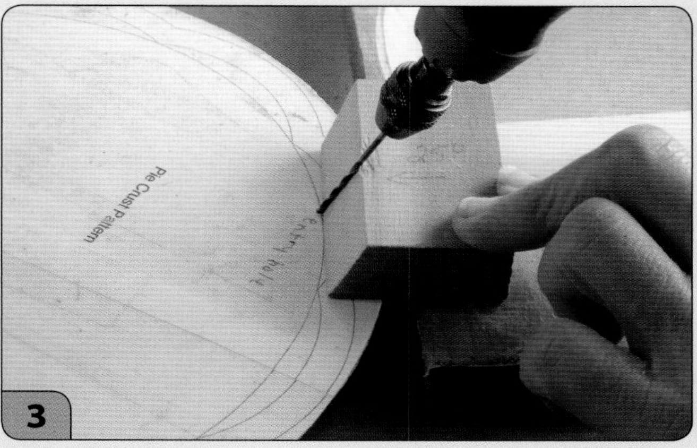

Drilling the entry hole. Use an awl to mark the entry hole where indicated on the pattern. Using a 25° angle guide or a drill press with a tilting table, drill a 25° entry hole with the 1⁄16" (2mm) drill bit, facing the center of the pattern.

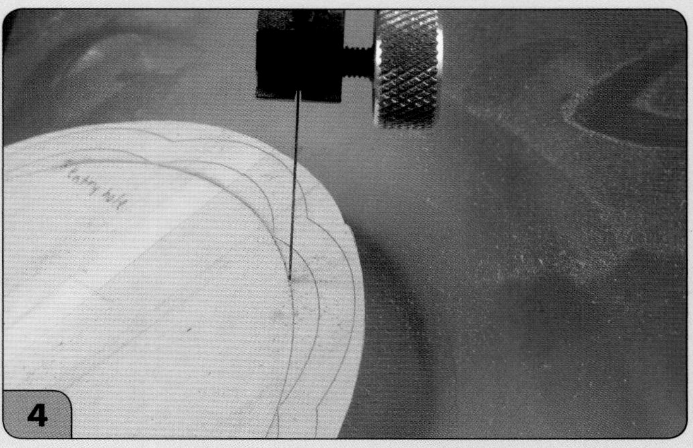

Completing the ring. Tilt the saw table to 25°, left side down. Insert the blade into the entry hole and cut clockwise around the circle to complete the ring. The ring will be about ¼" (6mm) wide at its lower edge. Save the remainder of the blank for another project.

Cutting the outside of the ripple. Tilt the saw table to 15°, left side down. Cut clockwise along the outside of the ripple. This is the preliminary shaping for the outer edge.

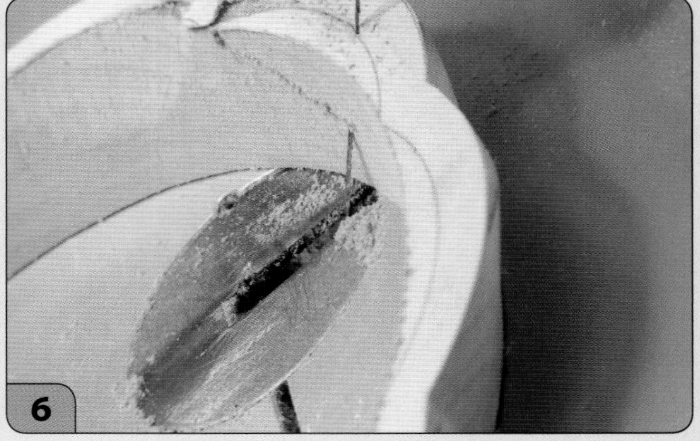

Cutting the inside of the ripple. Tilt the saw table to 45°, left side down. Cut along the inside of the ripple. Be careful not to cut into the lower edge. This is the preliminary shaping for the inside of the ripple.

7

Shaping the outside edge of the ripple. Use the hook-and-loop pad sander with a coarse grit to shape and smooth the outside of the ripple.

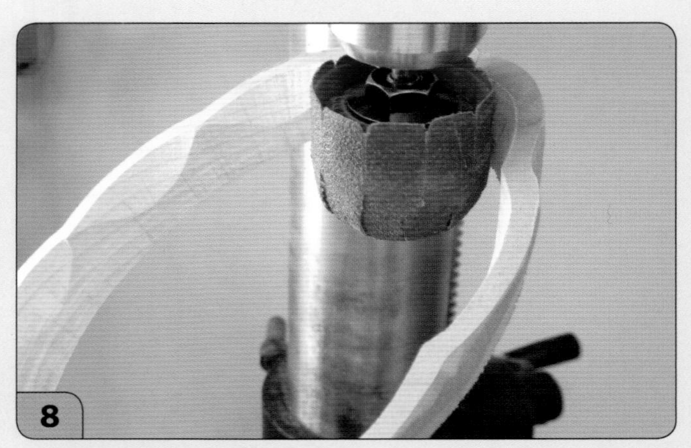

8

Shaping the inside edge of the ripple. Use the inflatable ball sander with a coarse grit to shape the inside of the ripple until the curves are smooth.

9

Completing the sanding. Using both sanders, sand with increasingly finer grits until the rim is well-shaped and smooth. Soften the upper edges.

10

Rounding over the edges. Round over the underside of the lower outer edge.

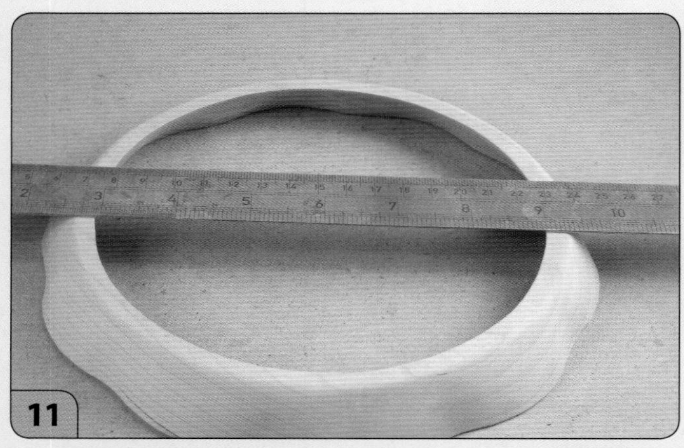

11

Measuring the diameter for the lid. Measure and record the diameter of the opening at the lower edge. It should be about 6" (150mm). You'll need this measurement for making the lid in Step 19.

12

Cutting the outside box body. Using repositionable adhesive, attach the box body pattern to the ⅞" (22mm)-thick piece of cherry. Drill a straight entry hole near a corner in each segment with the ⅛" (3mm) drill bit. Tilt the saw table to 15°, left side down, and cut clockwise around the outer circle.

13

Cutting out the segments. With the saw table level, insert the blade and cut out each segment. Sand the inside of the segments until they are smooth. Soften the upper edges. Do not sand the outside at this time.

14

Drawing the cutting line for the box bottom. Keeping the grain running in the same direction, place the box body on the piece of ¼" (6mm) cherry. Trace the lower edge. This is the cutting line for the box bottom.

15

Cutting and gluing on the box bottom. Tilt the saw table to 15°, left side down. Cut clockwise on the cutting line for the box bottom. Sand the upper surface smooth. Glue the bottom to the box body. Clamp and let dry.

Clamp Placement

Because there will be a lot of glue squeeze-out, it's a good idea to arrange the clamps so you can clean up the glue without removing the clamps.

16

Sanding the box body. Sand the outside of the box body smooth. Round the lower edge.

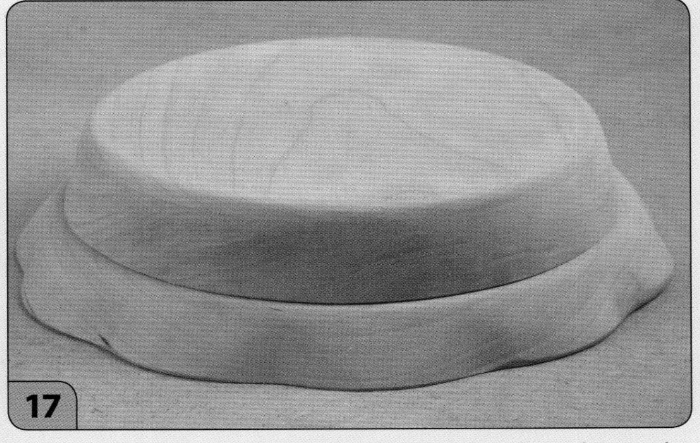

17

Gluing the ripple edge to the box body. Place the ripple edge on the box body. Invert the pieces so you can align them more easily, and glue them together. Clamp for five minutes. Remove clamps and clean off any glue squeeze-out. Re-clamp and let dry.

18

Applying the finish. Apply a coat of shellac to the entire box to seal the wood and reveal glue spots. Sand away any glue spots and sand the box until smooth. Apply several coats of shellac or clear lacquer, rubbing down with 0000 steel wool between coats as needed.

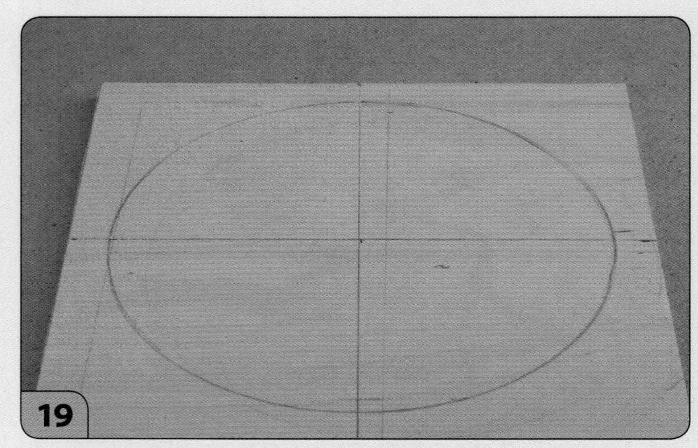

Drawing the cutting line for the lid. Draw a 6" (150mm) circle on the piece of ¼" (6mm) plywood. If the diameter you measured in Step 11 is different, use that figure instead.

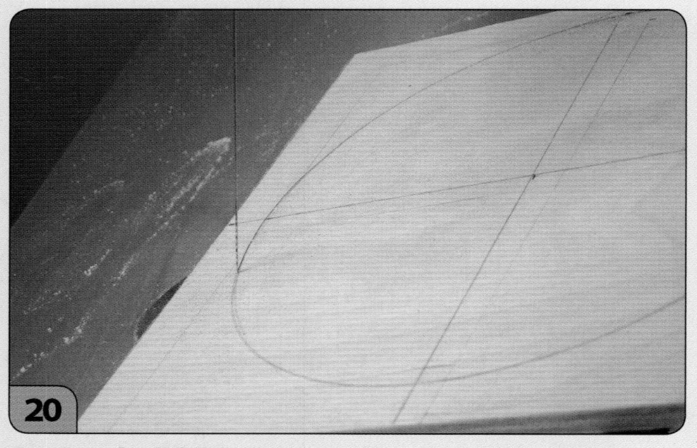

Cutting the lid. Tilt the saw table to 25°, left side down. Cut along the circle in a **counterclockwise** direction. This will give you a circle that is wider at the bottom than at the top. The wider face will be the top of the lid. Sand the edges and faces smooth.

Marking the strips for the "apple" slices. Place one piece of aspen on its ½" (13mm) edge. Draw a line ⅛" (2mm) from one of the longer edges. This is the cutting line for the strips that will be used for the apple slices.

Cutting the strips. Tilt the saw table to 10°, left side down. Cut along the line drawn in Step 21, using blocks and clamps if desired. Keep the wood flat on the saw table and the marked line on your right.

Sanding the strips. You will have two angled strips about the same size. Sand the faces of the strips until smooth. Repeat Steps 21 and 22 with the remaining three pieces of aspen.

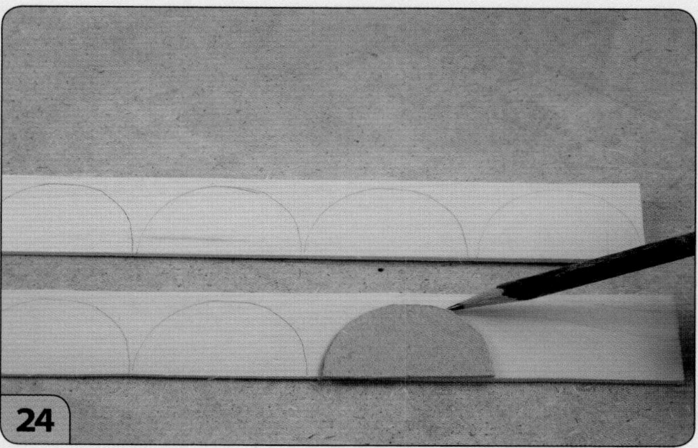

Drawing the "apple" slices. Make a cardboard copy of the apple slice pattern. Use this pattern to draw four half circles on each piece. For thin slices, place the flat side of the pattern on the thinner edge of the strip. For thicker slices, place the pattern higher up on the strip.

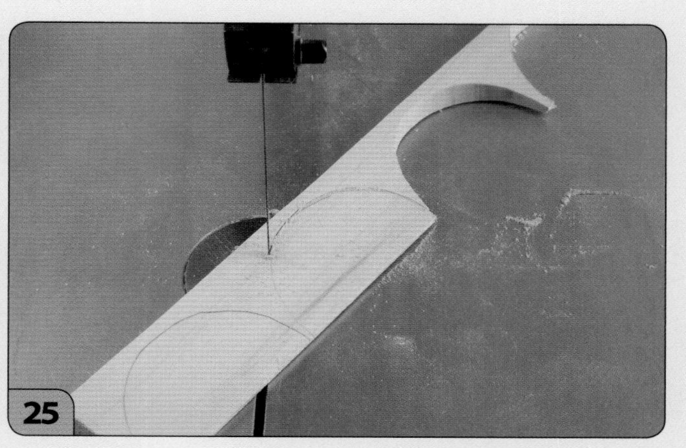

Cutting the slices. With the saw table level, use the #3 blade to cut out the slices. Sand the edges smooth and remove all "fuzzies."

Gluing the slices around the lid. Place the piece of plywood cut in Step 20 on the box body to help position the slices. Overlap the slices along the perimeter, rotating them to cover the edge of the plywood. When you are satisfied with your arrangement, glue the slices into place.

Gluing the center slices. Glue on the remaining slices, placed on edge, to fill the center of the lid. Sand to fit if necessary. You may have some slices left over.

Applying the finish. Remove the lid when the slices are completely dry. Finish with a coat of spray shellac or clear lacquer. Glue slices cut from a cinnamon stick, if desired.

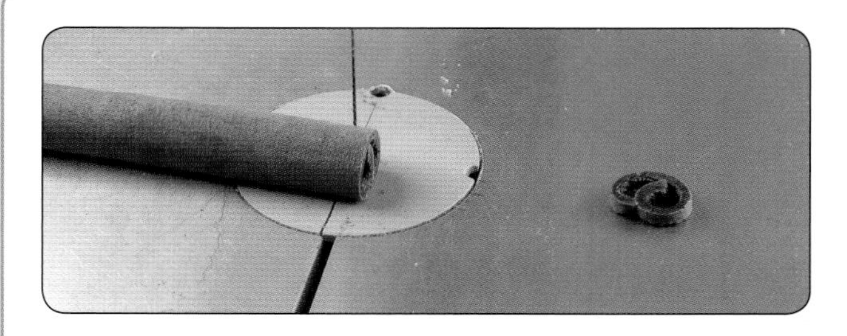

Cinnamon Apple Pie

To create a pie that smells as good as it looks, cut thin slices from a stick of cinnamon with an attractive pattern on its end, and glue them to the apple slices after finishing. You may need to make a zero clearance insert (see page 65, Cupcake Box) to prevent the slices from falling through the opening in the saw table.

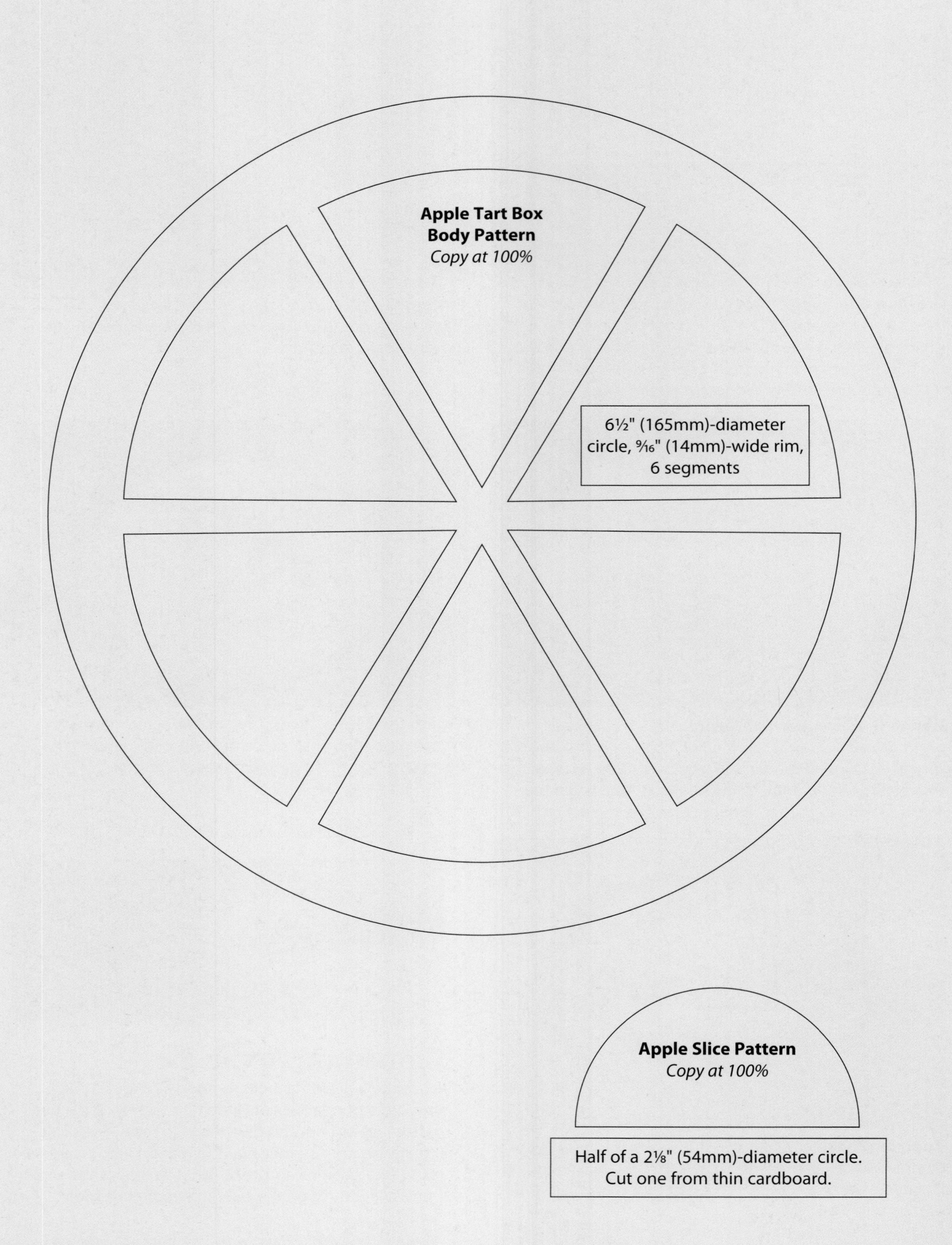
Apple Tart Box
Body Pattern
Copy at 100%
6½" (165mm)-diameter circle, 9⁄16" (14mm)-wide rim, 6 segments
Apple Slice Pattern
Copy at 100%
Half of a 2⅛" (54mm)-diameter circle. Cut one from thin cardboard.

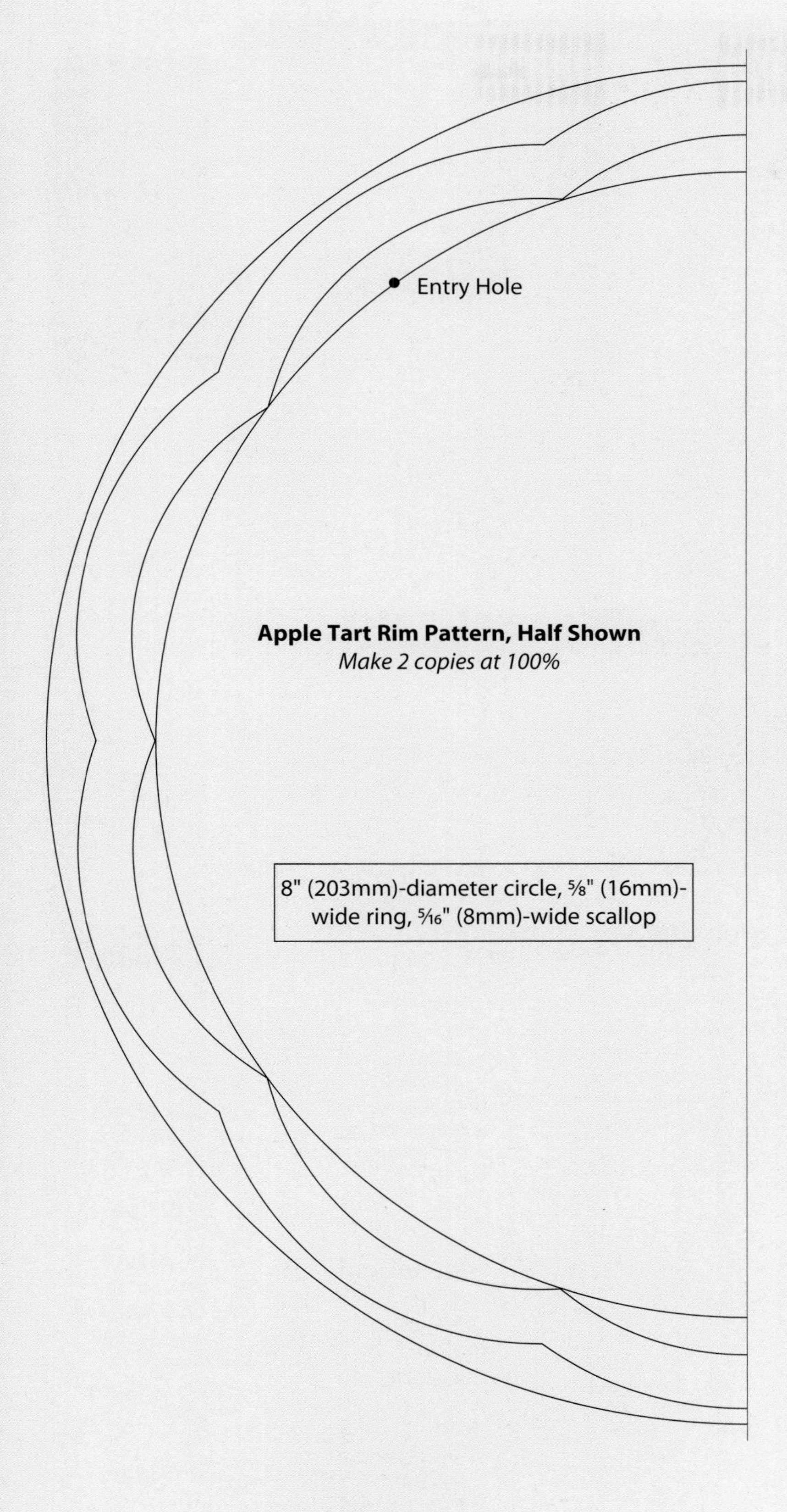
Entry Hole
Apple Tart Rim Pattern, Half Shown
Make 2 copies at 100%
8" (203mm)-diameter circle, ⅝" (16mm)-wide ring, 5⁄16" (8mm)-wide scallop

Coffee Cup Box

Difficulty Rating:

In my search for new ideas, I came across numerous versions of the "coffee cup" box. Most were lathe-turned or required use of a router. Unable to resist a challenge, I set out to create a coffee cup box that could be made with the scroll saw alone. Stacked rings, cut at a steep angle, were a natural for the basic shape, and for the inner rim, as well. If you're not familiar with this technique, see Chapter One for basic information, and the Apple Tart Box, page 52, for illustrated instructions.

I added two handles to the basic shape—one for the cup and one for the box lid—and an easy-to-make saucer. For a different look, you can replace the "steam" with a few rings of "cupcake icing" (page 63) for cocoa with "whipped cream."

Materials and Tools

Wood

- (1) 4½" x 4½" x ¾" (115 x 115 x 19mm) mahogany for cup
- (2) 4½" x 4½" x ¼" (115 x 115 x 6mm) mahogany for cup and saucer
- (1) 4½" x 4½" x ⅛" (115 x 115 x 3mm) bloodwood for cup
- (2) 4½" (115mm) squares of light-colored veneer for cup
- (1) 3" x 3" x ¼" (75 x 75 x 6mm) walnut for handle
- (1) 4" x 4" x ⅛" (100 x 100 x 3mm) walnut for lid
- (1) 4" x 2" x ¼" (100 x 50 x 13mm) aspen for "steam"

Materials

- Repositionable adhesive
- Glue (Weldbond recommended)
- Sanding discs for 2" (50mm) hook-and-loop pad sander, assorted grits 80 to 320
- Sanding sleeves for inflatable round sander, assorted grits 80 to 320
- Sandpaper for hand sanding, assorted grits
- 0000 steel wool
- Shellac
- Clear spray lacquer

Tools

- #3 scroll saw blade for thin wood
- #9 scroll saw blade for thick wood
- #54 or 1⁄16" (2mm) drill bit
- Awl
- Compass
- Ruler
- 15° shop-made angle guide (see page 18)
- 28° shop-made angle guide
- 35° shop-made angle guide
- 45° shop-made angle guide
- Press or clamps for gluing
- 2" (50mm) hook-and-loop pad sander
- Inflatable round sander and pump

7

Drawing the second ring.

11

Thinning the base.

1. Glue together one piece of ¼" (6mm)-thick mahogany, one piece of veneer, the piece of bloodwood, and the second piece of veneer. Clamp and let dry.
2. To make the top ring, attach the cup pattern to the mahogany side of the glued-up wood, using repositionable adhesive. Tilt the saw table to 15°, left side down. Cut along the outer circle in a clockwise direction.
3. Mark the entry hole with an awl. Using an angle guide or a drill press with a tilting table, drill a 15° entry hole, facing the center of the circle.
4. With the saw table at a 15° angle, left side down, insert the saw blade and cut along the inner circle in a clockwise direction to complete the top ring.
5. Sand the inside of the top ring just until smooth. Sand off any fuzzies on the bottom edge.
6. Place the top ring on the piece of ⅛" (3mm)-thick walnut and trace the inner diameter. Tilt the saw table to 15°, left side down, and cut around the circle in a **counterclockwise** direction. This is the lid. The wider face is the upper surface of the lid. Set it aside until Step 18.
7. Place the top ring on the piece of ¾" (19mm) mahogany. Be sure that the grain of both pieces runs in the same direction. Trace the outside circle. Remove the ring and draw an inner circle that is ¾" (19mm) smaller in diameter than the outside circle. This will create a ring that is ⅜" (10mm) wide. This wider ring, when glued to the top ring, will form a lip to support the cup lid.
8. Tilt the saw table to 28°, left side down. Using the #9 blade, cut along the outer circle drawn in Step 7, cutting in a clockwise direction.
9. Drill an entry hole on the inner circle at a 28° angle, facing the center of the circle. With saw table tilted at 28°, left side down, insert the saw blade and cut along the circle in a clockwise direction to complete the second ring.
10. Place the second ring on the remainder of the blank and trace the inside edge. This is the cutting line for the third ring. Drill a 35° entry hole on this line, facing the center of the circle. Tilt the saw table to 35°, left side down. Insert the saw blade and cut along this circle in a clockwise direction to make the third ring.
11. Draw a line on the side of the remainder of the blank that encircles the blank and is ¼" (6mm) from the upper face. Sand the smaller face of this piece evenly until the piece is about ¼" (6mm) thick. This is the base of the cup, and has been thinned for better proportion.
12. Sand the inside of the second and third rings lightly to remove drill marks. It is easier to do this before gluing up the rings.
13. Glue the top ring, second ring, and third ring together, keeping the grain running in the same direction. Clamp and let dry.
14. Sand the inside of the glued-up rings to remove excess glue and to smooth the seam between the second and third rings. Be careful not to sand away the lid support.
15. Glue on the base, clamp and let dry. Shape the outside of the cup, contouring the bottom and flaring the top ring in an outward direction. Sand until smooth.

16. Attach the cup handle pattern to the piece of ¼" (6mm) walnut using repositionable adhesive. Cut out the handle, shape it, and sand it smooth. Contour the ends of the handle, if necessary, to match the sides of the cup. Invert the cup and glue the handle into place. Remove excess glue before it dries.

17. Attach the "steam" pattern to the piece of aspen using repositionable adhesive. Cut along the lines, shape it, and sand it smooth.

18. Place the lid cut in Step 6 on the rim and sand to fit as needed. Glue the "steam" to the lid.

19. To make the saucer, attach the saucer pattern to the remaining piece of ¼" (6mm) thick mahogany. Cut along the outer circle at a 45° angle, saw table tilted left side down, cutting clockwise.

20. Drill a 45° entry hole on the inner circle, facing the center of the circle. Tilt the saw table to 45°, left side down. Insert the saw blade and cut along the circle in a clockwise direction. Sand the inside of the ring smooth.

21. Glue the ring to the remainder of the blank. Clamp and let dry. Shape the outside and sand the saucer until it is smooth.

Gluing on the cup handle.

22. Apply a coat of shellac to the box, lid, and saucer, to seal the wood and reveal any glue spots. Remove glue spots and sand smooth. Apply additional coats of shellac or lacquer and rub down with 0000 steel wool between coats, as needed.

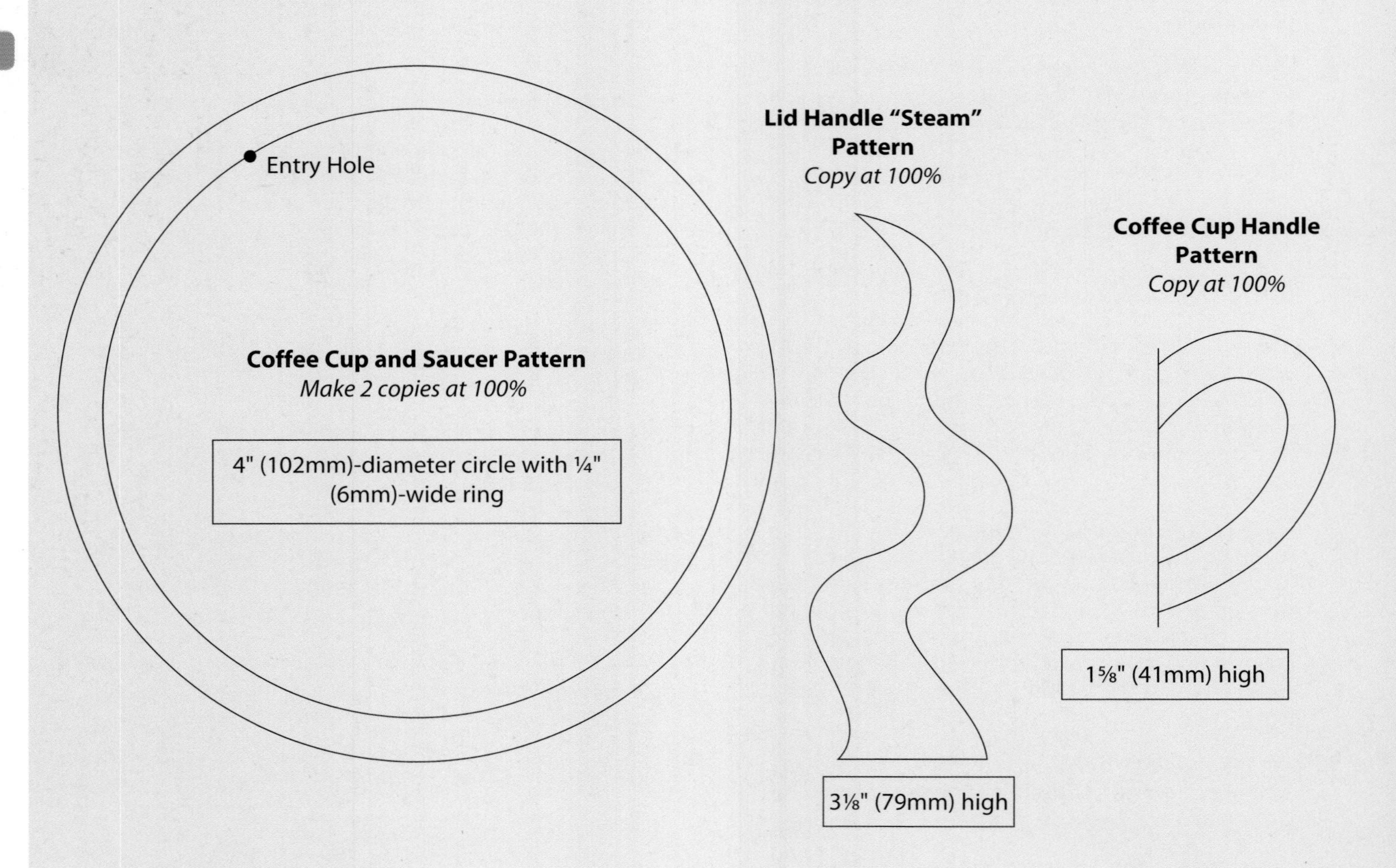

Cupcake Box

Difficulty Rating:

Everyone loves cupcakes, and these cute little boxes look just like the real thing. Standard tools, used in new ways, and techniques borrowed from other crafts, result in a box that is dramatic, different, and fun to make. I used aspen, walnut, and canarywood for vanilla, chocolate, and butterscotch "icing," topped by yellowheart, bloodwood, maple, and walnut "sprinkles."

A trio of cupcakes on a footed stand (see page 67) make a dramatic presentation, but each box, by itself, is a delicious little gift.

Materials and Tools

Wood

For each cupcake, you will need:

- (1) 3½" x 3½" x 1⅜" (90 x 90 x 35mm) mahogany for base
- (1) 4" x 4" x ½" (100 x 100 x 13mm) wood of choice for icing
- (1) 3½" x 3½" x ½" (90 x 90 x 13mm) wood of choice for icing
- (1) 3" x 3" x ½" (75 x 75 x 13mm) wood of choice for icing
- (1) 3" x 3" x ⅛" (75 x 75 x 3mm) wood for lid liner
- Small pieces of colorful ⅛" (3mm) wood for sprinkles

Materials

- Repositionable spray adhesive
- Glue (Weldbond recommended)
- Sandpaper for sanders of choice, assorted grits
- Sandpaper for hand sanding, assorted grits
- Playing card for zero clearance insert (optional)
- 1½" (40mm) circle of adhesive-backed velvet (actual size needed)
- Shellac
- Clear spray lacquer

Tools

- #12 scroll saw blade for the base
- #7 *spiral* scroll saw blade for the base
- #5 scroll saw blade for the circles
- #2/0 scroll saw blade for the sprinkles
- 2" (50mm) Forstner bit
- 1½" (40mm) Forstner bit
- 1⁄16" (2mm) bit for lid circles
- Awl
- Compass
- Clamps
- Sanders of choice (belt or disc sander recommended for the rings)

Helpful Cupcake Hints

Choose wood with color variations for interesting "icing."

Avoid padauk for sprinkles; the color will bleed.

To make multiple bases quickly, drill the holes (Steps 1 and 2) on a single strip of wood, then cut into individual 3½" (89mm) pieces.

Drilling the first hole.

1. Using an awl, mark the center point on the square of mahogany. Clamping the wood securely, drill a hole ⅛" (3mm) deep at that point with a 2" (50mm) Forstner bit. Be sure the depth is correct or the lid will not sit properly.
2. Using the same center point, drill the hole an additional ¾" (19mm) with a 1½" (40mm) Forstner bit. The total depth of the hole will be ⅞" (22mm).
3. Using repositionable adhesive, attach the base pattern to the piece of mahogany, lining up the pattern with the hole drilled in Step 1. Cut along the outer line of the pattern with the saw table tilted 20°, left side down, cutting clockwise. Sand the outside of the base smooth.

Cutting out the base.

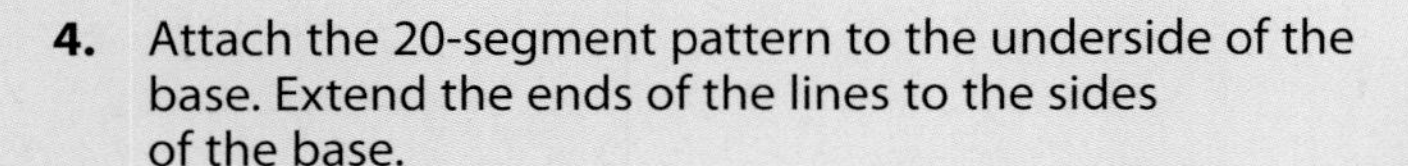

4. Attach the 20-segment pattern to the underside of the base. Extend the ends of the lines to the sides of the base.
5. Tilt the saw table to 20°, left side down. The indentations are cut with the #7 spiral blade, in one continuous motion that consists of three parts. First, place the base against the blade, to the right of the blade, aligned with one of the pencil marks, and push it gently into the blade to create an indentation. Second, push the base away from you slightly, toward the back of the scroll saw, to widen the indentation. Third, pull it to the right and away from the blade. Follow this procedure at each pencil mark until twenty indentations are made.

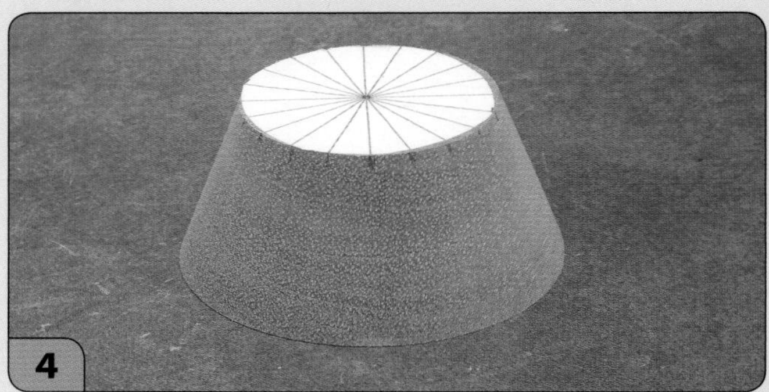

Marking the base.

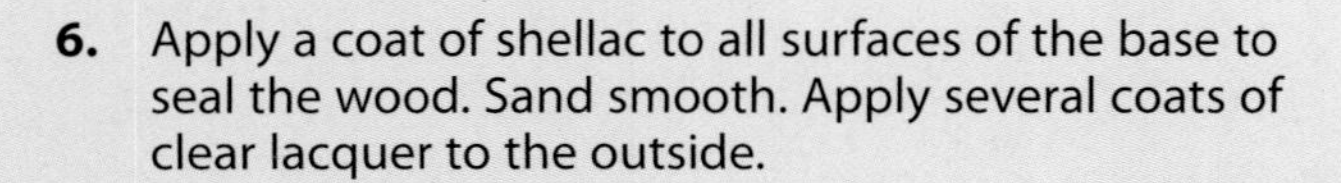

6. Apply a coat of shellac to all surfaces of the base to seal the wood. Sand smooth. Apply several coats of clear lacquer to the outside.
7. Attach the 1½" (38mm) circle of adhesive-backed velvet to the bottom of the hole to hide the drill mark.
8. Attach the lid patterns to the three pieces of wood for the icing, using repositionable adhesive. Cut along the outer circles for all three pieces. For pieces #2 and #3, drill an entry hole on the inner circles. Insert the saw blade and cut out the small circles. You will have five circles measuring 3¼" (85mm), 2¾" (70mm), 2¼" (60mm), 1¾" (45mm), and 1¼" (30mm) in diameter. Sand the circumference of each circle smooth.

Cutting the indentations in the base.

Marking the bevel.

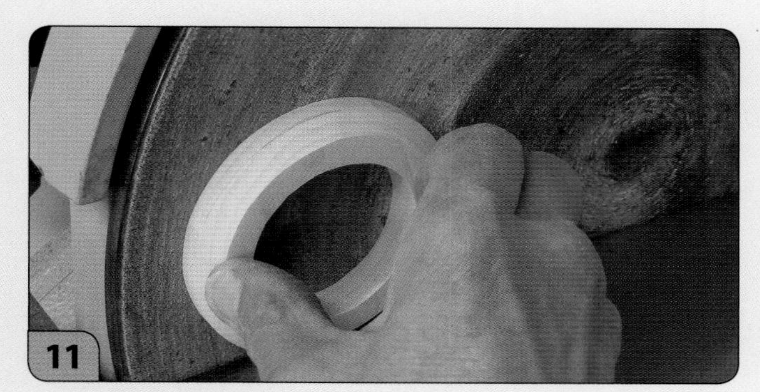
Sanding in the tilt.

Stacking the rings.

Completing the sprinkles.

9. Mark the side of each circle 3⁄16" (5mm) from the top edge.

10. Sand a 45° bevel on the top edge of each circle. The bevel should extend to the line drawn in Step 9.

11. Mark a point on each of the four smaller circles that is 1⁄8" (3mm) up from the bottom edge. Press each ring flat against a belt or disc sander, putting all pressure on the marked side until about 1⁄8" (3mm) of wood has been removed from that side. The result will be a ring that is flat on the bottom and higher on one side than the other by about 1⁄8" (3mm).

12. Stack the rings so the higher side alternates from one ring to the next. Check to be sure each ring sits flat against the one beneath. Adjust the bottoms by sanding, if necessary.

13. Sand the rings until they are smooth and the edges are rounded.

14. Draw a 2" (50mm) circle on the piece of 1⁄8" (3mm)-thick wood to make the lid liner. Cut along the line and sand the edges smooth. The piece should fit easily into the larger hole in the base.

15. Place the lid liner on the underside of the largest circle. Invert the base on top of the circle to position the lid liner. Glue the lid liner into place, being careful that it does not slip out of position when you clamp it.

16. Stack the four smaller circles on the largest one, rotating them so that the high and low sides alternate. Mark them so you can keep their orientation during glue-up. Remove the circles and glue them on, one at a time. To get a good bond, apply the glue to each circle, put it into place, and rub it back and forth until the glue is tacky.

17. To make the sprinkles, cut strips 1⁄16" (1.6mm) wide from the small pieces of 1⁄8" (3mm) thick wood. Cut each strip in half to form two strips measuring 1⁄16" (1.6mm) on each face.

18. Cut each strip into pieces about 1⁄4" (6mm) long, using a zero clearance insert to avoid losing any pieces. A playing card taped to the saw table works well for this purpose. Sand off any fuzzies and keep each color separate.

19. Spray a thin coat of shellac on the glued-up circles. Sand off any glue spots, and sand the entire top until smooth. Spray with several coats of clear lacquer. To stick on the sprinkles, spray a small section of the top and put on as many sprinkles as you can before the lacquer dries. If necessary, use tweezers for placement. Repeat until the top is covered evenly with the sprinkles. Finish the top with an additional coat of lacquer to secure them.

Cupcake Lid Pattern #1
Copy at 100%

3¼" (83mm)-diameter circle

Cupcake Base Pattern
Copy at 100%
Cut out center

3" (76mm)-diameter outer circle, 2" (51mm)-diameter inner circle

Cupcake Lid Pattern #2
Copy at 100%

2¾" (70mm)-diameter outer circle, 1 ¾" (44mm)-diameter inner circle

Cupcake Bottom Indentations Pattern
Copy at 100%

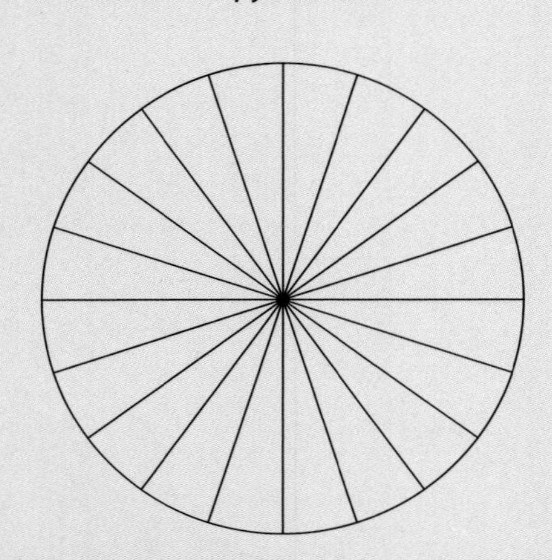

2" (51mm)-diameter circle with 20 segment pattern

Cupcake Lid Pattern #3
Copy at 100%

2¼" (57mm)-diameter outer circle, 1¼" (32mm)-diameter inner circle

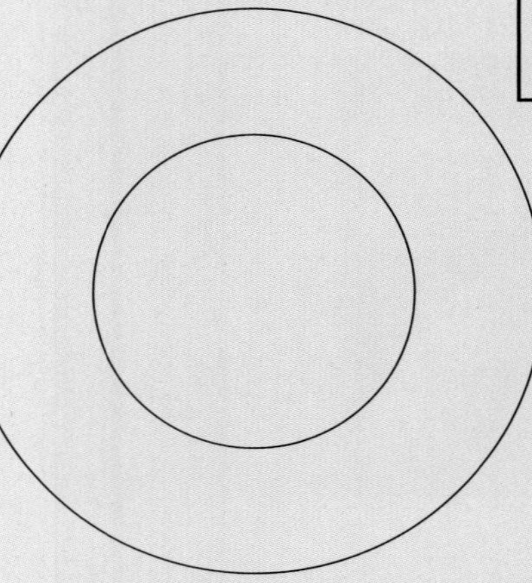

Cupcake Stand

Difficulty Rating:

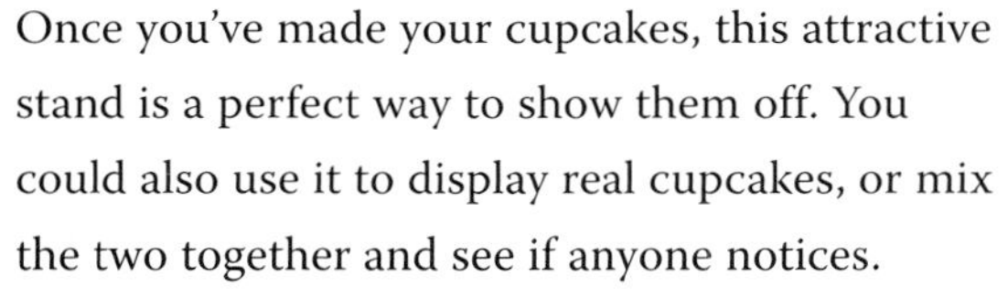

Once you've made your cupcakes, this attractive stand is a perfect way to show them off. You could also use it to display real cupcakes, or mix the two together and see if anyone notices.

The stand has a rippled "pie crust" edge, (made in the same way as the crust for the Apple Tart Box, page 52), and a contoured pedestal base. Hardwoods such as walnut, cherry, or maple all contrast nicely with the mahogany bases of the cupcakes.

Materials and Tools

Wood

- (1) 8" x 8" x ⅝" (205 x 205 x 16mm) walnut
- (2) 4" x 4" x ¾" (100 x 100 x 19mm) walnut

Materials

- Repositionable adhesive
- Glue
- Sanding discs for 2" (51mm) hook-and-loop pad sander, assorted grits 80 to 320
- Sanding sleeves for inflatable round sander, assorted grits 60 to 320
- Sandpaper for hand sanding, assorted grits
- 0000 steel wool
- Shellac
- Clear spray lacquer

Tools

- #9 scroll saw blade
- #54 or 1⁄16" (2mm) drill bit
- Awl
- Compass
- 25° shop-made angle guide (see page 18)
- Press or clamps for gluing
- 2" (50mm) hook-and-loop pad sander
- Inflatable round sander and pump

Alternate Version

For a less time-consuming alternative, you can adapt the base of the Pineapple Upside-Down Cake Box (page 81).

1. Using repositionable adhesive, attach the stand pattern to the 8" (203mm) piece of walnut.
2. Tilt the saw table to 40°, left side down. Cut along the outer circle in a clockwise direction.
3. Mark the entry hole with an awl. Using an angle guide or a drill press with a tilting table, drill an entry hole at a 25° angle. The hole should be drilled toward the center of the circle.
4. Tilt the saw table to 25°, left side down. Insert the saw blade and cut along the inner circle, cutting clockwise. The width of the lower ring will be about ¼" (6mm). Mark the top of the ring and the blank to help align them for gluing in Step 9.
5. Tilt the saw table to 15°, left side down. Cut along the outer edge of the ripple pattern, cutting clockwise. This cut will guide the sanding of the outside of the ripple in Step 7.
6. Tilt the saw table to 45°, left side down. Cut along the inner edge of the ripple pattern in a clockwise direction. Be careful not to cut into the lower edge. This cut will guide the sanding of the inside of the ripple in Step 8.
7. Using the hook-and-loop pad sander and a coarse grit disc, sand the outside of the rippled rim until the contours are smooth. Final sanding will be completed in Step 11.
8. Sand the inside of the rippled rim with the inflatable round sander, working from 80 to 220 grits until it is smooth. Be sure the lower inside edge is well shaped and smooth. You will not be able to sand this edge once the ring is glued to the remainder of the blank.
9. Glue the rippled rim to the remainder of the blank, keeping the grain aligned. Clamp for 5 minutes, remove clamps, and clean up excess glue inside the piece. Re-clamp and let dry.

10

Flaring the rippled rim.

13

Cutting the second pedestal piece.

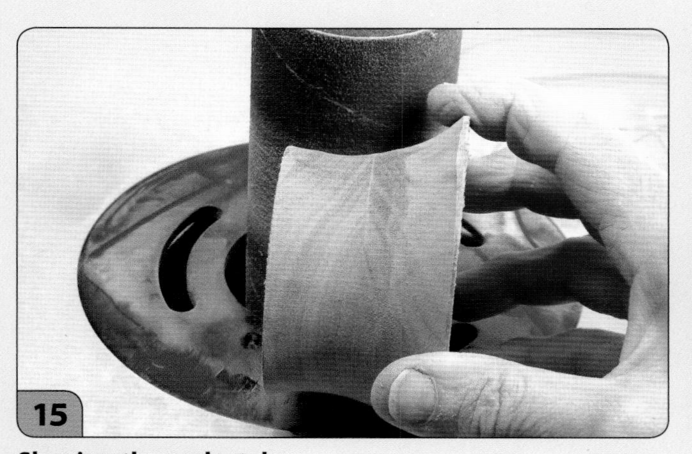

15

Shaping the pedestal.

16

Finishing the stand.

10. Using the hook-and-loop pad sander, thin the top edge of the ripple and flare it outward.

11. Use the hook-and-loop pad sander to finish sanding the outside of the pedestal top. Soften and round over the lower edge.

12. Using a compass, draw a 3½" (90mm) circle on one of the 4" (100mm) pieces of walnut. Tilt the saw table to 30°, left side down, and cut along the outline in a clockwise direction.

13. Trace the outline of the smaller face of the piece cut in Step 12 on the remaining 4" (102mm) piece of walnut, keeping the grain running in the same direction. Cut along this outline with the saw table level.

14. Glue the two pieces of the pedestal together, clamp and let dry.

15. Using a spindle sander, sand a curve into the pedestal. Finish the sanding with the inflatable round sander, if needed.

16. Glue the pedestal to the underside of the rippled top, making sure it is centered and sits flat. Weight it down until the glue is dry. Apply a coat of spray shellac to the entire piece to seal the wood and to reveal glue spots. Sand off glue spots, and sand the piece smooth. Apply several coats of shellac or clear lacquer, rubbing between coats with 0000 steel wool, as needed.

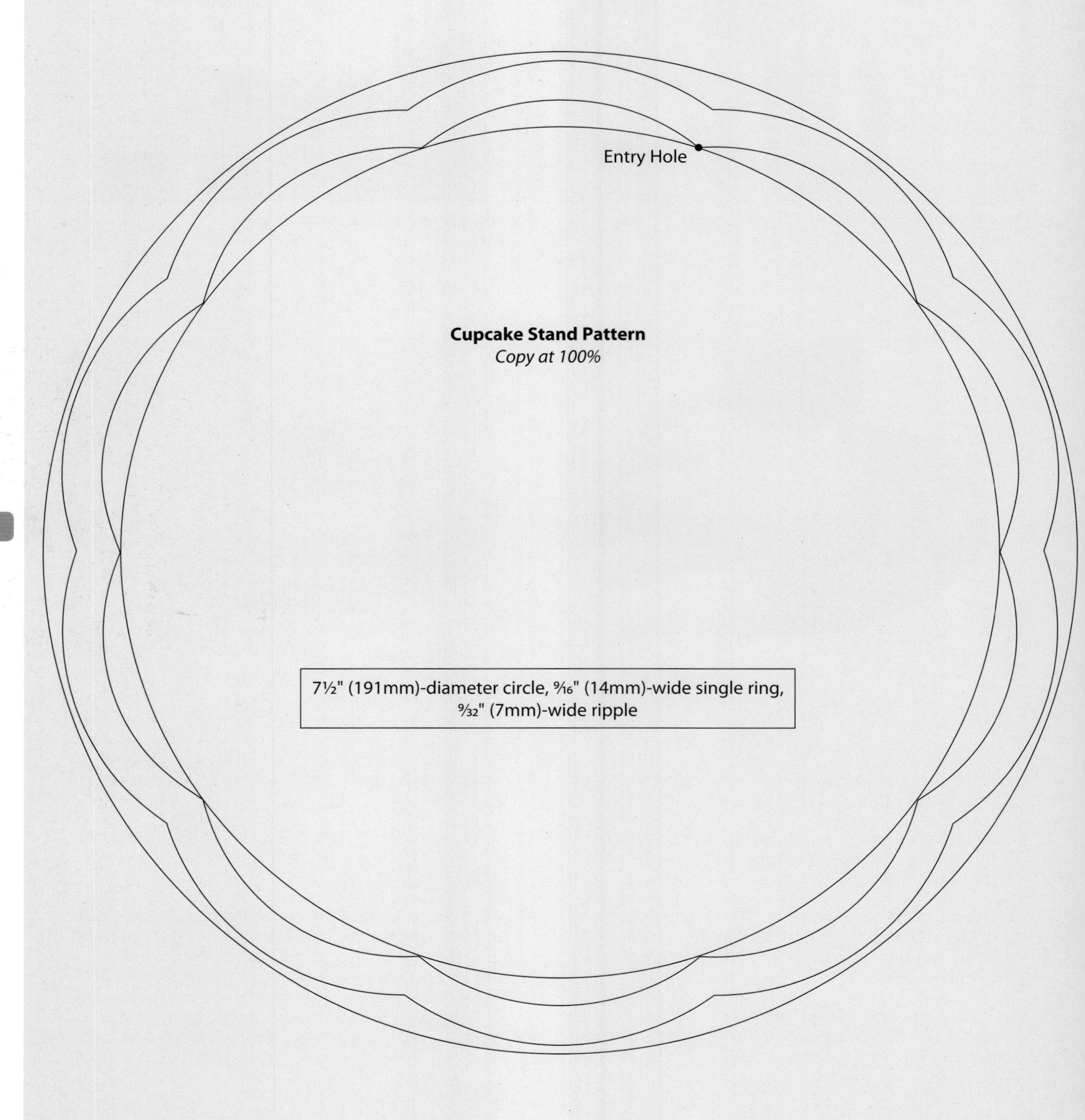
Entry Hole
Cupcake Stand Pattern
Copy at 100%
7½" (191mm)-diameter circle, 9⁄16" (14mm)-wide single ring,
9⁄32" (7mm)-wide ripple

Ice Cream Box

Difficulty Rating:

I always loved the look of swirled vanilla and chocolate soft ice cream, and decided to replicate that look in wood. If you prefer other "flavors," bloodwood makes a great raspberry sorbet, canarywood resembles butterscotch, and there's nothing wrong with a dish of "plain vanilla" made from aspen or maple.

I used mahogany for the box bottom, both for contrast and because it's easy to sand. Two different ring widths create a lip for the lid without using a router, (see Coffee Cup Box, page 60), and inverting and thinning the bottom piece creates a base with just the right proportions.

Materials and Tools

Wood

- (1) 6" x 6" x ¾" (150 x 150 x 19mm) mahogany for box
- (1) 4" x 3" x ¾" (100 x 75 x 19mm) yellowheart for lid
- (1) 5" x 3" x ¾" (130 x 75 x 19mm) yellowheart for lid
- (1) 4" x 3" x ¾" (100 x 75 x 19mm) walnut for lid
- (1) 5" x 3" x ¾" (130 x 75 x 19mm) walnut for lid
- (1) 1" x 1" x ⅜" (25 x 25 x 10mm) bloodwood for "cherry"

Materials

- Repositionable adhesive
- Glue (Weldbond recommended)
- Sandpaper for sanders of choice, assorted grits
- Sandpaper for hand sanding, assorted grits
- 0000 steel wool
- Spray shellac
- Clear spray lacquer

Tools

- #9 scroll saw blade
- ¹⁄₁₆" (2mm) or #54 drill bit
- 35° shop-made angle guide (see page 18)
- 40° shop-made angle guide
- Ruler
- Awl
- Compass
- Sanders of choice
- Clamps or press for gluing

1. Using repositionable adhesive, attach the box pattern to the square of mahogany. Tilt the saw table to 35°, left side down. Cut along the perimeter at a 35° angle, cutting clockwise.

2. Using a drill press with a tilting table or an angle guide, drill a 35° entry hole on the inner line, facing the center of the blank.

3. Insert the saw blade into the entry hole and cut on the inner line, at a 35° angle, cutting clockwise, to complete the first ring. Mark the top edges of the ring and the blank to keep their grain running in the same direction.

4. Center the first ring on the blank, keeping the grain oriented, and trace the outer and inner edges to create the outline for the second ring. At this point the ring is about ¼" (6mm) wide.

5. The ring drawn in Step 4 must be widened to about ⅜" (10mm) so it can support the lid. To do this, draw an additional circle on the blank that is ⅛" (3mm) inside the smaller circle. This new circle is the cutting line for the inside of the second ring. The cutting line for the outside of the second ring remains the same.

6. Tilt the saw table to 35°, left side down. Cut along the outside circle, cutting clockwise. Drill a 40°entry hole on the new inner cutting line drawn in Step 5. Tilt the saw table to 40°, left side down, and insert the saw blade. Cut along the line in a clockwise direction.

7. Draw a line around the side of the remaining piece that is halfway between the top and bottom faces. Sand the smaller face of this piece evenly until you reach the line. This piece, when placed smaller face up, is the base of the box.

8. Sand and shape the base as desired, softening the lower edge and rounding over the upper edge.

9. Sand the inside of each ring until it is smooth and the lower edge is well shaped.

10. Measure the inner diameter of the bottom of the first ring. The instructions for the largest ice cream ring assume that this diameter is 3½" (90mm) or slightly less. If you have a larger diameter, use that figure when you draw the cutting line for the largest circle in Step 16 to obtain a better fit.

11. Glue the two rings together, keeping the grain aligned and the inner lip even. Clamp and let dry, cleaning up any squeeze-out on the inside edge before the glue sets.

12. Sand the rings until smooth, shaping the lower edge as desired.

13. Center the rings on the base and glue the pieces together. Clamp or weight down until dry. Clean up any squeeze-out on the base before the glue sets.

6

Cutting the second ring.

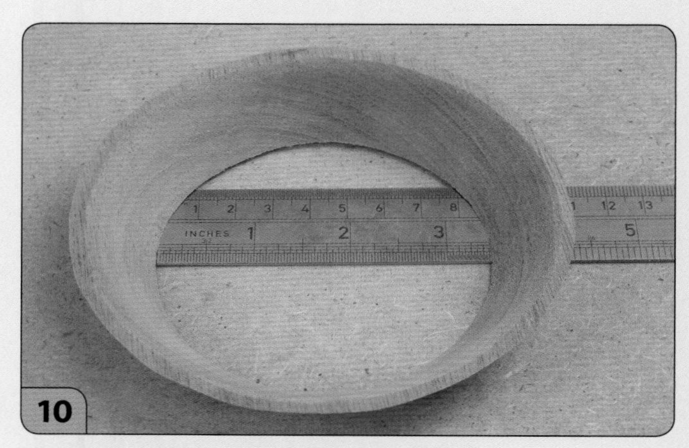

10

Measuring the inner diameter.

13

Gluing on the base.

14. For each piece of walnut and yellowheart, draw a line ¼" (6mm) from one long edge. Tilt the saw table to 45°, left side down, and cut along this line. The larger part of the wood should be to the left of the line.

15. Sand each bevel lightly so that the gluing surface is flat. Glue together the matching pieces of yellowheart and walnut. Rub the pieces back and forth until they start to drag, and then let them dry. If you prefer to clamp them, be careful they don't slip out of alignment. Sand the front and back faces smooth after the glue has dried.

16. Draw a line ⅜" (10mm) from the join of the two pieces of wood. This is the center of the blank. Draw a circle 3½" (90mm) in diameter on the 4" (100mm) piece of wood, and circles 2¾" (70mm) and 2" (50mm) in diameter on the 5" (130mm) piece of wood.

17. With the saw table level, cut out the three circles. Draw a line around each circle ⅜" (10mm) from the top face. Sand a 45° bevel to this line.

18. Sand each circle until it is smooth and the bevel is rounded. Stack the three circles and glue them together.

19. Cut a ⅞" (22mm) circle from the piece of bloodwood. Sand in a small bevel around the top. Soften and round the top and sides. Glue the "cherry" to the top of the circles.

20. Finish the box and lid with a coat of shellac to seal the wood and reveal glue spots. Sand off any glue spots, and apply several coats of clear lacquer, rubbing down between coats with 0000, as needed. If you'd like, you can add sprinkles (see Cupcake Box, page 63) while the finish is still wet.

Cutting the bevels.

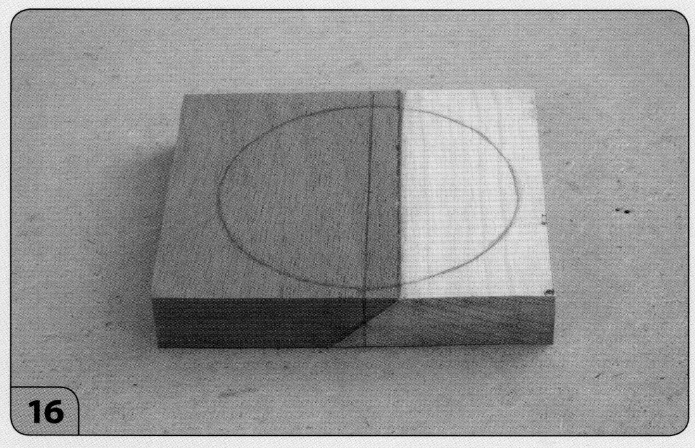

Marking the circles.

Cutting and beveling the circles.

Flip that Ring Over

Turning a ring upside down makes it easier to identify and correct rough or off-round places on the lower edge. Be sure to leave enough wood on the lower face for gluing.

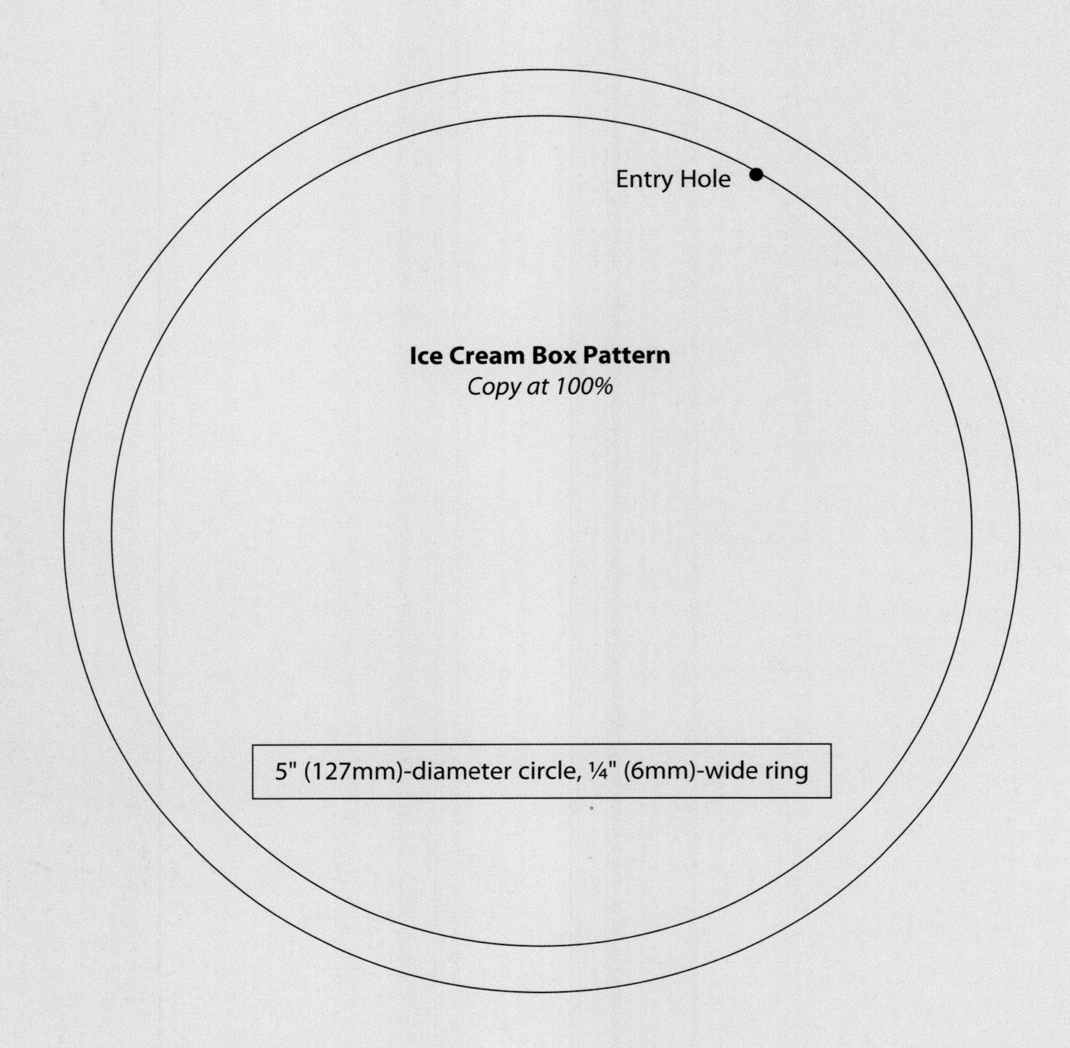
Entry Hole
Ice Cream Box Pattern
Copy at 100%
5" (127mm)-diameter circle, ¼" (6mm)-wide ring

Linzer Tart Box

Difficulty Rating:

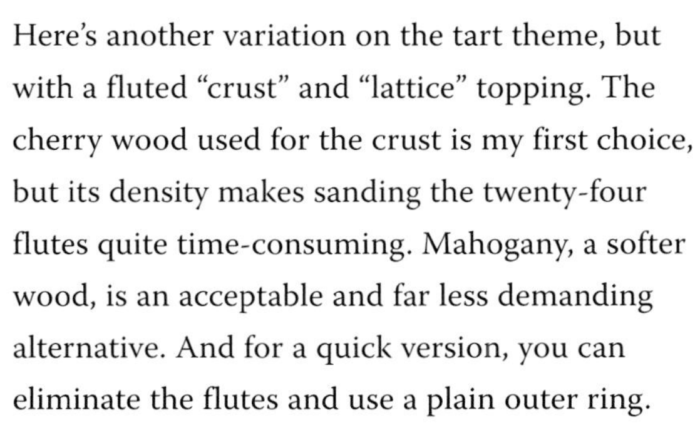

Here's another variation on the tart theme, but with a fluted "crust" and "lattice" topping. The cherry wood used for the crust is my first choice, but its density makes sanding the twenty-four flutes quite time-consuming. Mahogany, a softer wood, is an acceptable and far less demanding alternative. And for a quick version, you can eliminate the flutes and use a plain outer ring.

Two thicknesses of wood create the lattice. The pattern is placed under wax paper, making it easy to glue the strips into place. An egg-crate style divider provides support for the lid.

For different "flavors," try padauk for apricot and purpleheart for plum.

Materials and Tools

Wood

- (1) 8" x 8" x 1⅛" (205 x 205 x 30mm) cherry for box body
- (1) 7" x 7" x ¼" (180 x 180 x 6mm) cherry for box base
- (2) 6½" x 1" x ¼" (165 x 25 x 6mm) cherry for lid support
- (1) 7" x 7" x ⅛" (180 x 180 x 3mm) bloodwood for lid
- (3) 8" x ¾" x ¼" (205 x 19 x 6mm) cherry for lattice
- (3) 8" x ¾" x 3⁄16" (205 x 19 x 5mm) cherry for lattice
- Small piece of ¼" (6mm)-thick wood, about 3" x ¾" (75 x 19mm) for angle guide for lattice strips

Materials

- Repositionable adhesive
- Glue (Weldbond recommended)
- Clear packing tape
- Sandpaper for sanders of choice, assorted grits
- Sandpaper for hand sanding, assorted grits
- 0000 steel wool
- Wax paper
- Shellac
- Clear spray lacquer

Tools

- #3 scroll saw blade for thin wood
- #12 scroll saw blade for thick wood
- ⅛" (3mm) or larger drill bit
- 30-60-90 triangle or protractor
- Compass
- Clamps or press for gluing
- Sanders of choice

1. Attach the pattern to the 1⅛" (30mm)-thick piece of cherry using repositionable adhesive. Cover with clear packing tape to prevent burning. Tilt the saw table to 10°, left side down. Cut around the perimeter of the box, cutting clockwise.

2. Drill a straight entry hole about 1" (25mm) inside the perimeter, using a ⅛" (3mm) or larger drill bit. Tilt the saw table to 10°, left side down. Insert the blade and cut around the inner ring, cutting clockwise.

3. Sand the inside smooth. If using a spindle sander, be sure to sand at a 10° angle.

4. Place the ring on the 7" x 7" x ¼" (180 x 180 x 6mm) piece of cherry, keeping the grain of both pieces running in the same direction and trace the outer line. This is the cutting line for the base.

5. Tilt the saw table to 10°, left side down, and cut around the line drawn in Step 4, cutting clockwise.

6. Invert the fluted ring. Measure the inner diameter of the lower edge and record the measurement. You will use this figure for the lid supports in Step 14.

7. Glue the base to the ring. Clamp and let dry about 5 minutes. Remove clamps and clean up any glue squeeze-out. Re-clamp and let dry.

8. Sand the outside of the box until it is smooth. Soften the edges of the flutes.

9. Using a triangle or protractor, draw a line at a 60° angle to the straight edge of the small piece of ¼" (6mm)-thick wood. Cut the wood on this line and sand the cut surface smooth. This piece is the marking guide for the angled lattice pieces.

10. For each of the three 3⁄16" (5mm)-thick strips of cherry, place the angle guide at the left end of the strip, matching the bottom edges. Use the guide to draw a 60° angle at that end. From the bottom point of that line, mark additional points on the bottom edge of the strips as directed below, and draw 60° angles at those points.

    Strip 1: Six additional marks 1⅛" (30mm) apart. This will give you cutting lines for six short strips.

    Strip 2: Two additional marks 1⅛ (30mm) apart, and three additional marks 1½" (40mm) apart. This will give you cutting lines for two short strips and three long ones.

    Strip 3: Three additional marks 1½" (40mm) apart. This will give you cutting lines for three long strips with some extra wood left over.

11. Cut along each of the marked lines. You will have eight short strips, six long strips, and some wood left over.

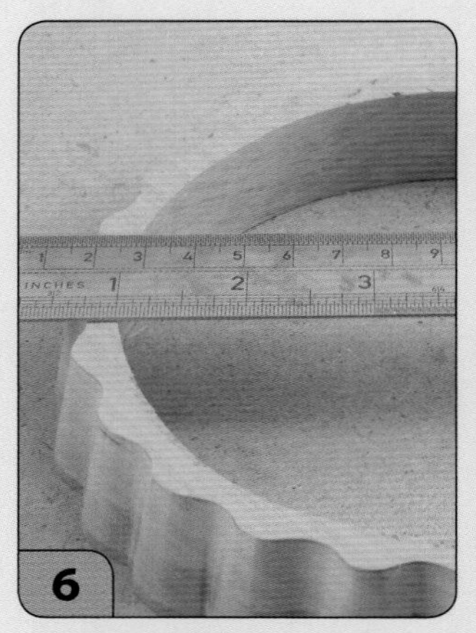

6 Measuring the bottom inner diameter.

9 Making the marking guide for the angled lattice pieces.

Alternate Cutting Instructions

If you are using mahogany, a softer wood than cherry, you can cut the box and bottom as one piece. Here's how:

A1. Cut around the inner ring, as in Step 2.

A2. Sand the inside of the ring, as in Step 3.

A3. Glue the ring to the wood for the base, as in Step 7.

A4. Cut around the perimeter of the box, as in Step 1.

10 Marking the cutting lines for the angled lattice pieces.

Completing the lattice.

12. Place the lattice pattern on a flat surface and put a piece of wax paper on top. Place the three ¼" (6mm)-thick strips of cherry on the wax paper, where indicated on the pattern.

13. Place the angled pieces where indicated on the pattern. You may need to try pieces in different locations, or sand the ends slightly, to get a good fit. Glue the pieces together, without clamping. Remove excess glue and let the lattice dry thoroughly. Sand the top edges of all strips to soften and sand the entire piece until smooth.

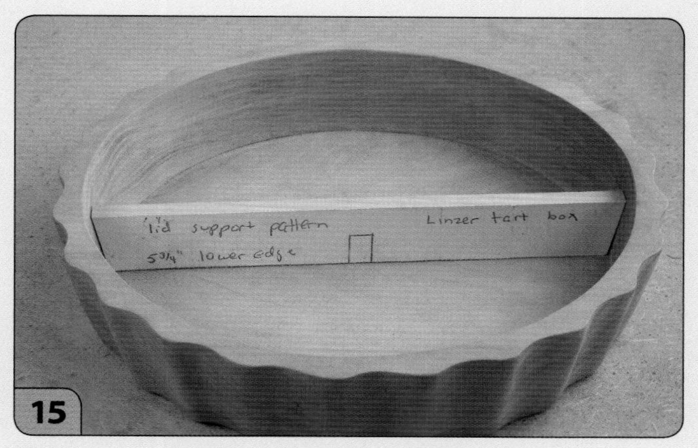

Checking the fit of the first lid support.

14. To make the lid supports, attach the patterns to the two 6½" (165mm)-long strips of cherry, using repositionable adhesive. The patterns are sized for a box bottom with an inner diameter of 5¾" (145mm). If your measurement from Step 6 is different, adjust the pattern, keeping the notched area centered.

15. Cut along the outline of one of the support pieces. Do not cut out the center notch yet. Place the strip in the center of the box and check the fit. Cut or sand on both ends of the strip, as needed, until it fits snugly against the sides of the box. The notch must remain in the center of the strip. Cut out the center notch. Measure the top edge of the strip and record that figure for use in Step 18. It should be about 6" (150mm).

16. Transfer any adjustments made on the first strip to the pattern for the second strip. Cut out the second strip. Sand both strips smooth.

17. Join the two strips at the center notched areas and place them into the box. The top of the support should be about 5⁄16" (8mm) below the top of the box. This will make the tops of the thinner pieces of lattice flush with the top of the box. The ends of thicker pieces will be rounded to meet the top of the box. Glue the lid support to the box.

Assembling the lid support.

18. To make the lid, place the point of a compass in the center of the ⅛" (3mm)-thick piece of bloodwood and draw a circle with a diameter the length of the strip you measured in Step 15. Tilt the saw table 10°, left side down, and cut along the circle, cutting **counterclockwise.** The bottom of the circle will be larger than the top. Place the circle, larger side up, on the lid supports and check the fit. Adjust by sanding if needed, until the lid fits easily into the box.

Gluing on the lattice.

Trimming the lattice.

19. Place the lid with its larger side up. Position the lattice on top of the lid, with its flat side against the top of the lid. Adjust the lattice until it is centered and glue it into place. Use a press or weights to get a good bond.

20. Tilt the saw table 10°, left side down. Place the lid, lattice side down, on the saw table. Using the edge of the bloodwood as a guide, cut around the lid, cutting **counterclockwise**, to trim the lattice. Do not cut into the bloodwood.

21. Sand the lattice flush with the bloodwood at a 10° angle. The lid should fit easily into the box.

22. Round over the ends of the thicker pieces of lattice. Soften the ends of the thinner pieces of lattice. Seal the box and lid with a coat of shellac to reveal glue spots. Remove glue spots and sand the pieces smooth. Finish with additional coats of shellac or clear lacquer, rubbing down between coats with 0000 steel wool as needed.

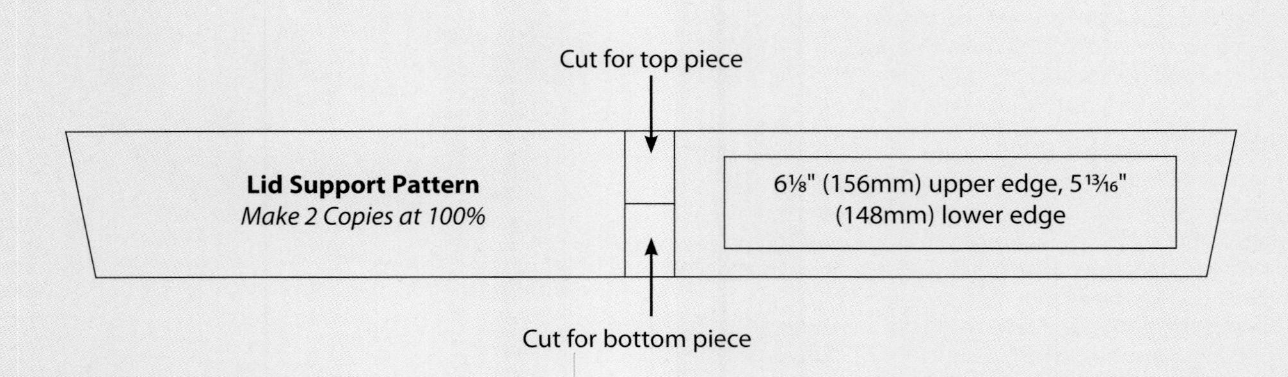

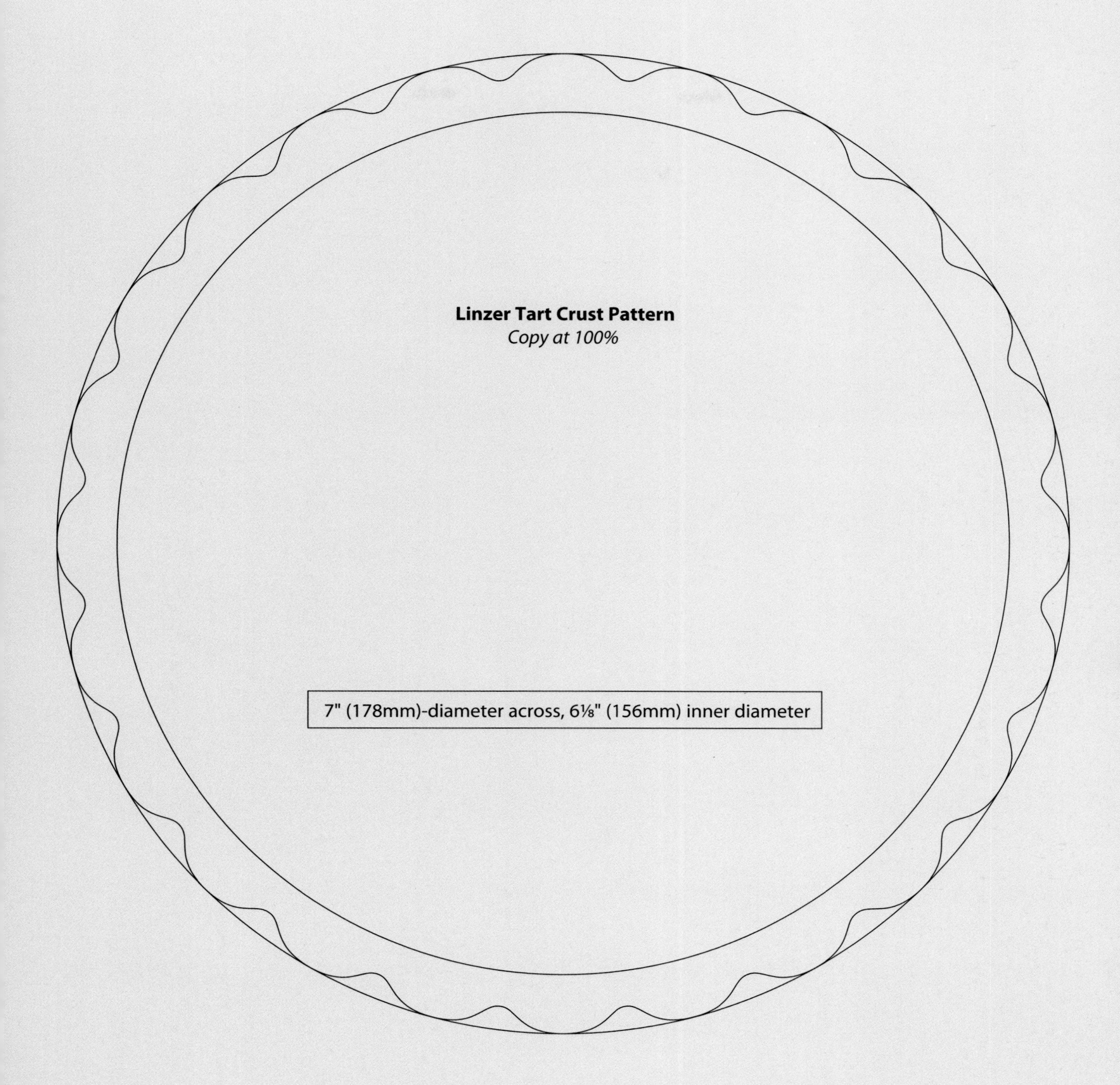
Linzer Tart Crust Pattern
Copy at 100%
7" (178mm)-diameter across, 6⅛" (156mm) inner diameter

Linzer Tart Box Lattice Pattern
Copy at 100%

8" x 7" (203 x 178mm) overall

Pineapple Upside-Down Cake Box

Difficulty Rating:

Pineapple upside-down cakes are a classic treat, and this box looks just like the real thing—until you remove the lid to reveal the elegant flocked interior. Techniques not typical for box-making—intarsia cherries and an angled-cut pedestal stand—lend impact to a project that is unusual, impressive, yet easy to make.

Materials and Tools

Wood

- (1) 16" x 2½" x ¼" (405 x 65 x 6mm) yellowheart for "pineapple slices"
- (1) 7" x 1" x ⅜" (180 x 25 x 10mm) bloodwood for "cherries"
- (1) 7" x 7" x ⅛" (180 x 180 x 3mm) mahogany for box lid
- (1) 7" x 7" x 1⅛" (180 x 180 x 30mm) mahogany for box body
- (1) 8½" x 8½" x ½" (215 x 215 x 13mm) oak for top of cake stand
- (1) 4½" x 4½" x ½" (115 x 115 x 13mm) oak for pedestal bottom
- (1) 3½" x 3½" x 1" (90 x 90 x 25mm) oak for pedestal top

Materials

- Repositionable adhesive
- Glue
- Sandpaper for sanders of choice
- Sandpaper for hand sanding, assorted grits
- 0000 steel wool
- Fibers for flocking and matching acrylic paint
- Thin cardboard for pineapple and cherry patterns
- Spray shellac
- Clear spray lacquer

Tools

- #3 scroll saw blade for thin wood
- #9 scroll saw blade for thick wood
- ¾" (19mm) Forstner bit
- 1/16" (2mm) or #54 drill bit
- Awl
- Compass
- 28° shop-made angle guide (see page 18)
- Clamps or press for gluing
- Sanders of choice
- Brush for acrylic paint

1. Attach the pattern for the pineapple slice to a piece of cardboard. Trace the circumference seven times on the piece of yellowheart. Mark the centers of the circles with an awl.

2. Place the Forstner bit on each center point and drill out the center of each circle.

3. Cut out the circles and sand them smooth. Choose one face for the top, and round all edges on that side.

4. Attach the cherry pattern to a piece of cardboard and trace the outline seven times on the piece of bloodwood. Cut out the circles.

5. Round the tops of the bloodwood circles to resemble cherries and sand the circles smooth. Place into the centers of the yellowheart circles. They will be glued on in Step 10.

6. Attach the box pattern to the piece of 1⅛" (30mm)-thick mahogany, using repositionable adhesive. Drill entry holes where indicated on the pattern with the 1⁄16" (2mm) or #54 drill bit. Insert the saw blade into the entry hole in the middle circle and cut around the circle. The outer piece will form the box lid and the inner piece will form the sides of the box. Do not remove the pattern from either piece.

7. Insert the saw blade into the entry hole on the inner piece. Cut along the circle to complete the ring that forms the sides of the box. Sand both sides of this ring until they are smooth. Do not remove too much wood from the outside of the ring or the lid will not fit snugly. Round the upper edges of the ring.

8. To complete the lid, sand the inside of the piece cut in Step 6 until smooth. Do not remove too much wood or the lid will not fit properly. Glue this piece to the piece of ⅛" (3mm)-thick mahogany. Clamp and let dry. Cut along the outer circle of the glued-up piece to complete the box lid.

9. Sand the outside of the lid until smooth and round over the upper edge. Soften the lower edge. Apply a thin coat of shellac to the outer and inner surfaces and sand again until smooth.

10. Place one of the pineapple rings, with a cherry, in the center of the lid and place the other six in a circle around it. Glue all the rings into place. Apply several coats of spray lacquer to the outside of the lid.

11. Attach the pattern for the cake stand to the 8½" (215mm) square of oak. Tilt the saw table to 28°, left side down. Cut along the circumference in a clockwise direction.

12. Mark the entry hole with an awl where indicated on the pattern. Drill a 28° entry hole, facing the center of the circle, using an angle guide or a drill press with a tilting table.

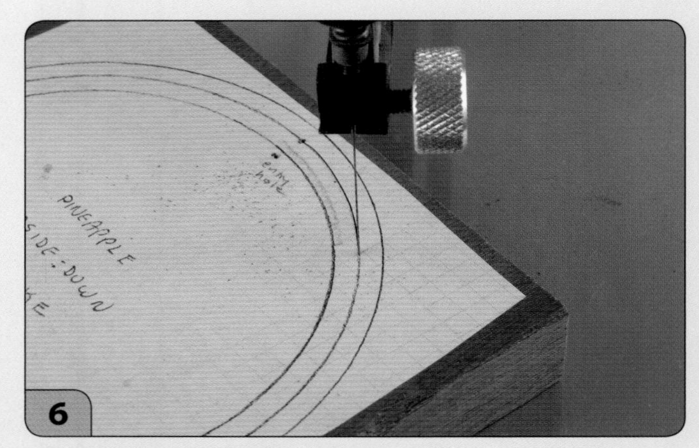

Separating the box lid and sides.

Completing the box lid.

Gluing on the pineapple rings.

13. Tilt the saw table to 28°, left side down. Insert the saw blade and cut along the inner circle in a clockwise direction to complete the rim.

14. Sand the inside of the ring smooth. Soften the inside of the upper edge. Sand away any fuzzies from the ring bottom.

15. Sand the upper surface of the remainder of the blank until smooth. Glue on the sanded ring. Clamp and let dry five minutes. Remove the clamp to clean up excess glue. Re-clamp and let dry.

16. Sand the outside of the glued-up piece, rounding the lower edge and softening the top edge.

17. To make the pedestal bottom, draw a 4" (100mm) circle on the 4½" (115mm) square of oak. Tilt the saw table 30°, left side down. Cut along the line, cutting clockwise. Shape the top and soften the lower edge.

18. To make the pedestal top, draw a 2¾" (70mm) circle on the 1" (25mm)-thick piece of oak and cut along the circle with the saw table level. Sand until smooth and glue to the pedestal bottom. Clamp and let dry.

19. Center the pedestal on the underside of the top of the cake stand. Glue it into place, weight down, and let dry.

20. Glue the ring that forms the box sides to the top of the cake stand. Make sure it is centered. Clamp or weight down and let dry. Clean up any excess glue before it sets.

21. Apply a coat of shellac to all surfaces of the cake stand and box sides, and let dry. Rub down the surfaces with 0000 steel wool and vacuum up all particles. Apply several coats of lacquer to the outside of the box sides, the pedestal, and the part of the cake plate not within the box.

22. To apply flocking to the inside of the box, follow the instructions on page 130, Fearless Flocking.

Gluing the top of the cake stand.

Shellac Before Flocking

The fibers of mahogany, a very porous wood, tend to raise when moistened. A sealer coat of shellac helps achieve a smooth finish, and prevents uneven absorption of acrylic paint during flocking.

Gluing on the pedestal.

Attaching the box sides.

Applying the flocking.

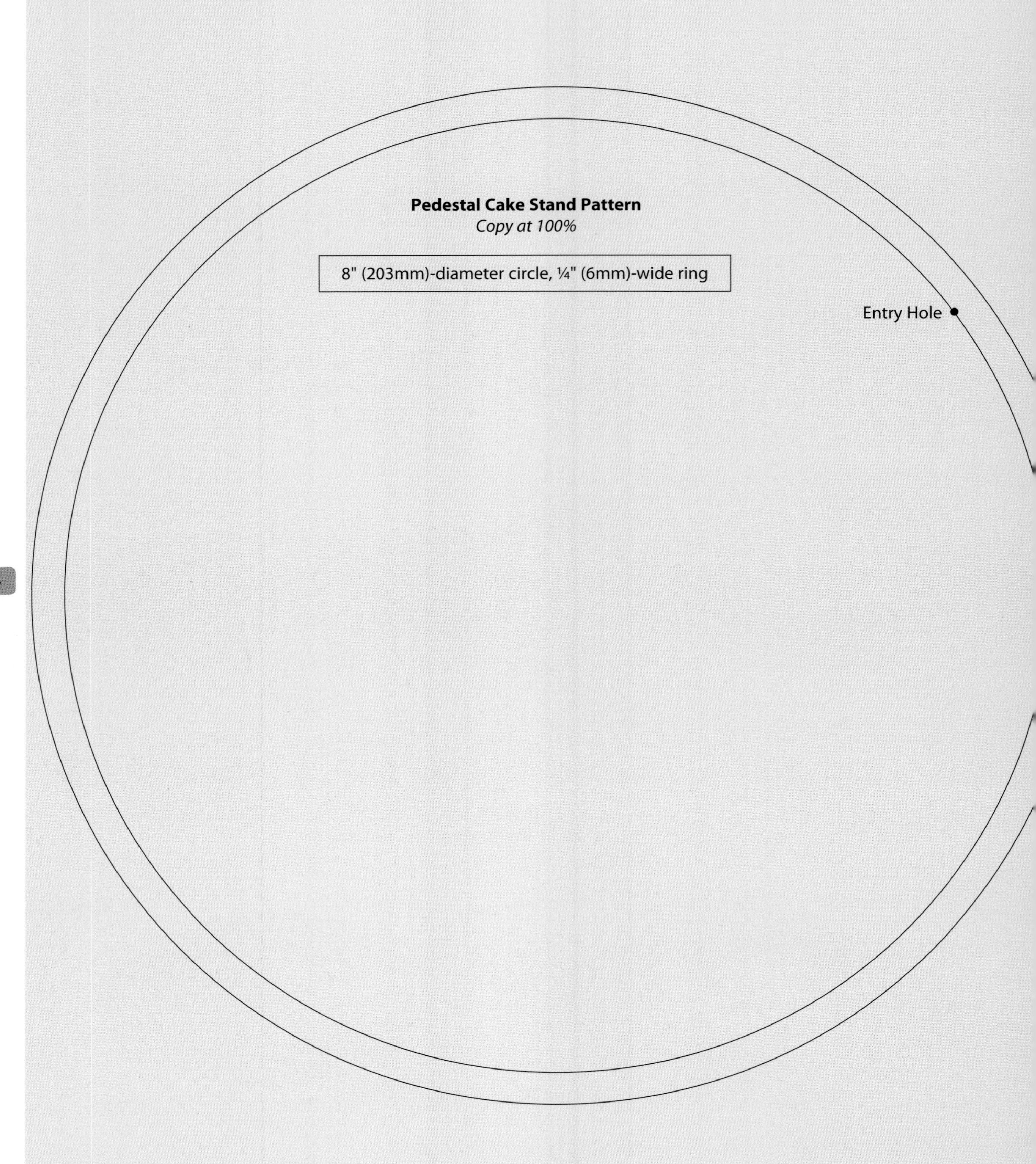
Pedestal Cake Stand Pattern
Copy at 100%
8" (203mm)-diameter circle, ¼" (6mm)-wide ring
Entry Hole

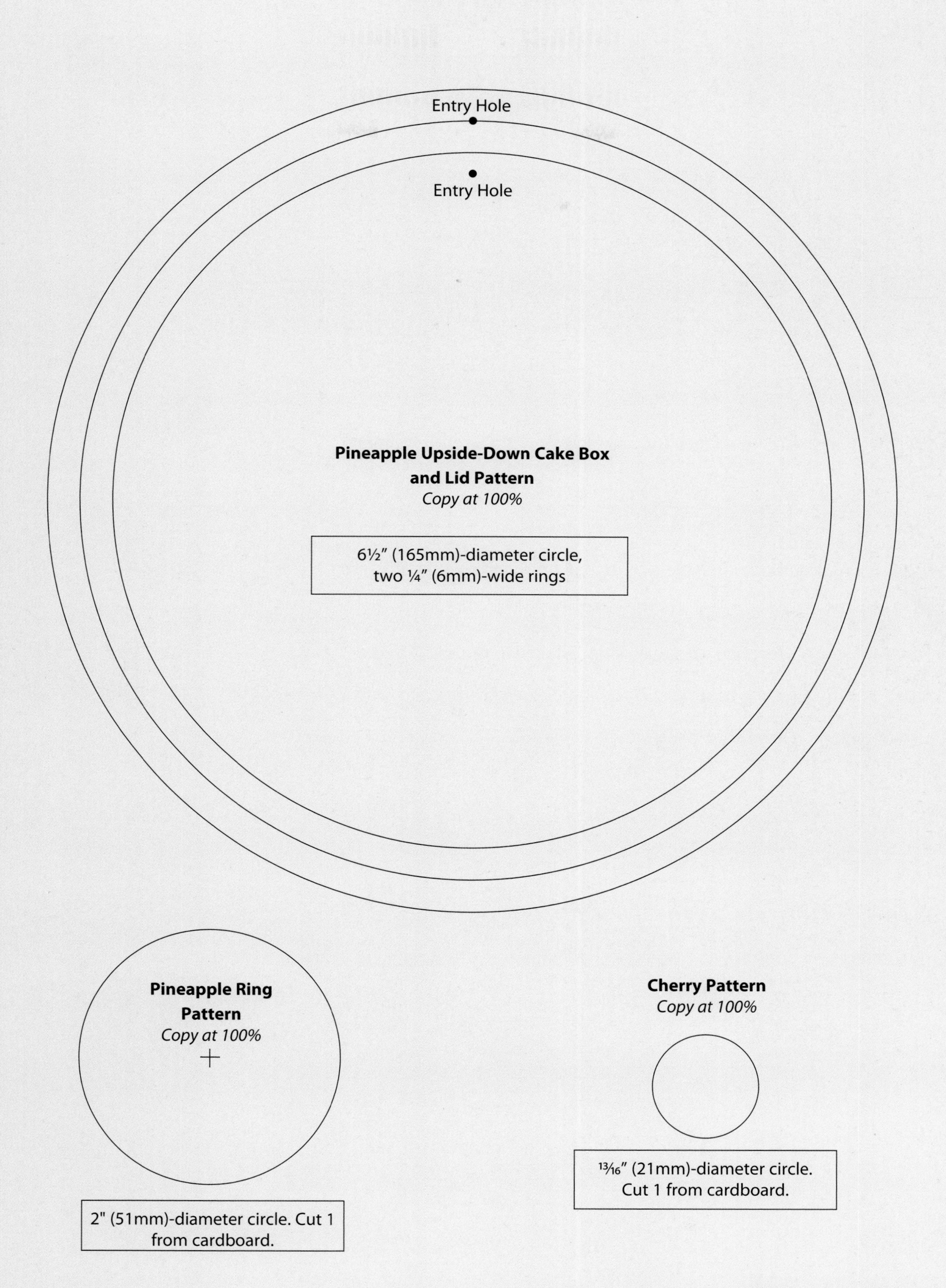
Entry Hole
Entry Hole
Pineapple Upside-Down Cake Box
and Lid Pattern
Copy at 100%
6½" (165mm)-diameter circle,
two ¼" (6mm)-wide rings
Pineapple Ring
Pattern
Copy at 100%
2" (51mm)-diameter circle. Cut 1
from cardboard.
Cherry Pattern
Copy at 100%
13⁄16" (21mm)-diameter circle.
Cut 1 from cardboard.

Barrel Hinge Jewelry Boxes

Here's an assortment of elegant boxes perfectly suited for rings and fine pieces of jewelry. All are lined with velvet or flocking, and those meant for rings have professional-looking inserts made from foam core and adhesive-backed velvet. Easy-to-install barrel hinges secure and operate the lids, and a Forstner bit creates inner spaces with speed and precision. Make them fancy, make them plain—all are winners, and the small ones are a great way to use up scraps from other projects.

Barrel Hinge Basics

Barrel hinges are an easy and attractive way to secure lids to small boxes. Regardless of specific project instructions, the hinge installation is always the same. Here's how to do it:

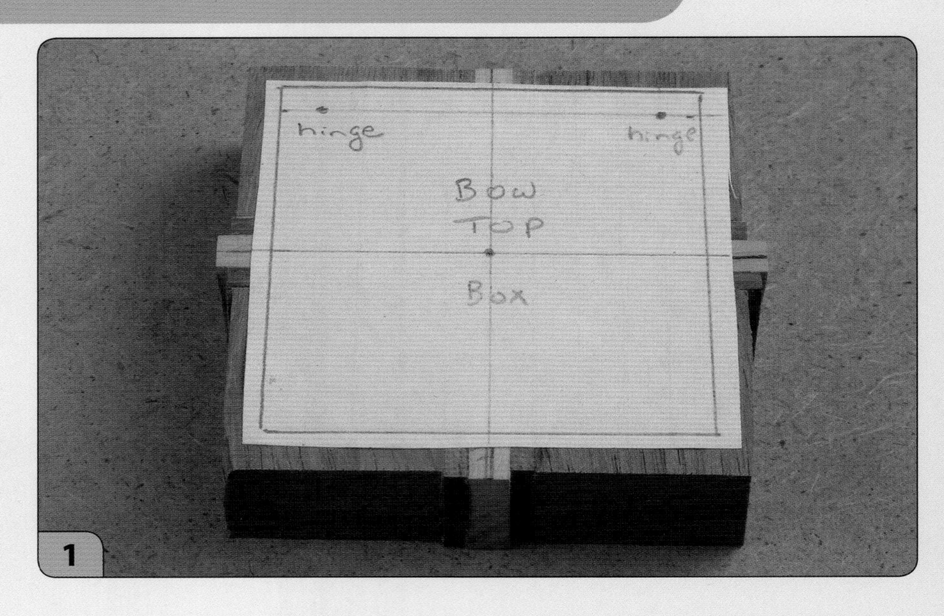

Attaching the pattern and marking the drilling points. Attach a copy of the box pattern to each half of the box. Use an awl to mark the drill points for the hinges and center hole.

Cutting the profile and drilling the center holes. Follow specific project instructions for drilling the center holes and cutting the profile of the box.

Matching the drilling marks. Place the box halves back-to-back, inner faces up, and check the placement of the drilling marks for the hinges. They must be directly opposite each other.

Measuring the hinge depth on the box exterior. For each box half, draw a line 7.5mm (19/64") from the top of the back edge to mark the depth of the holes for the hinges. Use a 5mm brad point bit to drill holes at each drilling point. It's better to drill too shallow a hole and "sneak" up on the proper depth than to drill too deep a hole.

Making a depth gauge. Mark a ⅛" (3mm) dowel 7.5mm (19/64") from one end to use as a depth gauge.

Checking the hole depth. Check the hole depth with the marked dowel. As a final check, insert the hinges and put the box pieces together to be sure that the box will close fully when the hinges are glued into place.

Marking the bevel for the hinges. Draw a line along the back edge of each piece that is 3/16" (5mm) down from the drilled face. This is the reference line for making the bevel for the lid.

8

Sanding in the bevel. For each piece, sand a 45° bevel to the reference line. The bevel will run through the center of the holes drilled for the hinges.

9

Preparing the box for the hinges. Sand the inner surfaces and the beveled edges of each piece until smooth. Apply shellac to interior surfaces to seal them and allow easy removal of excess epoxy. When the shellac is dry, rub the surfaces smooth with 0000 steel wool.

10

Gluing in the hinges. Using a toothpick or a #3 cake decorating tip, place a small amount of epoxy into each hinge hole. Insert the hinges, making sure they pivot from front to back. Let the epoxy dry the recommended time. If you used a cake decorating tip, clean it with acetone.

Basic Ring Box, Two Ways: A Step-by-Step Guide

Difficulty Rating:

The instructions for this small classic box contain everything you need to know about making ring boxes, including how to make one without using a Forstner bit. Its small size will accommodate bands and smaller decorative rings. If a deeper inner space is needed, increase the thickness of the primary wood to ⅝" (16mm) or ¾" (19mm).

Designing the ring insert was a challenge because I wanted it to be inexpensive, easy to make, yet professional in appearance. Pre-made inserts were costly; wood was too rigid; and cardboard was too flimsy. The solution was ½" (13mm)-thick foam core, cut into strips and notched, then covered with adhesive-backed velvet. Foam core is firm and cuts easily with a small scroll saw blade. Adhesive-backed velvet is simple to apply, and the finished unit has enough "give" to fit securely into the bottom hole.

Materials and Tools

Wood

- (2) 2½" x 2½" x ½" (65 x 65 x 13mm) walnut
- (2) 2½" x 2½" (65 x 65mm) pieces of veneer
- (2) 2½" x 2½" x ¼" (65 x 65 x 6mm) cherry
- (1) 2" (50mm) piece of ⅛" (3mm) dowel, marked at 7.5mm (19⁄64") to check depth of the hole for the hinges

Materials

- Repositionable adhesive
- Glue
- Epoxy
- Sandpaper for sanders of choice, assorted grits
- Sandpaper for hand sanding, assorted grits
- 0000 steel wool
- (2) 5mm brass barrel hinges
- (1) 2½" x 1⅝" x ½" (65 x 40 x 13mm) foam core for insert
- (1) 3" x 2" (75 x 50mm) adhesive-backed velvet for insert
- (1) 2" x 2" (50 x 50mm) adhesive-backed velvet for top recess (optional)
- Shellac
- Clear spray lacquer

Tools

- #7 scroll saw blade
- #2/0 scroll saw blade for cutting foam core
- 1⅜" (35mm) Forstner bit (for drilled version)
- 5mm brad point drill bit
- Awl
- Ruler
- Clamps for gluing
- Clamps to hold wood for drilling
- Sanders of choice
- Toothpick or #3 cake decorating tip for epoxy
- Craft knife, such as X-Acto, for thinning the insert

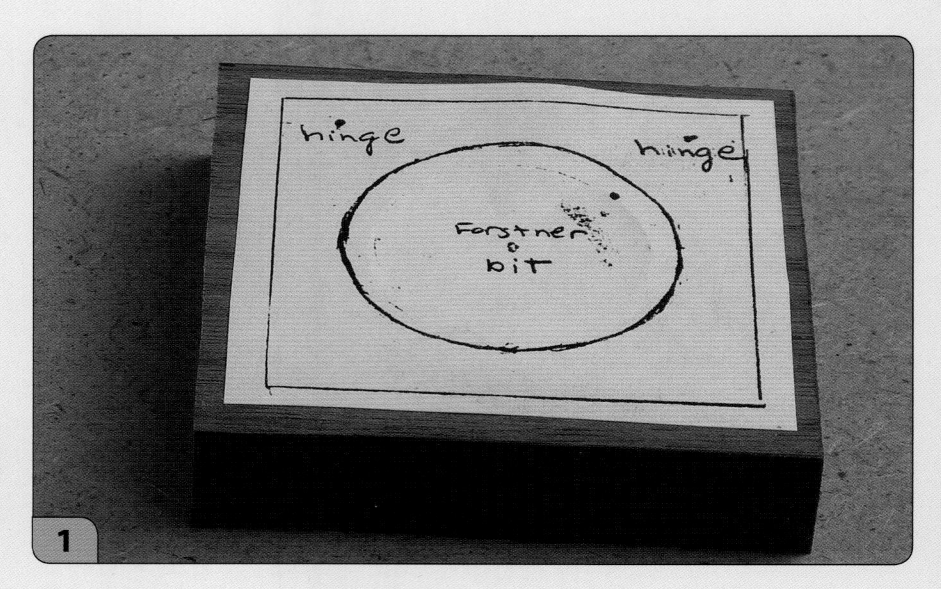

Attaching the pattern. Attach a copy of the pattern to each piece of walnut, using repositionable adhesive. Using the awl, mark the drilling points for the barrel hinges.

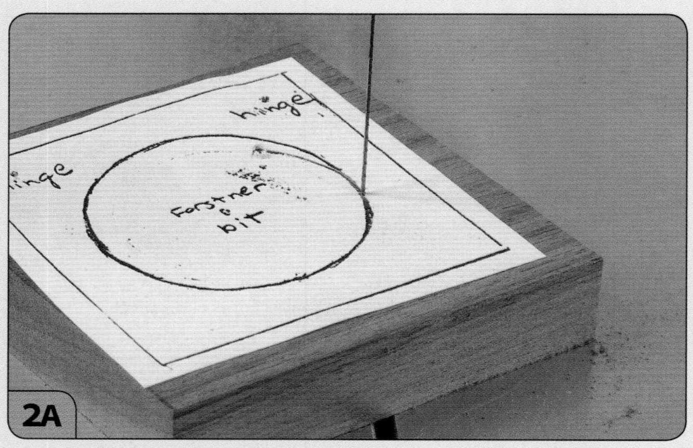

Scrolled version: Cutting out the centers. For each piece, drill an entry hole just inside the circle. Cut out the circles. Remove the patterns and set aside for use in Step 4. Sand the inside of the circles smooth.

Drilled version: Drilling out the centers. For each piece, mark the drilling point in the center of the circle with an awl. Remove the pattern and set aside for Step 4. Using a 1⅜" (35mm) Forstner bit, drill completely through the wood. Use a clamp and keep your fingers away from the bit.

Gluing up the lamination. Glue the pieces of veneer and the ¼" (6mm)-thick cherry to the bottom of each piece of walnut. Clamp and let dry.

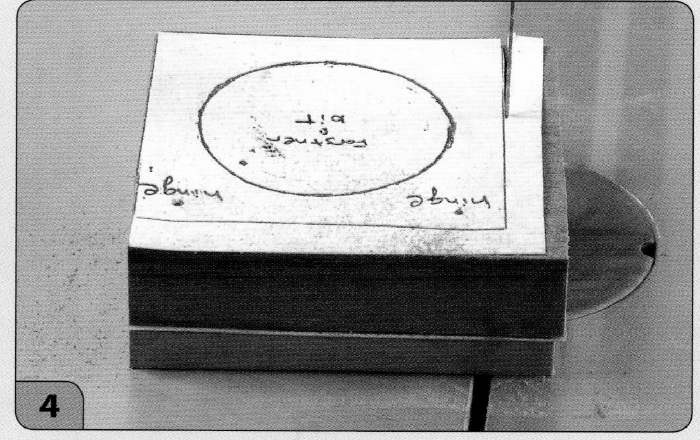

Cutting the outside of the box. Reattach the patterns, using the hinge drilling points to align them. Cut along the outer lines to form two 2" x 2" (50 x 50mm) squares. (Note: the picture refers to the drilled version, as the center of the pattern would have been cut out in the scrolled version.)

Installing the barrel hinges. To insert the barrel hinges, follow Steps 3–10 of Barrel Hinge Basics, page 88. Apply a coat of shellac to the recesses for a finished look.

Sanding the sides of the box. With the box closed, sand the outside so that top and bottom sides are completely even with each other. If desired, sand in a bevel at the front corners and a small bevel around the top edge of the box.

Finishing the box. Sand the box until completely smooth; soften all edges. Finish with several coats of shellac or clear lacquer, rubbing down between each coat as needed with 0000 steel wool until the desired finish is obtained. To make the ring insert, follow the instructions in the sidebar Making the Ring Insert, below.

Making the Ring Insert

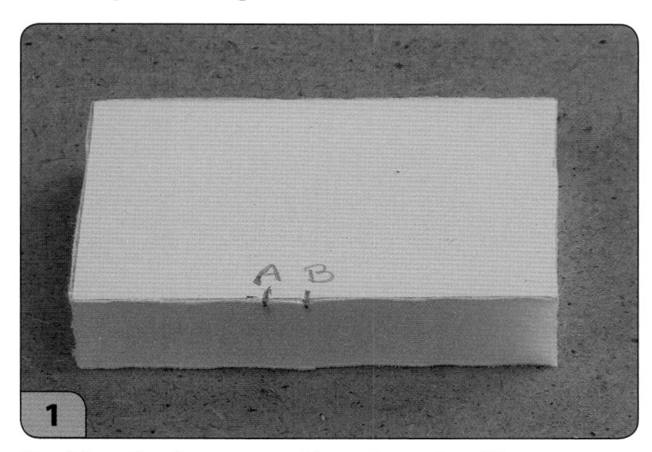

Marking the foam core. Place the strip of foam core flat, with a long side facing you, and make marks at 1" (25mm) (point A) and 1³⁄₁₆" (30mm) (point B) along the top edge, measuring from the left side.

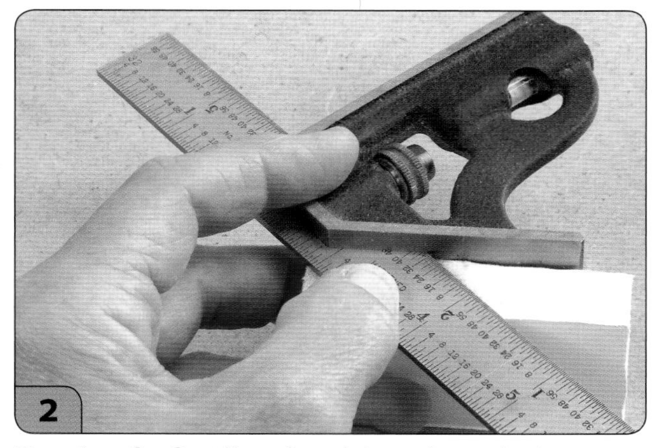

Drawing the first line. Stand the strip on the long edge opposite the one on which you made your marks. The marks should be on top, away from you. Draw a line at a 45° angle from point A to the opposite side, going left to right. This is line A.

Making the Ring Insert

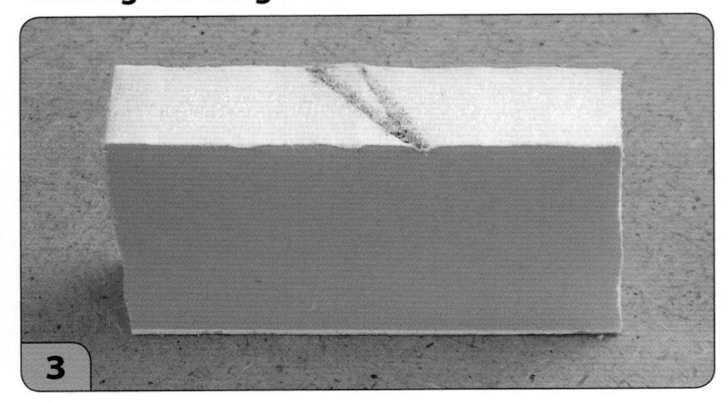

Drawing the second line. Draw a line from point B to the end of line A. This is line B. Together, the two lines form an angled wedge.

Making the first wedge cut. Stand the strip on the unmarked long edge, and using a #2/0 blade, cut along line A just until you reach the rigid paper on the other side of the foam core. Do not cut through the paper.

Making the second wedge cut. Cut along line B until you reach the paper. This will give you a wedge-shaped cut, as seen from the side, and a $\frac{3}{16}$" (5mm) wide channel, as seen from the top.

Cutting out the insert. Place the foam core with the wide side of the channel facing up. Fold the insert pattern along the center line. Attach the pattern with repositionable adhesive so the center line is centered on the channel. Cut along the circle.

Thinning the insert. If the depth of the center recess is ½" (13mm) or less, you must thin the insert slightly or it will be too thick. To do this, remove the top layer of paper and a small amount of foam, $\frac{1}{16}$" to ⅛" (2 to 3mm), with an X-Acto knife. If the recess is deeper than ½" (13mm), this step is not needed.

Inserting the velvet. Remove the backing from the 3" x 2" (75 x 50mm) adhesive-backed velvet. Fold the piece in half widthwise, adhesive side out. Open the foam core at the wedge so you can insert the velvet and place the folded edge of the velvet into the bottom of the wedge.

Trimming the velvet. Smooth the velvet in place on the top and sides, working from the wedge outward. Trim off excess velvet.

Completing the insert. Place the insert into the hole in the bottom of the box, wedge angled toward the back. If desired, use the insert pattern to cut a circle from the 2" x 2" (50 x 50mm) square of adhesive-backed velvet and place it into the recess in the top of the box.

Basic Ring Box Pattern
Make 2 Copies at 100%

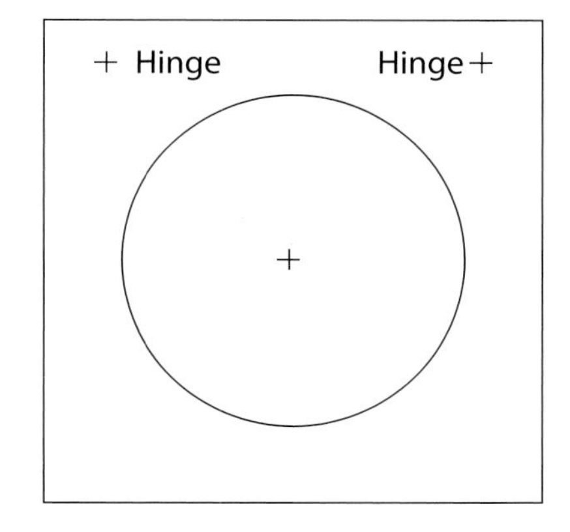

2" (51mm) square with 1⅜" (35mm)-diameter circle for Forstner bit

Foamcore Insert Pattern
Copy at 100%

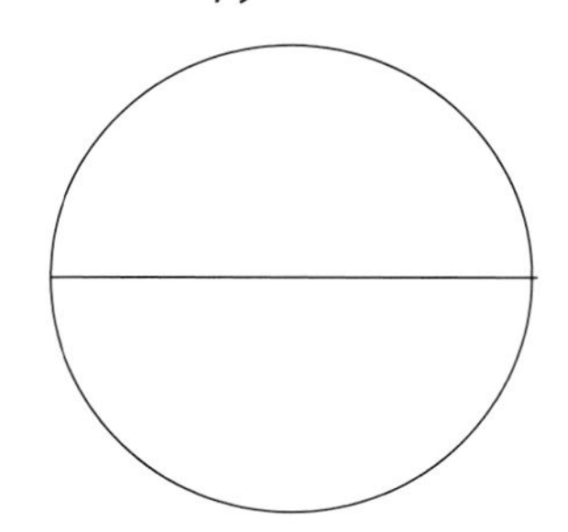

1⅜" (35mm)-diameter circle with center line

Flower Top Jewelry Box

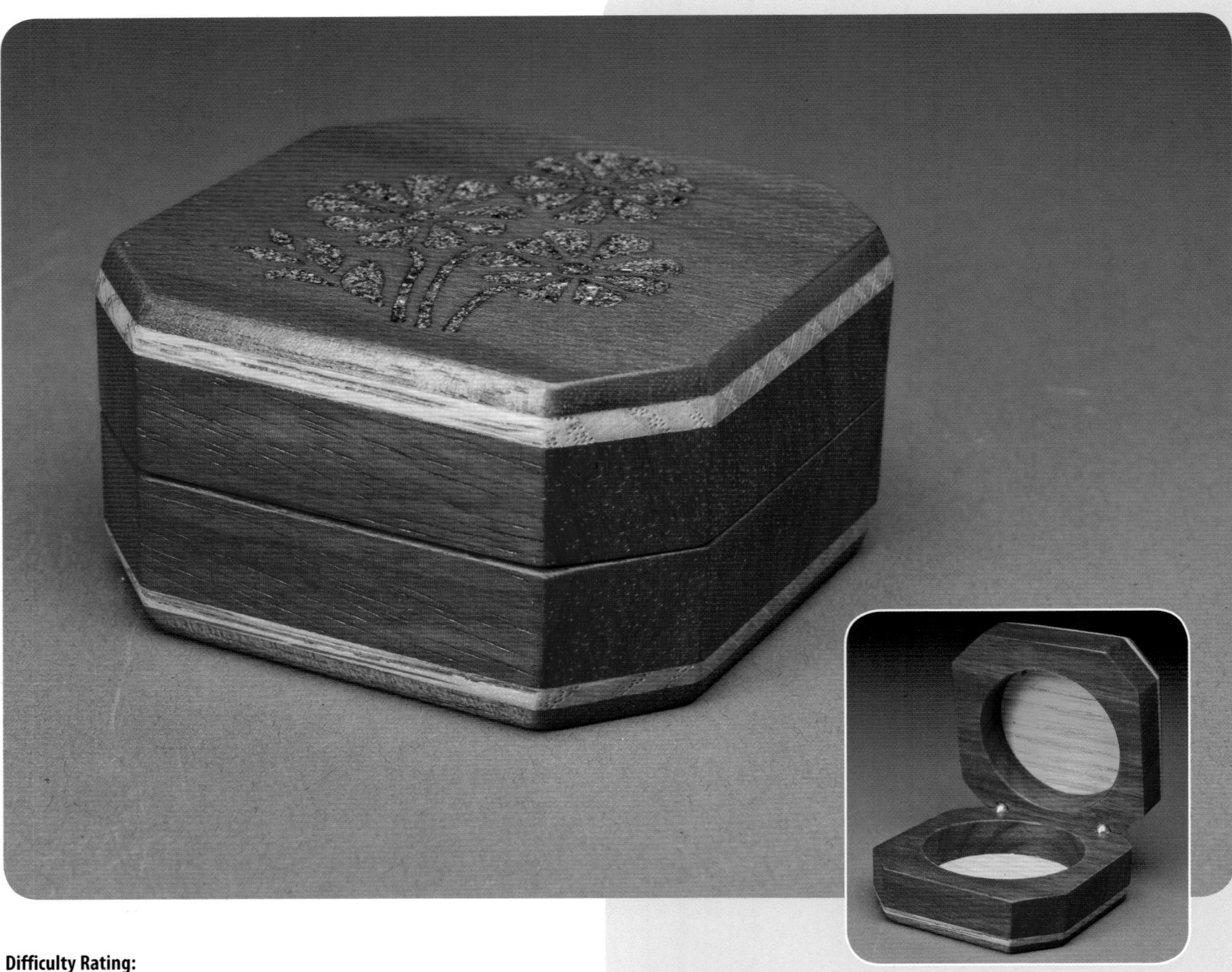

Difficulty Rating:

I'd been looking for an opportunity to use InLace, a pourable resin that looks like stone, and this flower pattern seemed just the place. Instead of flowers, you can substitute a favorite fretwork pattern, or customize the box with a name or initials. If you choose, the cutout areas can be left unfilled.

To turn this jewelry box into a large ring box, reduce the size of the center holes to 1⅝" (40mm). Make a 1⅝" (40mm) ring insert, using a piece of 2 ½" x 2" x ½" (65 x 50 x 13mm) foam core, and a 3 ½" x 2½" (90 x 65mm) piece of adhesive-backed velvet. The increased width of the foam core does not affect the instructions on page 93.

Materials and Tools

Wood

- (2) 3" x 3" x ¾" (75 x 75 x 19mm) padauk
- (2) 3" x 3" x ⅛" (75 x 75 x 3mm) walnut
- (2) 3" x 3" x ⅛" (75 x 75 x 3mm) oak
- (1) 2" (50mm) piece of ⅛" (3mm) dowel, marked at 7.5mm (19⁄64") from one end

Materials

- Repositionable adhesive
- Glue
- Epoxy
- Sandpaper for sanders of choice, assorted grits
- Sandpaper for hand sanding, assorted grits
- 0000 steel wool
- (2) 5mm barrel hinges
- InLace resin
- (2) 2" (50mm) circles of adhesive-backed velvet (actual size needed, optional)
- Shellac
- Clear spray lacquer

Tools

- #9 scroll saw blade
- #2/0 blade for fretwork
- 2" (50mm) Forstner bit
- 5mm brad point bit
- #56 or smaller bit for fretwork
- Awl
- Ruler
- Clamps for gluing
- Clamps to hold wood for drilling
- Sanders of choice
- Toothpick or #3 cake decorating tip for epoxy

1. Attach the flower pattern to one of the pieces of walnut with repositionable adhesive. Drill entry holes and cut out the pattern. Clean up any fuzzies on the underside of the wood.

2. Attach one box pattern with repositionable adhesive to each piece of padauk. Mark the center and hinge drilling points with an awl. Remove the patterns and set them aside until Step 5.

3. For each piece of padauk, drill a hole through the wood at the awl mark in the center of the wood with the Forstner bit. Use a clamp to hold the wood. Sand the bottom edge of the hole to remove fuzzies.

4. Glue one piece of walnut and one piece of oak to each piece of padauk, sandwiching the oak between the padauk and walnut, and keeping the grain of all pieces running in the same direction. Be sure to place the fretwork piece so that the top of the design is on the same edge as the drill marks for the hinges. Avoid getting glue in the fretwork openings and in the center holes. Clamp the pieces and let them dry.

5. Reattach the patterns to the padauk side of each piece, using an awl and the hinge drill marks to align the patterns properly. Cut around the outline of each piece with the #9 blade. Remove the pattern.

6. To insert the barrel hinges, follow Steps 3–10 of Barrel Hinge Basics, page 88. Apply a coat of shellac to the recesses for a finished look.

7. Sand the outside of the box until the sides match perfectly.

8. Sand a bevel of about 20° on the upper and lower edges, using the oak layer as a guide to keep the bevel even.

9. Soften and even out the beveled edges. Soften other edges as desired. Sand progressively from coarser to finer grits until the box is smooth.

10. Mix one tablespoon of InLace resin with 13-15 drops of hardener. Using a toothpick, generously fill the holes in the flower pattern. Let the InLace dry overnight or longer, until fully hardened.

11. Sand the InLace flush with the top of the box. Fill in any voids with additional InLace, mixed in the same proportion, and let dry thoroughly. Sand smooth.

12. Finish the box with several coats of clear lacquer, rubbing down between coats with 0000 steel wool, as needed.

13. Insert the 2" (50mm) circles of velvet into the recesses (optional).

Cutting out the flower pattern.

Sanding a bevel on the top and bottom edges.

Sanding the InLace.

Fretwork Flower Pattern
Copy at 100%

3" (76mm) square

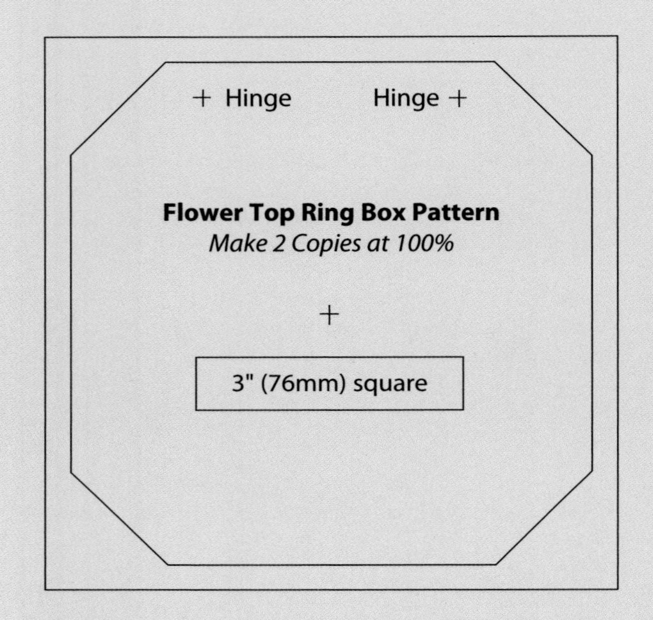

Octagonal Jewelry Box

Difficulty Rating:

A friend who designs jewelry provided the inspiration for this box, which is shaped to resemble a large, faceted gemstone. The bevels are created by sanding, not cutting, which makes the shaping of this box fast and easy. The softened edges add elegance, and the generous interior is the perfect size for a bracelet or small necklace.

Materials and Tools

Wood

- (2) 4" x 4" x ¾" (100 x 100 x 19mm) cherry
- (1) 2" (50mm) piece of ⅛" (2mm) dowel, marked 7.5mm (19/64") from one end

Materials

- Repositionable adhesive
- Epoxy
- Sandpaper for sanders of choice, assorted grits
- Sandpaper for hand sanding, assorted grits
- 0000 steel wool
- (2) 5mm barrel hinges
- (2) 2" (50mm) circles of adhesive-backed velvet (actual size needed)
- Shellac
- Clear spray lacquer

Tools

- #9 scroll saw blade
- 2" (50mm) Forstner bit
- 5mm brad point bit
- Awl
- Ruler
- Clamps to hold wood for drilling
- Sanders of choice
- Toothpick or #3 cake decorating tip for epoxy

Drawing the guideline for the first decorative bevel.

Sanding in the first decorative bevel.

Drawing the guideline for the second decorative bevel.

Completing the box.

1. Using repositionable adhesive, attach the pattern to each piece of cherry. Mark the centers and hinge drilling points with an awl.
2. Using the #9 blade, cut around the outline of each piece. Remove the pattern and discard it.
3. For each piece, place the point of the Forstner bit on the center point marked with the awl and drill a hole ½" (13mm) deep. Use a clamp to hold the wood securely.
4. To insert the barrel hinges, follow Steps 3–10 of Barrel Hinge Basics, page 88. Apply a coat of shellac to the recesses for a finished look.
5. Sand the outside of the box until the sides match perfectly.
6. Draw a line ⅜" (10mm) down from the top edge of the box. Extend this line around the entire top of the box. This will guide the sanding of the first bevel.
7. Sand a 20° bevel to the line drawn in Step 6 on each of the eight facets of the top of the box.
8. Draw a line ¼" (6mm) down from the top edge of the box. Extend this line around the entire top of the box. This will guide the second bevel.
9. Sand a 45° bevel to this line on each of the eight facets of the top of the box.
10. Sand to soften and even out the beveled edges on the top. Sand with progressively finer grits until smooth. Finish with several coats of lacquer, rubbing down between coats with 0000 steel wool, as needed.
11. Insert the two 2" (50mm) velvet circles into the recesses in the top and bottom of the box.

Variation

Try cutting this versatile box from other woods, such as sapele, as I have done here. Because the design of the box is so simple, this project is an excellent opportunity to feature the grain of a beautiful wood.

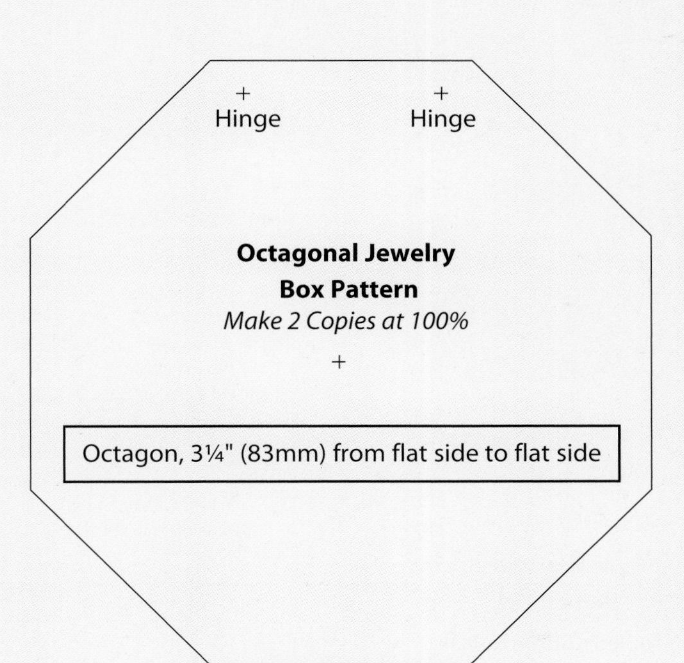

Double Heart Ring Box

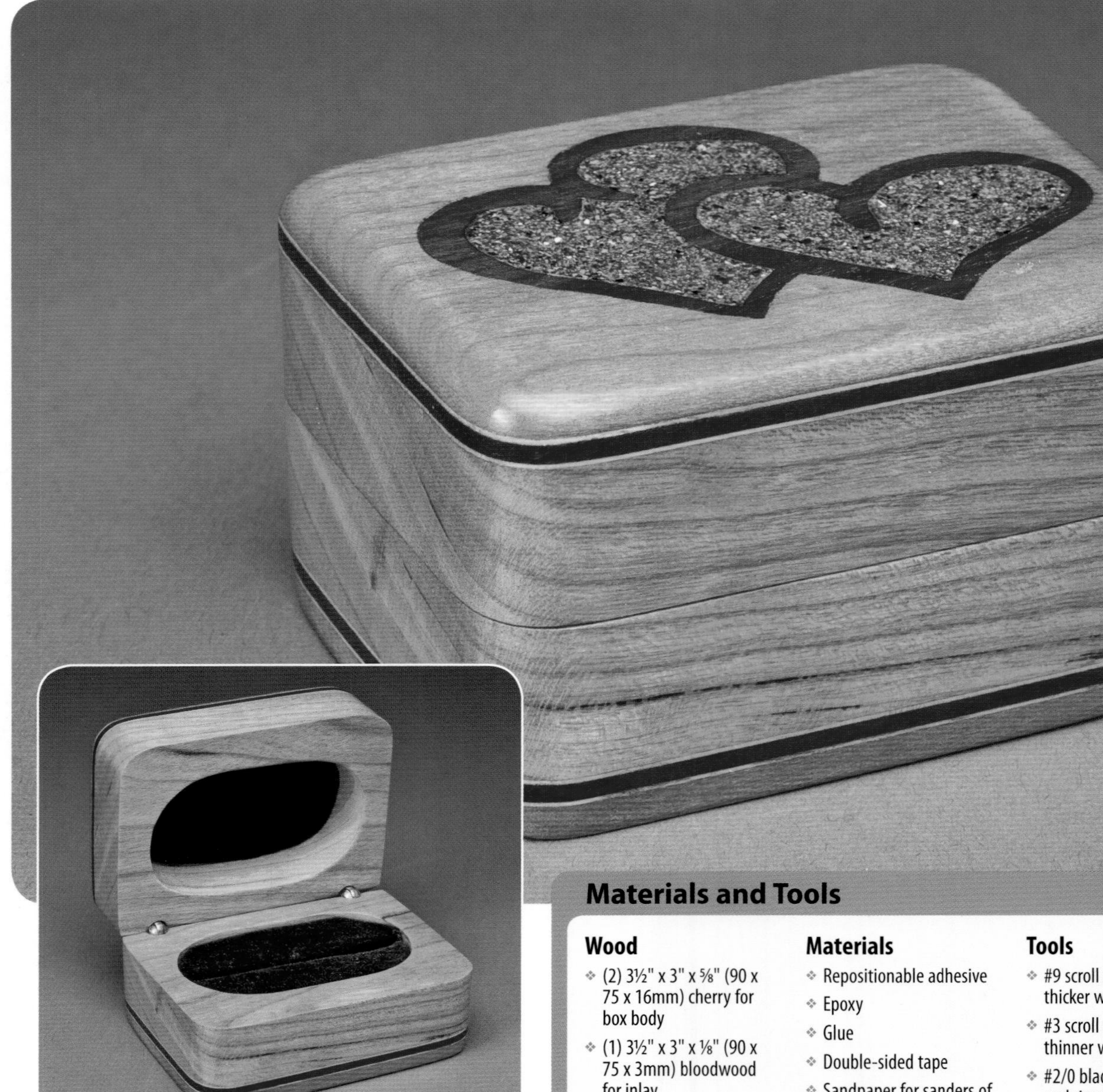

A double ring box is the perfect showcase for a set of matching wedding bands. Trying to be different, I considered pairings like yin and yang, sun and moon, even peanut butter and jelly, but none seemed right. In the end, I created an updated version of the popular double hearts, using cherry and bloodwood, with an InLace center for a jolt of color.

Difficulty Rating:

Materials and Tools

Wood

- (2) 3½" x 3" x ⅝" (90 x 75 x 16mm) cherry for box body
- (1) 3½" x 3" x ⅛" (90 x 75 x 3mm) bloodwood for inlay
- (2) 3½" x 3" x ⅛"(90 x 75 x 3mm) cherry for top and bottom pieces
- (2) 7" x 3" (180 x 75mm) ash veneer
- (1) 7" x 3" (180 x 75mm) bloodwood veneer, about 1/16" (2mm) thick
- (1) 2" (50mm) piece of ⅛" (2mm) dowel, marked 7.5mm (19/64") from one end

Materials

- Repositionable adhesive
- Epoxy
- Glue
- Double-sided tape
- Sandpaper for sanders of choice, assorted grits
- Sandpaper for hand sanding, assorted grits
- 0000 steel wool
- (2) 5mm barrel hinges
- InLace resin
- (2) 2½" x 1½" x ½" (65 x 40 x 13mm) pieces of foam core
- (1) 3½" x 3" (90 x 75mm) piece of adhesive-backed velvet for insert
- (1) 3" x 2" (75 x 50mm) piece of adhesive-backed velvet for the lid recess
- Shellac
- Clear spray lacquer

Tools

- #9 scroll saw blade for thicker wood
- #3 scroll saw blade for thinner wood
- #2/0 blade for fretwork and ring insert
- 5mm brad point bit
- 1⅜" (35mm) Forstner bit
- Tiny drill bit for #2/0 blade
- Awl
- Ruler
- Clamps for gluing
- Clamps to hold wood for drilling
- Sanders of choice
- Toothpick or #3 cake decorating tip for epoxy

1. Attach the heart pattern to the ⅛" (3mm)-thick piece of bloodwood. Drill an entry hole just inside the inner cutting line of each heart. Insert the #2/0 blade and cut along the inner line of each heart to remove the insides.
2. Attach the piece cut in Step 1 to one of the ⅛" (3mm)-thick pieces of cherry with small strips of double-sided tape. Cut along the outer rectangle.
3. Drill a small entry hole on the outer cutting line of the hearts. Insert the blade and cut around the perimeter.
4. Carefully separate the pieces of wood and glue the bloodwood heart into the open area in the middle of the piece of cherry. Fill any spaces where the two pieces join with a mixture of sawdust and white glue.
5. Attach one copy of the box pattern to each piece of ⅝" (16mm)-thick cherry. Cut along the outer line of each piece. Use an awl to mark the drill points for the hinges and for the center drilling holes, as indicated on the pattern. Remove the patterns and set them aside until Step 12.
6. For each piece, using a clamp to hold the wood, place the point of the Forstner bit on one of the center drilling marks and drill a hole completely through the wood. Repeat with the other center drilling mark. The two circles will overlap each other.
7. For each piece, draw two lines to connect the overlapping circles. Cut along these lines to form an oval opening. Sand the inside of the opening until smooth.
8. Glue together the three pieces of veneer with the bloodwood between the pieces of ash. Clamp and let dry. Cut the piece in half, crosswise.

Cutting the outside of the hearts.

Gluing the hearts in place.

Cutting out the centers.

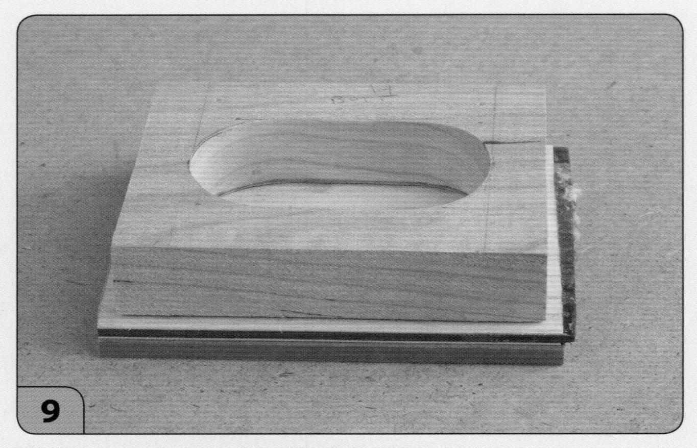
9

Making the bottom half of the box.

10

Making the top half of the box, first part.

11

Making the top half of the box, second part.

9. Make the bottom half of the box by gluing, in order, the remaining piece of ⅛" (3mm) cherry, one piece of the lamination, and one piece of the ⅝" (16mm) cherry. Be sure the side of the cherry with the drill marks for the hinges is facing up. Clamp the pieces together and let them dry.

10. Glue the second laminated piece to the remaining piece of ⅝" (16mm) cherry. Be sure the side of the cherry with the drill marks for the hinges is facing up. Clamp the pieces together and let them dry. Sand the sides to make the lamination flush with the cherry.

11. Glue the piece with the inlaid hearts to the laminated piece. Be sure that the hinge marks and the top of the hearts are on the same edge, and that all edges are aligned. Clamp the pieces and let them dry.

12. For each half of the box, reattach the pattern removed in Step 5, using the hinge drilling points for alignment. Cut along the line to form the perimeter of the box. Remove the patterns.

13. Follow Steps 3–10 on page 88 (Barrel Hinge Basics) to insert the 5mm barrel hinges. Apply a coat of shellac to the recesses for a finished look.

14. Sand the outside of the box until the sides match perfectly.

15. Mix one tablespoon of InLace with 13-15 drops of hardener. Fill the inside of the hearts, overfilling slightly to allow for shrinkage. Let dry overnight or longer until fully hard, and sand flush with the wood. Fill any voids with additional InLace, mixed in the same proportion, and let dry thoroughly. Sand flush when dry.

16. To complete the box, sand in a slight bevel at the top edge, soften all edges, and sand the entire box until smooth. Finish the outside of the box with several coats of clear lacquer, rubbing between coats with 0000 steel wool, as needed.

17. Because of its length, the insert is made in two pieces. Using the two pieces of foam core, follow the instructions on page 93 for cutting each piece. Glue the pieces together to form one long piece, aligning the slots.

18. Follow the instructions on page 93 to cover and complete the insert, using the insert pattern and the 3 ½" x 3" (90 x 75mm) piece of adhesive-backed velvet.

19. Using the insert pattern, cut the remaining piece of adhesive-backed velvet so it fits into the recess in the lid of the box.

Making the ring insert.

Variation

You can vary this design to make a small jewelry box. Here's how:

1. Instead of using a Forstner bit, cut a rectangular opening into each piece of ⅝" (16mm) cherry. Round the corners for ease in sanding.

2. Assemble the box according to instructions, but instead of velvet inserts, apply flocking to the top and bottom recesses. (See Fearless Flocking, page 130.)

Double Heart Inlay Pattern
Copy at 100%

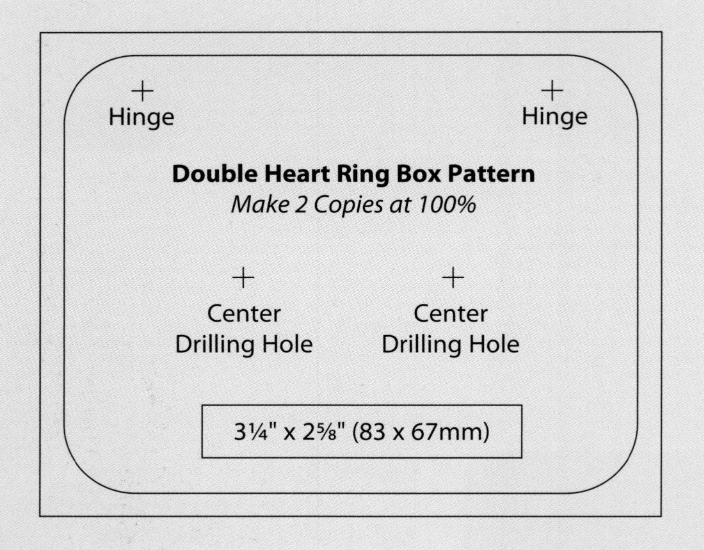

3¼" x 2⅝" (83 x 67mm)

Double Heart Ring Box Insert Pattern
Copy at 100%

2⁵⁄₁₆" x 1⅜" (59 x 35mm) oval

Rectangular Jewelry Box

Difficulty Rating:

Here's an easy way to create an attractive jewelry box with multiple compartments, using just three pieces of wood and some veneer. Small barrel hinges attach the lid and keep it from falling backward. I finished the recesses with flocking, but you can glue velvet to the bottoms if you prefer, or they can be left natural with their coat of shellac.

Materials and Tools

Wood

- (1) 7" x 4" x 1" (180 x 100 x 25mm) maple burl for the box body
- (1) 7" x 4" x ¼" (180 x 100 x 6mm) purpleheart for the box bottom
- (1) 7" x 4" x ½" (180 x 100 x 13mm) purpleheart for the lid
- (2) 7" x 4" (180 x 100mm) maple veneer
- (1) ¾" (19mm)-long piece of ⅛" (3mm) dowel, marked 7.5mm (19/64") from one end

Materials

- Repositionable spray adhesive
- Glue
- Epoxy
- Sandpaper for sanders of choice, assorted grits
- Sandpaper for hand sanding, assorted grits
- 0000 steel wool
- (2) 5mm brass barrel hinges
- Flocking fibers
- Acrylic paint to match the flocking fibers
- Shellac
- Clear spray lacquer

Tools

- #9 or #12 scroll saw blade for thick wood
- #3 scroll saw blade for thinner wood
- 5mm brad point drill bit
- Awl
- Ruler
- Clamps
- Toothpick or #3 cake decorating tip for epoxy
- Sanders of choice
- Brush for acrylic paint

Aligning the hinge marks.

Sanding the outside of the box.

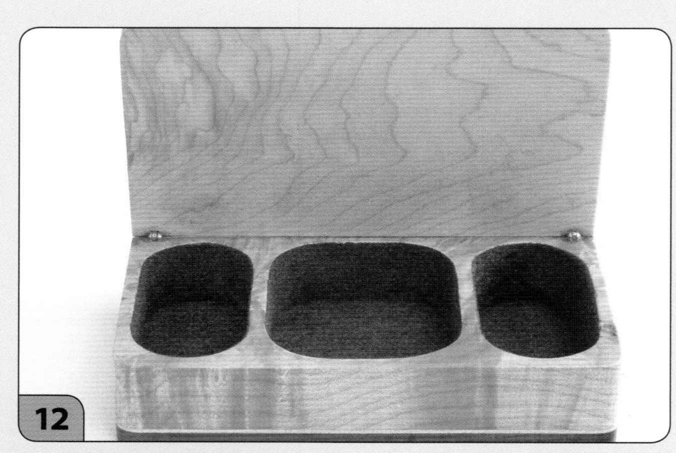

Applying the flocking.

1. Using repositionable adhesive, attach the pattern to the 1" (25mm)-thick piece of maple burl. Mark the hinge drilling points with an awl.
2. Drill entry holes where indicated on the pattern. Insert the saw blade through each entry hole and cut out the compartments. Remove the pattern and save it for Step 5.
3. Sand the sides of the cut-out areas and round over the upper edges. Sand off any fuzzies on the lower edges.
4. Glue one piece of maple veneer and the ¼" (6mm)-thick piece of purpleheart to the bottom of the box body. Clamp the pieces for five minutes, remove from the clamps, and clean up any glue squeeze-out. Re-clamp the box and let it dry.
5. Re-attach the pattern, using the hinge marks for alignment, and cut along the outer line.
6. Glue the remaining piece of veneer to the ½" (13mm)-thick piece of purpleheart. Clamp and let dry.
7. Attach a second copy of the pattern to the veneer side of the lid. Mark the hinge drilling points with an awl. Cut along the outline to form the lid.
8. Support the lid so it is level with the top of the box body. Check to be sure the hinge holes on the box and lid are aligned.
9. To insert the barrel hinges, follow Steps 3–10 of Barrel Hinge Basics, page 88. Because of the larger size of this box, the guideline for the bevel drawn in Step 7 of the hinge instructions should be ¼" (6mm) from the drilled face of each piece, not 3⁄16" (5mm).
10. Sand the outside of the box until the base and top are perfectly matched. Bevel the top of the lid, if desired.
11. Soften all edges slightly and sand the box until completely smooth. Apply several coats of shellac or clear lacquer, rubbing down each coat with 0000 steel wool, as needed.
12. Apply flocking to the inner compartments (See Fearless Flocking, page 130).

Rectangular Jewelry Box and Lid Pattern
Make 2 Copies at 100%

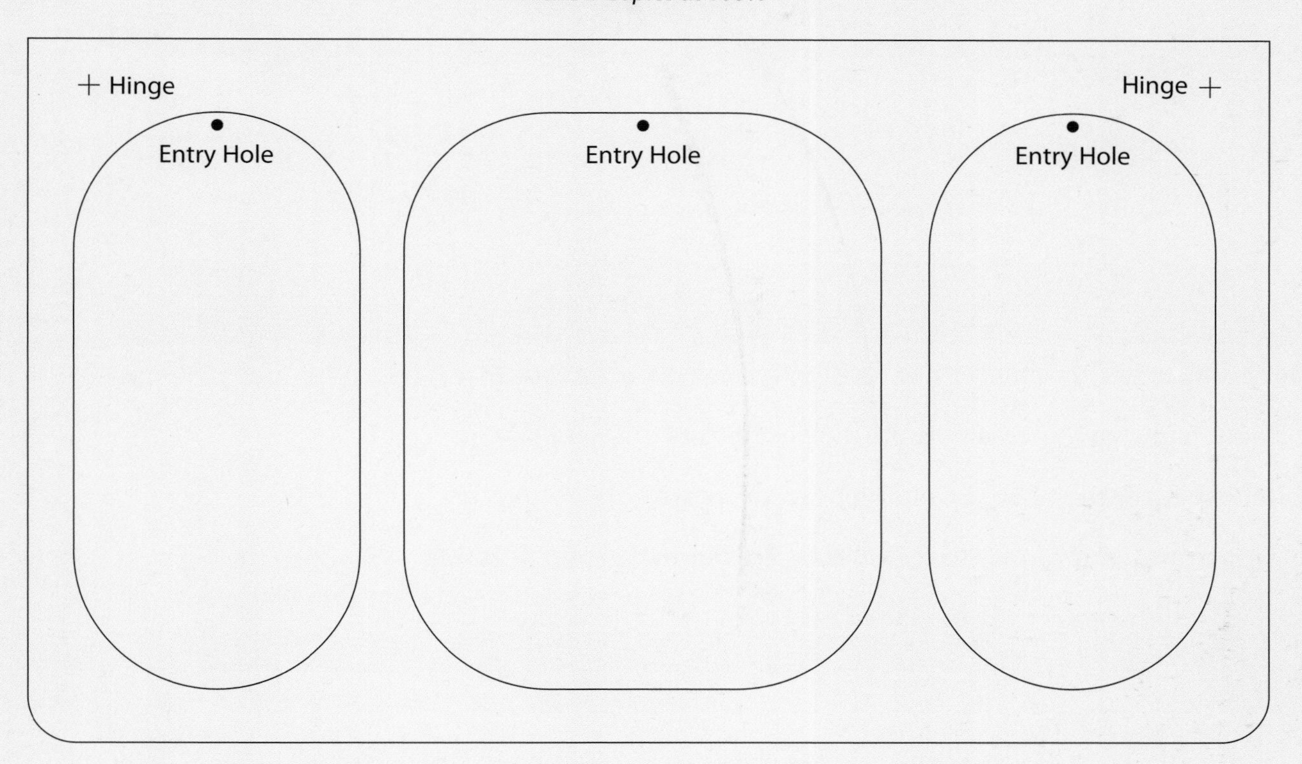

6½" x 3 13⁄16" (165 x 99mm) rectangle with two rounded corners and three oval cutouts. Hinge drilling holes are ¼" (6mm) from the back edge and 5⁄16" (8mm) from the sides.

Chapter 5

Miniature Furniture Boxes

The projects in this chapter use techniques usually associated with the band saw to create multi-purpose boxes that look like dollhouse furniture. The novel touches—decorative bases, overlay drawer fronts, and miniaturized objects—result in a group of boxes that are unique, easy to personalize, and a lot of fun to make.

China Cabinet: A Step-by-Step Guide

Materials and Tools

Wood

Bottom section: Box

- (3) 6½" x 3½" x ¾" (165 x 90 x 19mm) mahogany for box
- (1) 6¼" x 3¼" x ¼" (160 x 85 x 6mm) mahogany for back
- (1) 6½" x 3" x ¾" (165 x 75 x 19mm) mahogany for decorative base
- (1) 5¾" x 3" x ¼" (145 x 75 x 6mm) mahogany for drawer fronts
- (1) 6½" x 2¾" x ¼" (165 x 70 x 6mm) mahogany for top (actual size needed)

Hutch

- (2) 3⁵⁄₁₆" x 1⅜" x ¼" (84 x 35 x 6mm) mahogany for sides (actual size needed)
- (1) 5" x 1⅜" x ¼" (127 x 35 x 6mm) mahogany for shelf (actual size needed)
- (1) 5½" x 3⁵⁄₁₆" x ¼" (140 x 84 x 6mm) mahogany for back (actual size needed)
- (1) 6" x 1" x ¼" (150 x 25 x 6mm) mahogany for trim
- (1) 6" x 2⅛" x ¼" (152 x 54 x 6mm) mahogany for top (actual size needed)

Decorations

- See Making Decorative Miniatures, page 119, for wood and patterns

Materials

- Repositionable adhesive
- Glue
- Masking tape
- Sandpaper for sanders of choice, assorted grits
- Sandpaper for hand sanding, assorted grits
- 0000 steel wool
- (4) Small steel screws, same size or smaller than those for the brass knobs
- (4) ⁵⁄₁₆" (8mm) brass knobs that screw directly into the wood
- Flocking fibers
- Acrylic paint to match flocking
- Shellac
- Clear spray lacquer

Tools

- #7 scroll saw blade for thicker wood
- #3 scroll saw blade for thinner wood
- ³⁄₃₂" (2mm) or other small drill bit for brass knobs
- ¹⁄₁₆" (2mm) drill bit for entry holes
- Awl
- Clamps
- Wide rubber bands for clamping the base
- Sanders of choice
- Brush for acrylic paint

Difficulty Rating:

 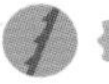 

Most boxes with drawers use conventional joinery, such as box joints or miters. By cutting both carcass and drawers from the same piece of wood, then adding overlay drawer fronts, I created a box with a traditional appearance, but without the fuss. The easy-to-make compound-cut base and matching hutch add a touch of realism. For convenience, all wood, except for the optional decorative objects, is either ¼" or ¾" (6 or 19mm) thick.

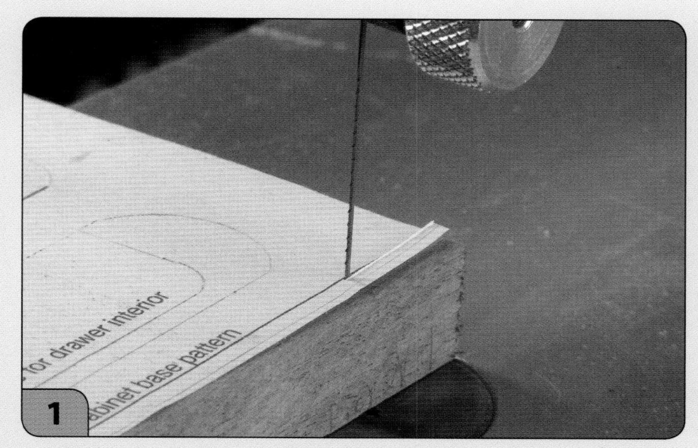

Cutting the outside of the box. Using repositionable adhesive, attach a copy of the box pattern to each piece of 6½" x 3½" x ¾" (165 x 90 x 19mm) mahogany. Mark which piece will be used for the front, middle, and back of the box. Cut along the outer line of each piece.

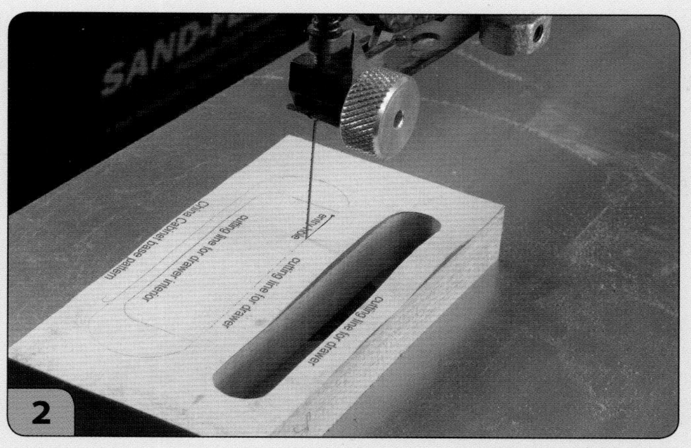

Cutting out the drawer pieces. For each piece, drill entry holes where indicated on the pattern. Insert the saw blade and cut out the drawers. Mark the drawer pieces "front," "middle," and "back" to correspond to the piece they were cut from. Do not remove the drawer patterns.

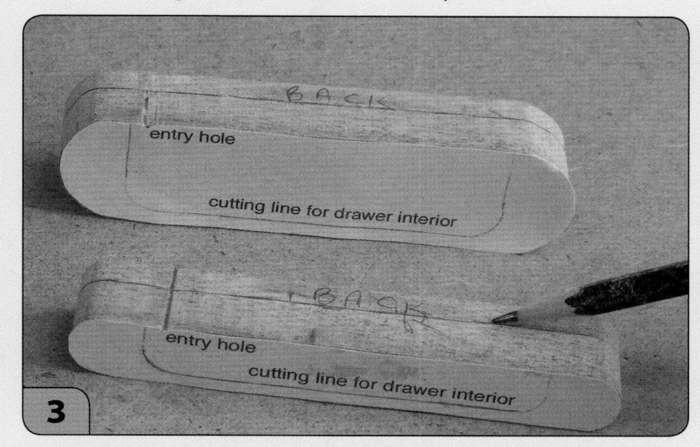

Drawing the cutting lines for the backs of the drawers. On both "back" drawer pieces, draw a line that is ¼" (6mm) from the rear face of that piece.

Cutting the backs of the drawers. Cut along the lines drawn in Step 3. The thin pieces are the backs of the drawers. Mark each back so you can glue it to the corresponding drawer in Step 7.

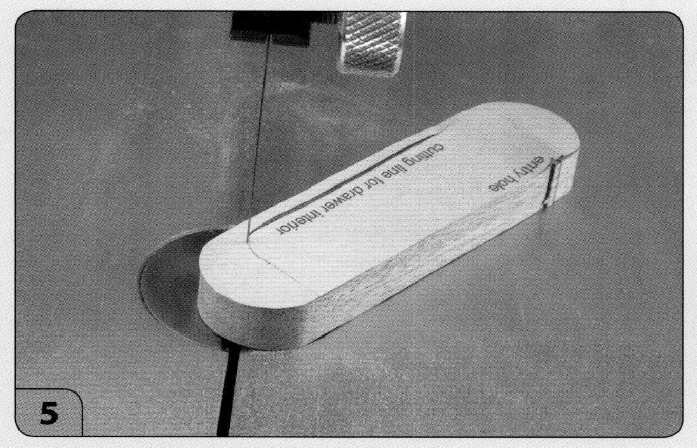

Cutting the drawer interiors. Cut along the inner lines of the six drawer pieces to create the interiors. Remove the patterns and discard the cut-out pieces.

Gluing the drawer pieces together. Glue together the drawer pieces from Step 5, keeping them in order, to make the two drawers. Do not glue on the back pieces. Clamp and let dry.

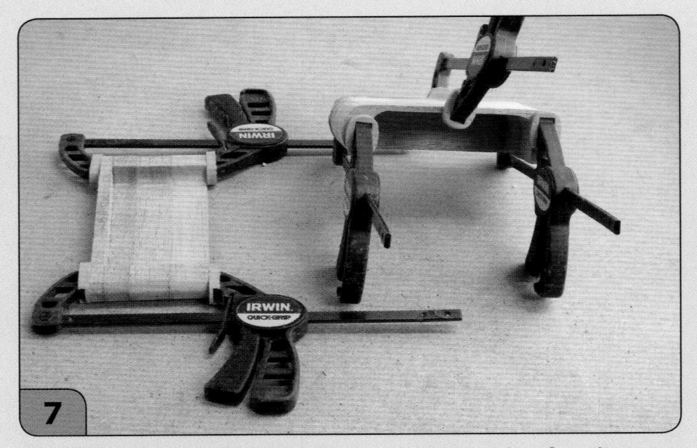

7

Attaching the drawer backs. Sand the inside of each drawer until it is smooth. Glue the back of each drawer into place. Clamp and let dry. Clean up any squeeze-out inside each drawer. Sand the drawer outsides just until smooth.

8

Gluing the body of the box. Glue the three box pieces together, keeping them in marked order. Clamp and let dry.

9

Sanding the drawer openings. Sand the drawer openings to smooth the glue joint between the pieces.

10

Adjusting the fit of the drawers. Check the fit of each drawer by inserting it into its corresponding opening in the box. Sand as needed so that each drawer slides in easily.

11

Making the back of the box. Place the box, face up, on the 6¼" x 3¼" x ¼" (160 x 85 x 6mm) piece of mahogany and trace the outline. Cut along the outside of this line to make the back of the box. Glue it into place, clamp, and let dry.

12

Sanding the box. Sand the back flush with the box sides, top, and bottom. Sand all surfaces smooth. Check to make sure the box is square and the top and bottom faces are flat.

Cutting the drawer fronts. Attach the drawer front patterns to the 5¾" x 3" x ¼" (145 x 75 x 6mm) piece of mahogany. Cut along the perimeters.

Beveling and drilling the drawer fronts. Drill appropriately sized holes for the drawer knobs where indicated on the patterns. Remove the patterns and sand a small 45˚ bevel on the front edge of all four sides of each drawer.

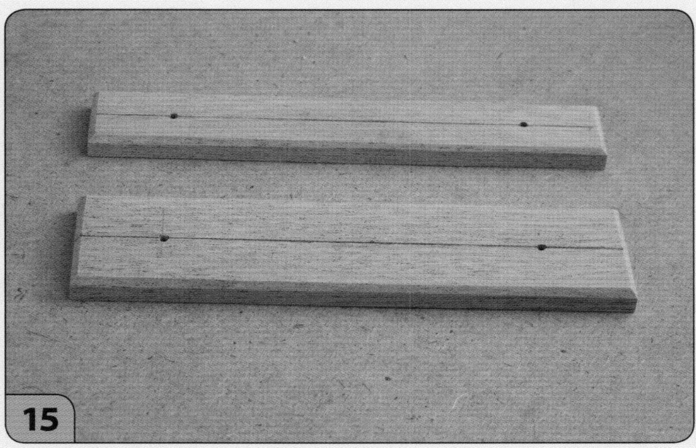

Marking the drawer fronts. Draw a pencil line across each drawer front through the drilled holes. Continue the line down the side edges. This will help guide the drawer front placement.

Drawing alignment lines for the drawer fronts. Mark the front of the box from the top down on both sides at 11/16" (17mm) and 2 1/16" (52mm). Draw lines across the box at these points. This will help you align the drawer fronts.

Securing the drawers. Insert the drawers, without their fronts, into their corresponding places in the box. With the box upright, secure each drawer with a small piece of masking tape to keep its position.

Marking the drilling holes. Place the box on its back and position the drawer fronts, using the lines drawn in Steps 15 and 16. Insert an awl through the holes in each drawer front to mark the knob locations. Remove the drawer fronts and drill holes into the drawers for the screws.

19

Attaching the drawer fronts. Screw the drawer fronts into place with small steel screws to be sure they are positioned properly. If spaces between the fronts are not even, remove the screws, reposition the fronts, adjust the drilling holes, and re-check the alignment. When you are satisfied, remove the screws and glue the drawer fronts to the drawers. Insert the screws to hold the fronts firmly against the drawers until the glue dries. Remove screws.

Using Steel Screws

Small brass screws are prone to breakage, and some small knobs attach with hanger bolts, making removal difficult. For this reason, attach the knobs after the box is completed and use steel screws for positioning and gluing on the drawer fronts.

20

Making the top for the bottom section. Place the piece of 6 ½" x 2 ¾" x ¼" (165 x 70 x 6mm) mahogany on top of the bottom section of the box, back edge flush and side overhangs even. If needed, adjust the size by cutting or sanding. Sand the upper and lower edges of the front and sides to soften. Glue to the top of the box. Clamp and let dry.

21

Cutting out the decorative base. Attach the pattern for the decorative base to the remaining piece of ¾" (19mm)-thick piece of mahogany. Cut along all lines. Remove the pattern. Number and mark the top of each piece as shown for ease in re-assembly.

22

Cutting the sides of the decorative base. Attach the side patterns to each side of the decorative base. Cut along the lines.

Gluing up the decorative base. Glue the four pieces of the base together. Clamp with wide rubber bands and let dry. Sand smooth and soften all edges.

Gluing on the decorative base. Glue the decorative base to the bottom of the box, keeping the spacing on the sides and front even. Clamp securely and let dry.

Making the Hutch

Assembling the hutch. To position the shelf properly, draw a line across the inside face of the back and the two side pieces. The line should be 1 5⁄16" (33mm) from the bottom edge. Place the shelf and sides into position on the back to check the length of the shelf, aligning the bottom of the shelf with the pencil lines. If the shelf is too long, shorten it until the sides of the hutch are flush with the edges of the back. (If the shelf is too short, your best option is to cut a new piece to fit.) Glue together the shelf, the sides, and the back. Use blocks of wood to stabilize the assembly, and press firmly on the pieces to get a good bond.

Cutting and attaching the trim. Attach the pattern for the decorative trim to the 6" x 1" x ¼" (150 x 25 x 6mm) piece of mahogany and cut along the lines. Glue the trim to the front edge of the sides, at the top of the hutch. Sand off any overhang when the glue is dry.

27

Attaching the top. Sand a small 45° bevel along one long and both short sides of the 6" x 2 ⅛" x ¼" (152 x 54 x 6mm) mahogany piece. Glue it to the hutch top, bevel side down, flat side flush with the back, and the overhang even on both sides. Clamp or use weights to ensure a good bond.

28

Attaching the hutch to the base. Glue the hutch to the base, keeping the back edges flush and the sides even. Clamp securely to ensure a good bond.

29

Applying the finish. Sand all surfaces smooth. Shellac all surfaces to seal the wood. Sand smooth and remove glue spots. Apply additional coats of shellac or clear lacquer, smoothing surfaces between coats with 0000 steel wool as needed. Screw in the brass knobs. To flock the drawer interiors, see Fearless Flocking, page 130.

30

Adding the decorations. To decorate the china cabinet, see the sidebar on Making Decorative Miniatures, right.

Making Decorative Miniatures

Apply your finish of choice to the objects before gluing them into place. Lightly sand the area where the object will be glued so it can adhere properly.

Photos, book covers, or periodicals. Scan in the desired picture or cover and print it out about 1" (25mm) high, using photo paper. Glue the scans to ⅛" (3mm) or thinner pieces of wood. For standing photos, glue a small angled piece of wood to the back of the frame as a support.

Books. Cut a piece of ¼" (6mm)-thick aspen or maple to the size desired for the pages. Make shallow parallel cuts with the scroll saw in one long and both short sides of this piece to simulate pages. Cut two pieces of ⅛" (3mm) or thinner wood the same size as the pages for the covers. Cut a spine from the same wood and glue the parts together. Sand a curve where the spine and covers meet for a more realistic effect.

Bowls. Attach a bowl pattern (page 123) to a small piece of ¼" to ½" (6 to 13mm)-thick wood. Drill an angled entry hole, between 15° and 25°, just inside the inner ring, drilling toward the center of the pattern. Tilt the saw table to that same angle, left side down. Insert the saw blade and cut clockwise along the inner ring. Discard the center. Sand the cut surface smooth, and glue the piece to a matching or contrasting piece of thin wood, ranging from ⅛" to ¼" (3 to 6mm) thick. Cut along the outer ring to form the bowl. Sand smooth.

Vase. Cut out two identical angled circles from ½" (13mm)-thick wood (plain or laminated) and glue them together at the larger faces. Cut a smaller angled circle to match the top of the glued-up circles and glue it into place. Drill a hole in the center with a countersink bit to create the appearance of an opening.

Basket. Attach one of the basket patterns (page 123) to a piece of ⅛" (3mm)-thick wood. Cut out the rings and base and glue them together.

Collapsible basket. Attach the patterns (page 123) to a piece of ⅛" (3mm)-thick wood. Cut out the pieces and glue them together. Cut out thin strips from matching wood and glue them to the underside of the basket at right angles to each other and positioned under the handle.

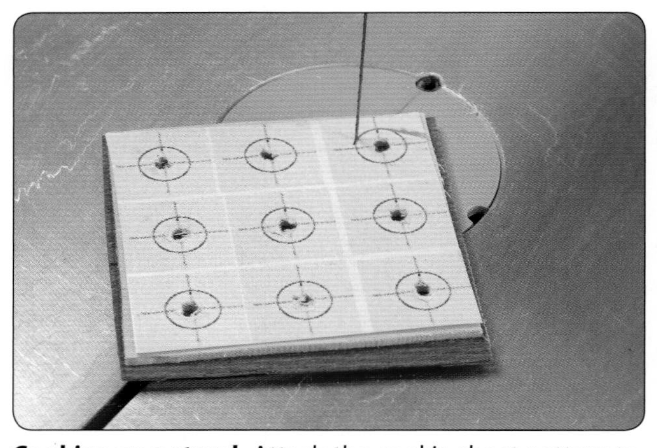

Cookies on a stand. Attach the cookie sheet pattern to a 2" x 3" (50 x 75mm) piece of 1⁄16" (2mm)-thick maple. Drill ⅛" (3mm) holes at the center of each circle. Glue a piece of red veneer between the drilled piece and a matching solid piece of maple. Clamp firmly and let dry. Cut along the circles to form the cookies. To make the stand, follow the instructions for making a bowl, using ⅛" (3mm)-thick wood for the sides and the bottom and a 15°cutting angle. Cut a small circle at a 15° angle from ⅛" or ¼" (3 or 6mm)-thick piece of matching wood to form the pedestal; glue it to the underside of the top piece. Choose the ten best cookies and glue them into place, using seven on the bottom and three on the top.

Bread in basket. Follow the instructions for making a bowl, using ¼" (6mm)-thick wood for the ring, ⅛" (3mm)-thick wood for the base, and a 15° cutting angle. To make the bread, cut a piece of walnut to about 1¼" x ½" x ⅜" (32 x 13 x 10mm), or to fit the basket. Round the top edges and the ends. Cut off two thin pieces from one end. Make parallel cuts along the rest of the piece, cutting almost to the bottom, to form slices. Glue the bread inside the basket, positioning the cut pieces at the end of the loaf.

China Cabinet Decorative Top Edge Pattern
Copy at 100%

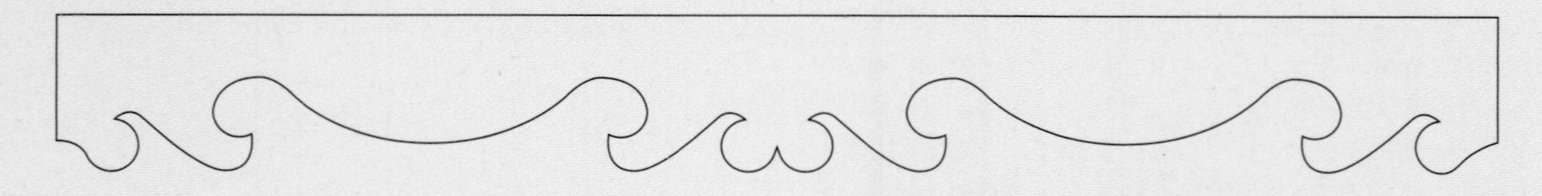

5 9⁄16" x ⅝" (141 x 16mm)

China Cabinet Box Base

Make 3 Copies at 100%

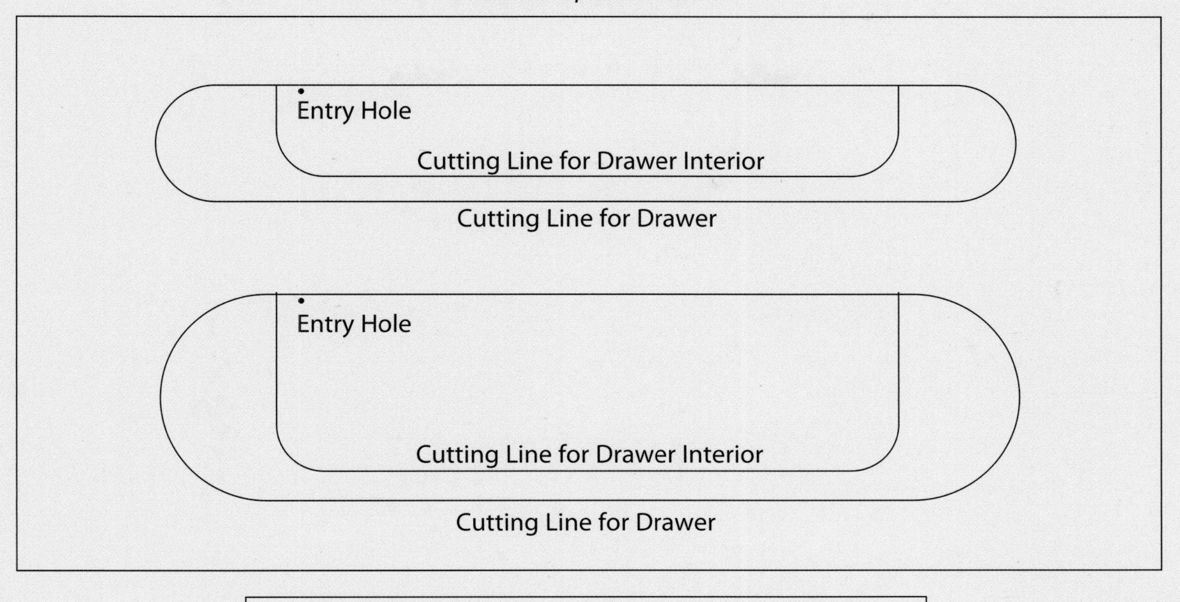

6" x 3" (152 x 76mm), drawers are ⅜" (10mm) from top and bottom edges and ½" (13mm) apart.

China Cabinet Drawer Front Patterns

Copy at 100%

Top Drawer is 5 7/16" x ⅞" (138 x 22mm).

Bottom Drawer is 5 7/16" x 1⅜" (138 x 35mm).

Decorative Base, Long Side Pattern

Make 2 copies at 100%

6⅛" x ¾" (156 x 19mm)

Decorative Base, Top Pattern

Copy at 100%

6⅛" x 2⅝" (156 x 67mm)

Decorative Base, Short Side Pattern

Make 2 copies at 100%

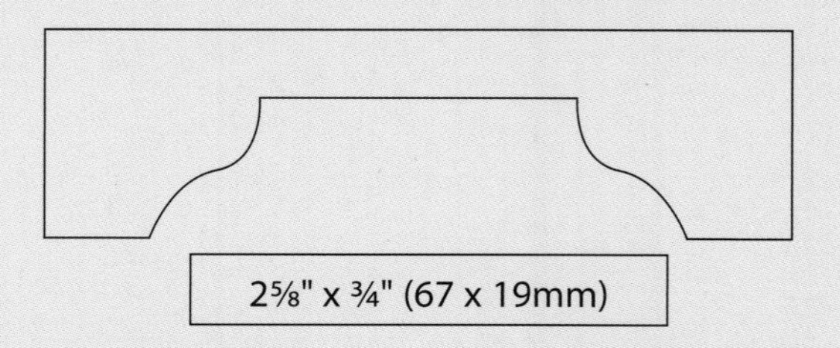

2⅝" x ¾" (67 x 19mm)

Miniature Object Patterns

Seven-Wave Basket Pattern
Copy at 100%

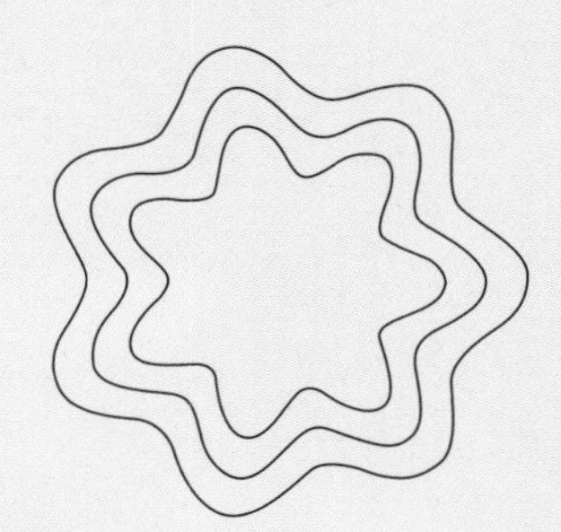

Nine-Wave Basket Pattern
Copy at 100%

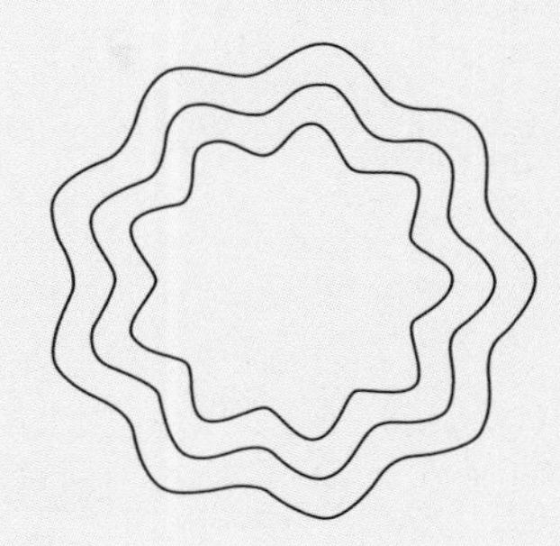

Collapsible Basket Pattern
Copy at 100%

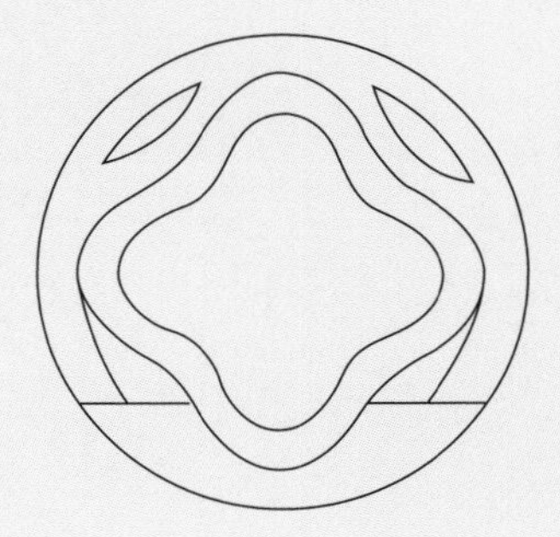

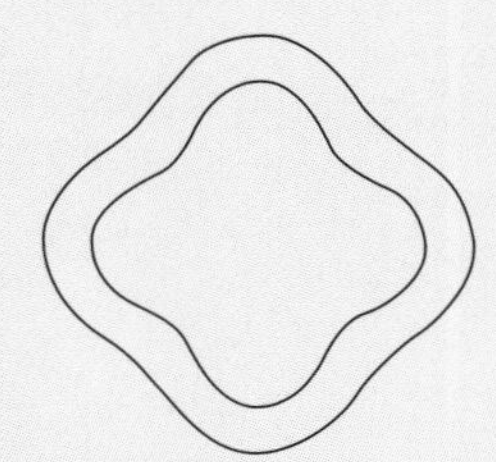

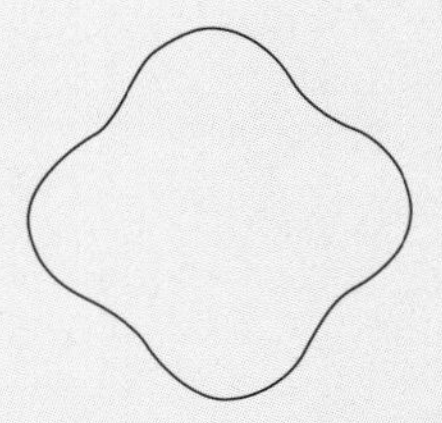

Cookie Sheet Pattern
Copy at 100%

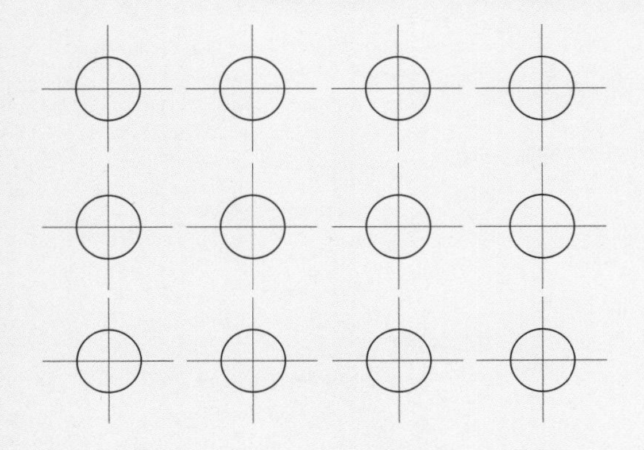

Top of Cookie Stand Pattern
Copy at 100%

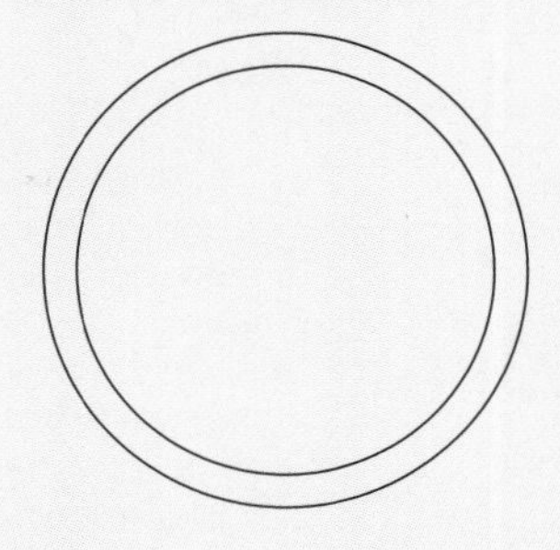

Bread Basket Pattern
Copy at 100%

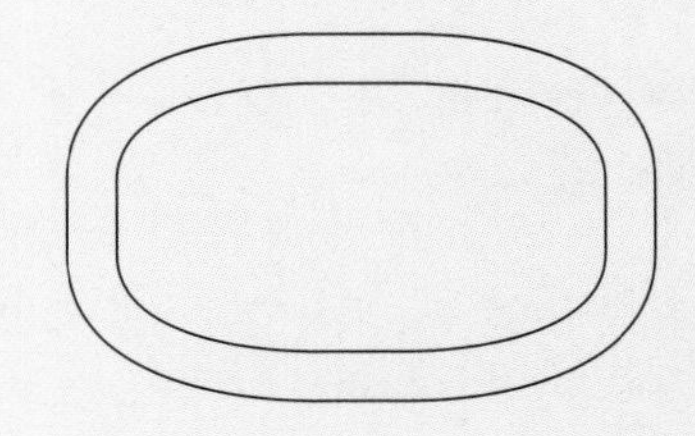

Oval Bowl Pattern
Copy at 100%

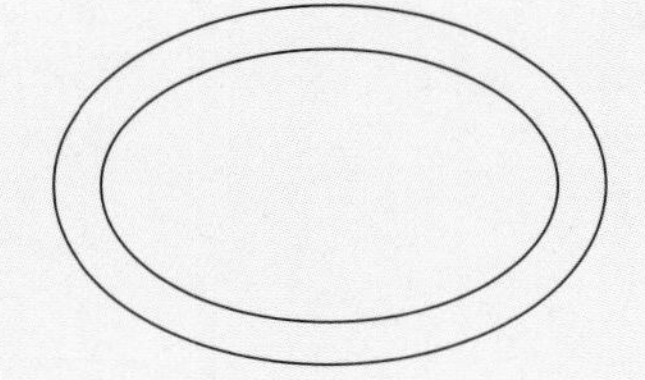

Round Bowl Pattern
Copy at 100%

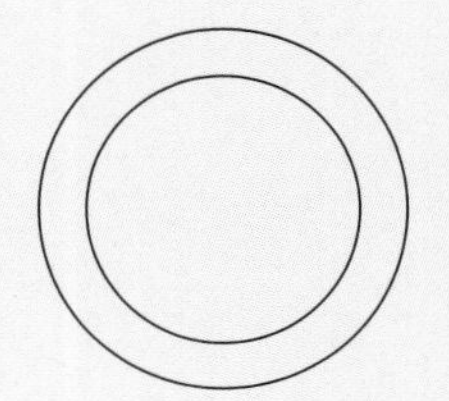

Chest of Drawers Box

Difficulty Rating:

Mahogany, an attractive softer hardwood, is ideal for this project. The box and drawers are cut from two 1" (25mm)-thick pieces of wood, glued together to achieve attractive proportions. The beveled top piece and compound-cut base complete the furniture effect, and the brass knobs and flocked drawer interiors lend a touch of class.

Materials and Tools

Wood

- (2) 5½" x 6" x 1" (140 x 150 x 25mm) mahogany for box body
- (1) 6¼" x 2¾" x ½" (159 x 70 x 13mm) mahogany for box top (actual size needed)
- (1) 6¼" x 3" x ¾" (160 x 75 x 19mm) mahogany for base
- (1) 5½" x 6" x ¼" (140 x 150 x 6mm) mahogany for box back
- (1) 5½" x 5½" x ¼" (140 x 140 x 6mm) mahogany for drawer fronts

Materials

- Repositionable adhesive
- Glue
- Masking tape
- Sandpaper for sanders of choice, assorted grits
- Sandpaper for hand sanding, assorted grits
- 0000 steel wool
- (6) Steel screws, same size or smaller than for knobs
- (6) 7⁄16" (11mm) brass knobs that screw directly into the wood
- Flocking fibers
- Acrylic paint to match flocking
- Shellac
- Clear spray lacquer

Tools

- #9 scroll saw blade for thick wood
- #3 scroll saw blade for thin wood
- 3⁄32" (2.5mm) or other small drill bit for brass knobs
- 1⁄16" (2mm) drill bit for entry holes
- Awl
- Clamps
- Wide rubber band for clamping the base
- Sanders of choice
- Brush for acrylic paint

1. Attach a copy of the box body pattern to each piece of 1" (25mm) mahogany. Cut along the outer line of each piece. Mark the top of each piece and whether it is for the front or back half of the box.
2. For each piece, drill three entry holes where indicated on the pattern. Cut out the drawer pieces, keeping the patterns attached. Mark each with its location in the box and the piece it was cut from.
3. For each drawer that was cut from the back half of the box, mark a line that is ¼" (6mm) from the rear face, and cut along the lines to make the drawer backs.
4. Cut along the inside lines of the six drawer pieces to create the interiors.
5. Glue together the two pieces for each drawer. Sand the insides smooth.
6. Glue the back of each drawer into place. Sand the outsides just until smooth.
7. Glue the two box pieces together, keeping them in their marked positions.
8. Sand the drawer openings until smooth and check the fit of each drawer. Sand, as needed, until each drawer slides easily.
9. Trace the outline of the back of the box on the 5½" x 6" x ¼" (140 x 150 x 6mm) piece of mahogany. Cut along the outside of this line to make the back of the box. Glue it into place.
10. Sand the back flush with the box sides, top, and bottom. Sand all surfaces until smooth.
11. Sand a small 45° bevel on the two vertical edges of the front of the box. Be sure to keep the bevel the same size on each side.
12. Attach the drawer front patterns to the remaining ¼" (6mm)-thick piece of mahogany. Cut out the fronts.
13. Drill small holes for the drawer knobs where indicated on the patterns. Remove the patterns and sand a small 45° bevel on the front edge of all sides of the drawers.
14. Draw a line across both drawer fronts through the drilled holes.
15. Mark the front of the box from the top down on both sides at 1" (25mm), 2⁹⁄₁₆" (65mm), and 4⅛" (105mm). Draw lines across the box at these points.
16. Insert the drawers into their corresponding places in the box and secure them with masking tape.
17. Place the box on its back and align the drawer fronts with the lines drawn in Steps 14 and 15. Insert an awl through the holes drilled in each drawer front to mark the knob locations on the drawer. Remove the drawer fronts and drill holes into the drawers at the marks.
18. Screw the drawer fronts into place with small steel screws. Check the position of the drawer fronts and adjust them if needed. Remove the screws, glue the drawer fronts to the drawers, and insert the screws to clamp the drawer fronts. Remove the screws when the glue has dried.
19. Draw a line ¼" (6mm) from the top and bottom faces on one long and both short sides of the piece of ½" (13mm)-thick mahogany. Sand a 45° bevel to this line. Sand the bevel to soften slightly.

Sanding in the front bevels.

Making the top of the box.

20. Glue the top to the box body with the bevel side down, the straight edge flush with the back, and the side overhangs evenly spaced.

21. Attach the pattern for the base to the ¾" (19mm)-thick piece of mahogany. Cut along all lines. Remove the pattern. Discard the center piece. Number and mark the top of the four remaining pieces.

22. Attach the side patterns to each side of the base and cut along the lines.

23. Glue the base pieces together. Sand smooth and soften all edges when dry.

24. Glue and clamp the base to the box body. Shellac all surfaces and sand smooth. Finish with several coats of shellac or clear lacquer. Screw in the brass knobs.

25. Follow the instructions for Fearless Flocking, page 130, to flock the drawer interiors.

Chest of Drawers Box Body Pattern
Make 2 copies at 100%

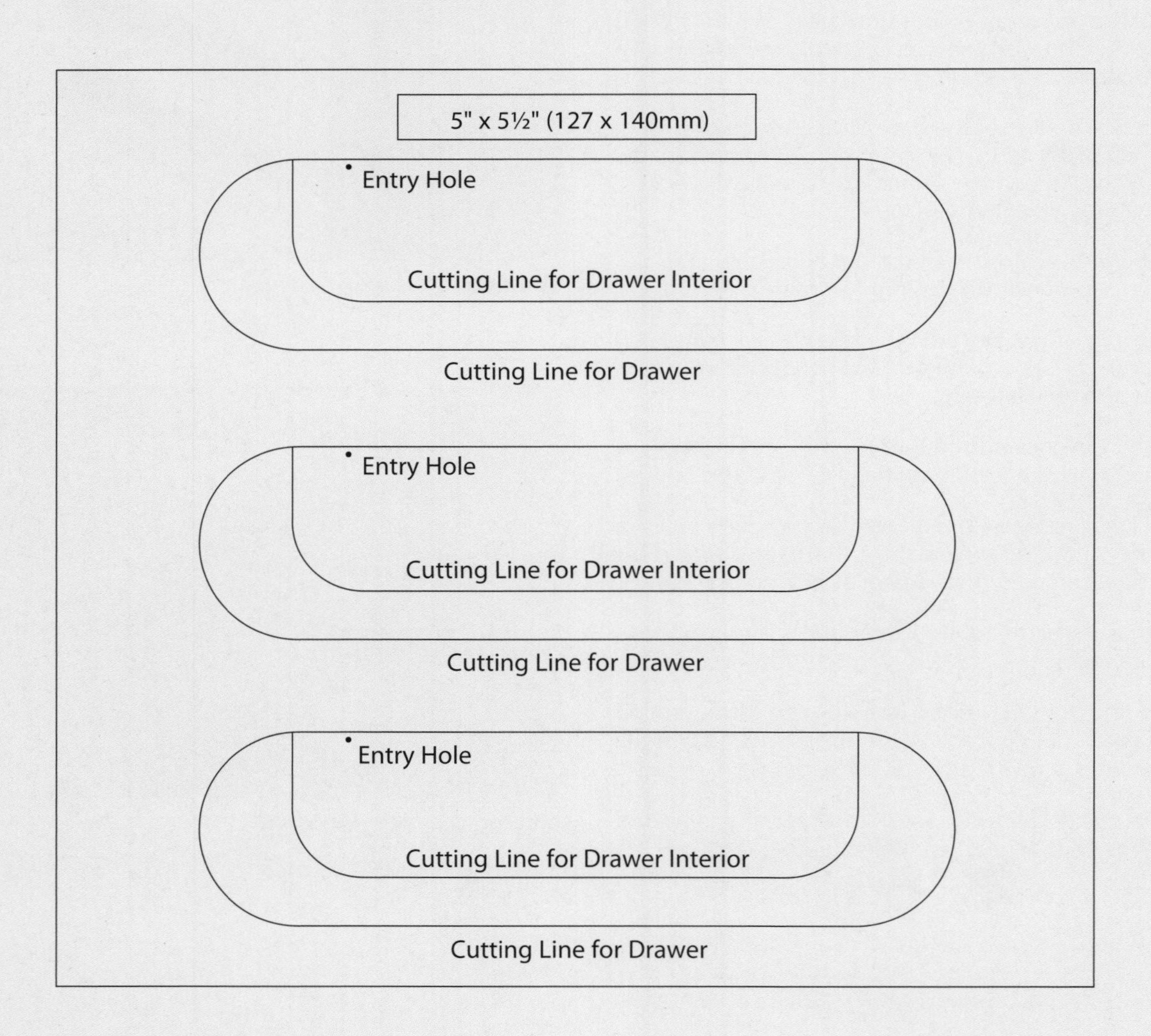

Drawer Front Pattern

Make 3 copies at 100%

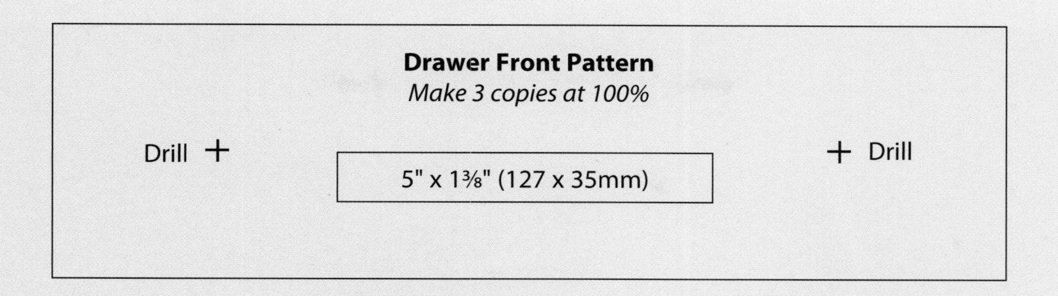

Base, Top Pattern

Copy at 100%

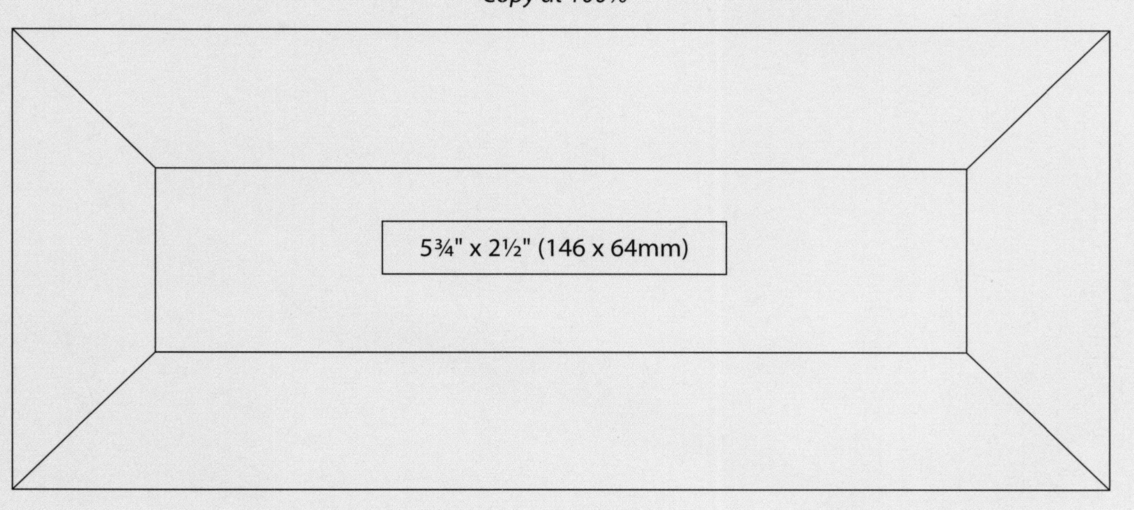

Base, Long Side Pattern

Make 2 Copies at 100%

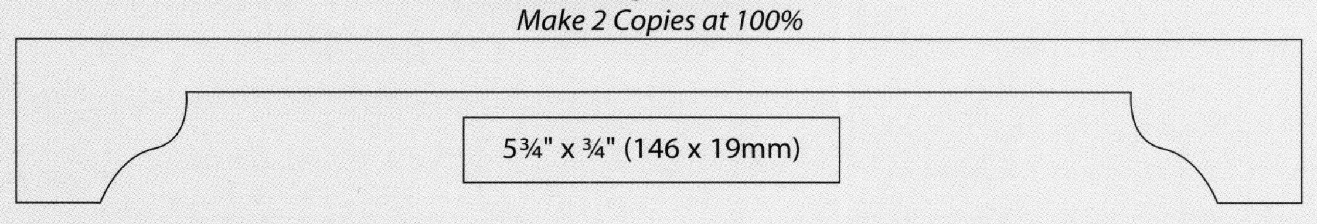

Base, Short Side Pattern

Make 2 copies at 100%

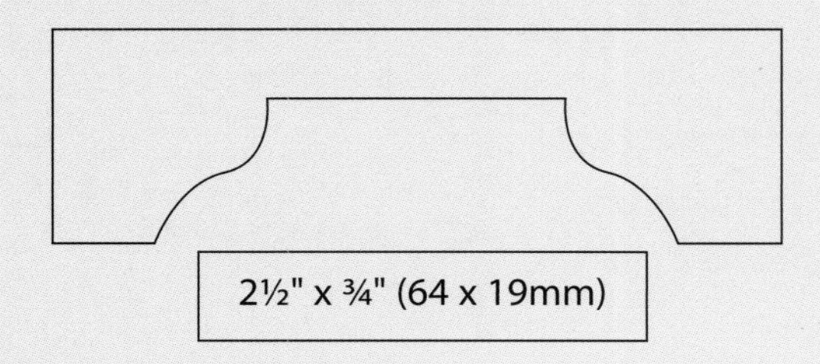

Blanket Chest Box

Difficulty Rating:

I thought that a blanket chest would be a nice addition to my "furniture suite." Making it, however, required fairly thick wood, and I was concerned about blade deflection. The outer cut was not the problem, because irregularities could easily be sanded smooth, but I wanted a reliable way to handle the interior cut. The solution was to use a Forstner bit to remove most of the wood, leaving very little interior cutting. A decorative base, beveled lid, oval basket, and some "blankets" complete the effect.

Materials and Tools

Wood
- (1) 5¼" x 2½" x 1 13⁄16" (135 x 65 x 46mm) mahogany for box
- (1) 5½" x 2¾" x ½" (140 x 70 x 13mm) mahogany for base
- (1) 5" x 2¼" x ¼" (127 x 57 x 6mm) mahogany for lid (actual size needed)
- (2) 4¾" x 2" x ⅛" (120 x 50 x 3mm) wood of choice for box bottom and lid insert
- Small pieces of colorful wood for "blankets" and other decorative objects

Materials
- Repositionable adhesive
- Glue
- Sandpaper for sanders of choice, assorted grits
- Sandpaper for hand sanding, assorted grits
- 0000 steel wool
- Flocking fibers
- Acrylic paint to match flocking fibers
- Shellac
- Clear spray lacquer

Tools
- #9 scroll saw blade for thick wood
- #3 scroll saw blade for thin wood
- #7 *spiral* scroll saw blade for "blankets"
- 1½" (40mm) Forstner bit
- Awl
- Clamps for gluing
- Clamps for holding wood for drilling
- Wide rubber band for clamping the base
- Sanders of choice
- Brush for acrylic paint

1. Using repositionable adhesive, attach the pattern. Cut out the perimeter and mark the holes for drilling with an awl. Remove the pattern.

2. Clamp the wood firmly. Using a drill press and the Forstner bit, drill through the wood at each drilling point to form the box interior.

3. Draw lines ¼" (6mm) from each outside edge.

4. Cut along the lines to complete the box interior. Sand the inside and outside surfaces smooth.

3 **Drawing the interior lines.**

Interior Flat Sanding

A detail sander with a small extension makes quick work of sanding flat interior surfaces.

5. Invert the box on one of the ⅛" (3mm)-thick pieces of wood and trace the inside edge of the upper face. Cut along the line. This is the liner for the lid. Sand it smooth and put it aside until Step 8.

6. Place the box, right side up, on the remaining ⅛" (3mm)-thick piece of wood and trace the inside edge of the lower face. Cut along the line. This will be the bottom of the box. Set it aside until Step 13.

7. Sand the piece of mahogany designated for the box lid until smooth. Sand a small bevel all around on the lower edge.

8. Place the liner on the underside of the box lid. Invert the box on the lid to position the liner correctly. Mark its location. Remove the box and glue the liner into place.

9. Attach the pattern for the base to the ½" (13mm)-thick piece of mahogany and cut along the lines. Remove the pattern. Discard the center piece. Number and mark the remaining four pieces so you can glue them up correctly in Step 11.

10. Attach the side patterns to the base pieces. Cut along the lines to complete the pieces of the base.

11. Glue the pieces of the base together. Clamp with the rubber band and let dry. Sand smooth.

12. Glue the box to the base. Clamp and let dry.

13. Glue the bottom of the box cut in Step 6 to the inside of the box, attaching it to the top of the base.

14. Sand the box and lid. Place small pieces of blue tape on the lid to mask the places where decorative objects will be glued. Apply a coat of shellac to all surfaces of the box, including the inside and the lid, to seal the wood. Sand until smooth. Apply several coats of shellac or lacquer to the outside of the box, rubbing down between coats with 0000 steel wool as needed. Remove the blue tape.

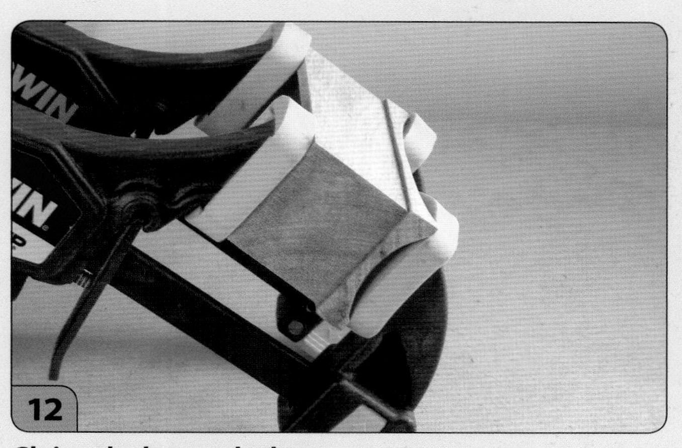

12 **Gluing the box to the base.**

15. To make blankets, see sidebar, 131. To make baskets or other decorations, see Making Decorative Miniatures, page 119. If you decide to add decorations after applying the finish, sand away the finish carefully at the gluing points.

16. Follow the instructions in the sidebar, Fearless Flocking, page 130, to apply flocking to the box interior.

Fearless Flocking

It's easy to obtain a perfect interior finish with flocking fibers. Here's how:

Gather the materials. You'll need a bag of flocking fibers, a plastic bottle with a large hole to contain and dispense them, matching acrylic paint, and a brush. You do not need special adhesive or a flocking gun.

Coat the interior with acrylic paint. If you've not already done so, seal the inside of the box with shellac and let it dry before applying the paint. Thoroughly coat the box interior with an even layer of acrylic paint. Be sure all surfaces are completely covered and that there are no pools of paint.

Apply the flocking fibers. Using the plastic bottle, apply a generous coating of fibers. You cannot apply too much since only the bottom layer will stick. Do not tap out excess or try to even out the fibers.

Remove excess fibers. Let the flocked coating dry thoroughly (about 10 hours), then invert the box and tap out the excess. Gather up excess fibers to re-use for another project. Avoid handling the flocked surface until it has dried for several days and set completely.

Making Blankets

Here's how to create small "blankets" from pieces of wood:

1. Cut pieces of ¼" (6mm)-thick wood into squares or rectangles of desired size.
2. Clamp each piece on edge, short side down, between two pieces of wood.
3. Using a #7 spiral blade, cut a line through the middle of the wood, stopping about ¼" (6mm) from the end. Back the blade out of the wood.
4. Sand the cut edges to simulate folds, and round and soften all edges.
5. Glue several blankets in a pile, rotating each slightly for a more realistic effect.
6. Apply a coat of shellac or lacquer to the blankets, if desired, before gluing them to the top of the blanket chest.

Cutting the blanket.

Blanket Chest Box Pattern
Copy at 100%

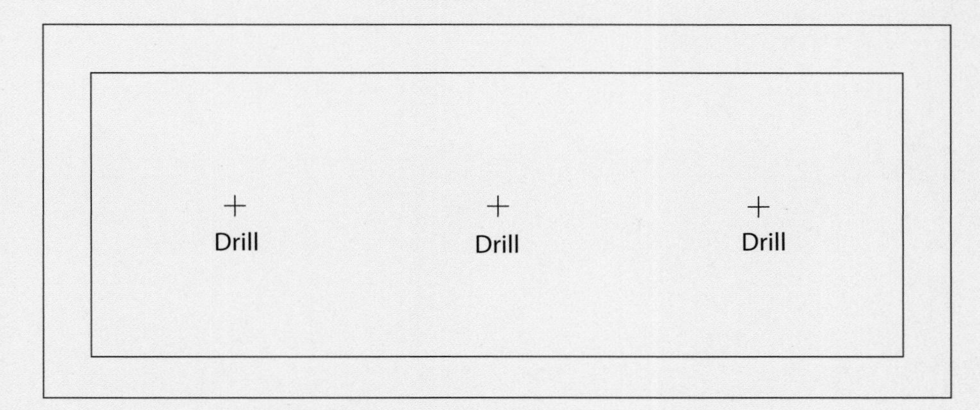

4¾" x 2" (121 x 51mm), ¼" (6mm)-wide wall

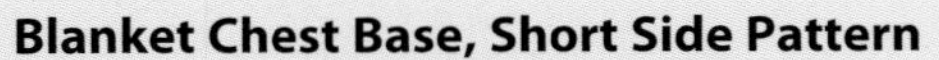

Blanket Chest Base, Short Side Pattern
Make 2 copies at 100%

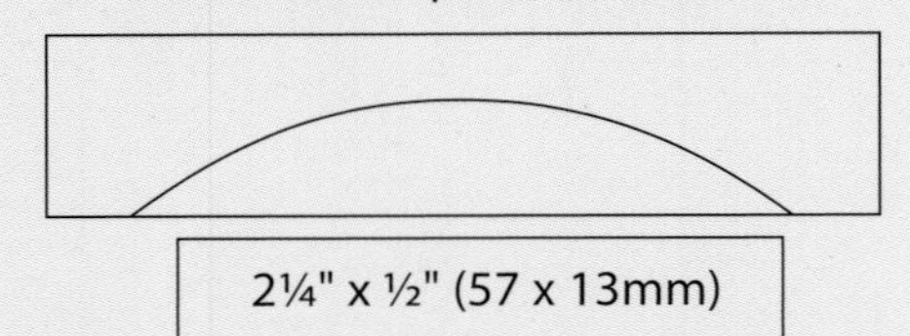

2¼" x ½" (57 x 13mm)

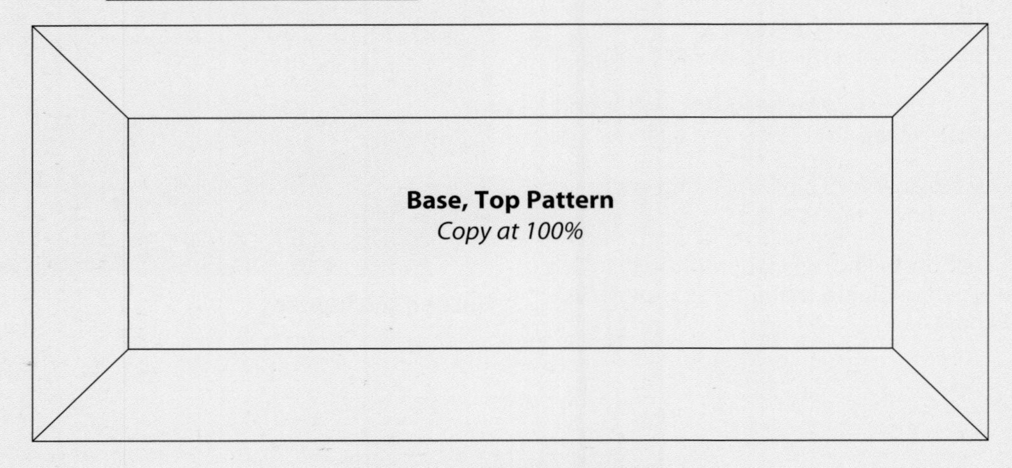

Base, Top Pattern
Copy at 100%

5" x 2¼" (127 x 57mm)

Blanket Chest Base, Long Side Pattern
Make 2 copies at 100%

5" x ½" (127 x 13mm)

Bookcase Box

Difficulty Rating:

Similar in construction to the Chest of Drawers Box, the overlay drawer fronts of this project completely disguise the front of the box. This box is actually a wooden version of a cake I created some years ago, decorated with "books" and small objects made from fondant icing. Miniature photos were used for a personal touch.

Most scroll saw projects are customized with names or initials. I think scans of meaningful pictures, books, or invitations are a simple yet far more creative, and unusual, alternative.

Materials and Tools

Wood

- (1) 5½" x 5" x 1⅜" (140 x 130 x 35mm) mahogany for box
- (1) 4¼" x 1⅞" x ¼" (108 x 48 x 6mm) mahogany for base (actual size needed)
- (1) 4¾" x 2¼" x ¼" (121 x 57 x 6mm) mahogany for top (actual size needed)
- (2) 5½" x 5" x ¼" (140 x 130 x 6mm) mahogany for drawer fronts and box back
- Small pieces of ⅛" (3mm)-thick colorful wood for "books"
- Small pieces of wood for bowls, books, or frames to decorate the top

Strips of mahogany for drawer trim, cut to actual size as follows:

- (2) 4½" x ⅜" x ¼" (115 x 10 x 6mm)
- (4) 1½" x ⅜" x ¼" (40 x 10 x 6mm)
- (2) 1¼" x ⅜" x ¼" (30 x 10 x 6mm)
- (2) 3¾" x ¼" x ¼" (95 x 6 x 6mm)

Materials

- Repositionable adhesive
- Glue (Weldbond recommended)
- Masking tape
- Sandpaper for sanders of choice, assorted grits
- Sandpaper for hand sanding, assorted grits
- 0000 steel wool
- (6) Small steel screws to position drawer fronts
- Flocking fibers
- Acrylic paint to match flocking
- Photo paper and picture to scan for the top decoration
- Shellac
- Clear spray lacquer

Tools

- #9 scroll saw blade for thick wood
- #3 scroll saw blade for thin wood
- ¹⁄₁₆" (2mm) drill bit for entry holes
- Drill bit for small screws
- Awl
- Clamps
- Sanders of choice
- Brush for acrylic paint

Patterns Have Their Limits

Although patterns are convenient, it's often helpful to use the project itself as the pattern for certain components. For example, if cutting or sanding has altered the expected size or shape of a box, you will obtain a better fit for the back piece by tracing the sanded profile of the box directly on the wood than if you used a pattern or a precut piece of wood. When many separate parts are involved, as with the decorative pieces for the drawer fronts of the Bookcase Box, many small adjustments are usually needed before the pieces fit snugly against each other.

1. Using repositionable adhesive, attach the pattern for the box body to the 1⅜" (35mm)-thick piece of mahogany and cut along the outer line. Mark the top of the box.
2. Drill entry holes with the 1⁄16" (2mm) bit where marked on the pattern. Cut along the outlines to form the drawers.
3. Mark each drawer with its location in the box. Do not remove the pattern from each drawer yet.
4. Sand the three drawer openings in the box body until smooth.
5. Draw a line ¼" (6mm) from the rear face of each of the three drawers.
6. To make the drawer backs, cut along the line drawn in Step 5. Mark each back to correspond with its matching drawer. The drawer backs will be glued on in Step 8.
7. Place each of the drawer pieces on its back, pattern side up. Cut along the inner line to make the drawer interior. Sand the inside of each drawer. Sand off fuzzies on the rear edge.
8. Glue on the back of each drawer. Clamp and let dry. Clean up any squeeze-out inside each drawer.
9. Check the fit of each drawer by inserting it into its corresponding opening in the box. Sand the outside of each drawer just until it is smooth and slides easily.
10. Trace the outline of the back of the box on one of the 5½" x 5" x ¼" (140 x 130 x 6mm) pieces of mahogany. Cut along the outside of this line. Glue the back of the box into place. Clamp and let dry.
11. Sand the back flush with the box sides, top, and bottom. Sand all surfaces until smooth.
12. Attach the drawer fronts pattern to the remaining 5½" x 5" x ¼" (140 x 130 x 6mm) piece of mahogany and cut along the lines to form the drawer fronts. Drill holes for the small screws where indicated on the pattern, using an appropriately sized bit.
13. Insert the drawers into their corresponding places in the box. Keeping the box upright, secure each drawer in place with a small piece of masking tape. The tape will keep the drawers from moving out of position.

14. Place the box on its back and position the drawer fronts over the drawers. Insert an awl through each hole in the drawer fronts to mark drilling holes on the drawers. Set the drawer fronts aside and remove the tape.

15. Drill holes into the drawers deep enough for the screws to hold the drawer fronts in place during glue-up.

16. Glue the drawer fronts to the drawers and screw in the six small screws to clamp the pieces together. Clean up any glue squeeze-out. Let dry and remove the screws. Stand the box upright. Sand the top and bottom edges of the drawers as needed until they move freely.

17. Glue the pieces of ¼" (6mm)-thick mahogany for the box top and box bottom into place, keeping the back of each piece flush with the back of the box and the sides evenly spaced.

18. Place the mahogany strips for the drawer fronts (see "Wood" section) in place, using the drawer fronts pattern as a guide. You may need to make minor adjustments in length. Glue the strips into place.

19. Cut small strips from ⅛" (3mm)-thick contrasting woods to resemble books. Glue into place on the shelves. Sand away any fuzzies.

20. Apply a coat of spray shellac to all surfaces, including drawer insides, to seal the wood and reveal any glue spots. Smooth the box with 0000 steel wool. Apply several coats of lacquer to the outer surfaces, rubbing between each coat with 0000 steel wool as needed.

21. To finish drawer interiors, see Fearless Flocking, page 130.

22. For decorations for the top of the bookcase, see Making Decorative Miniatures, page 119.

Attaching Miniatures

If you are making objects to decorate the top, and know their size and location, place small pieces of blue tape at those spots before applying the finish. This will allow the glue to adhere properly when you attach the objects. If you decide to attach objects after the box is finished, carefully rough up the finish at the gluing spots so the decorations will stick.

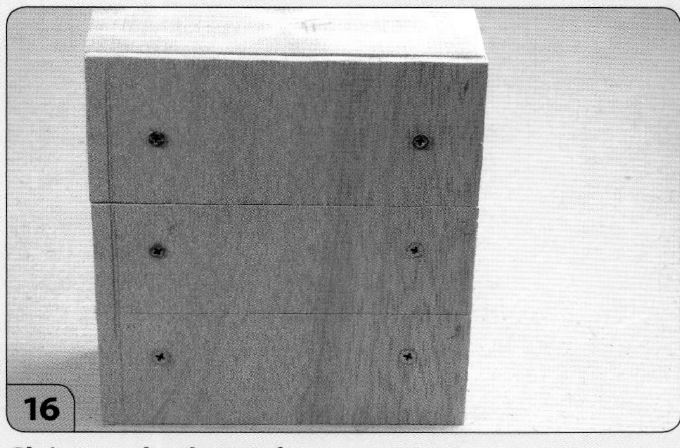

Gluing on the drawer fronts.

Gluing on the top and bottom pieces.

Positioning the strips.

Bookcase Box Body Pattern
Copy at 100%

5" x 4½" (127 x 114mm)

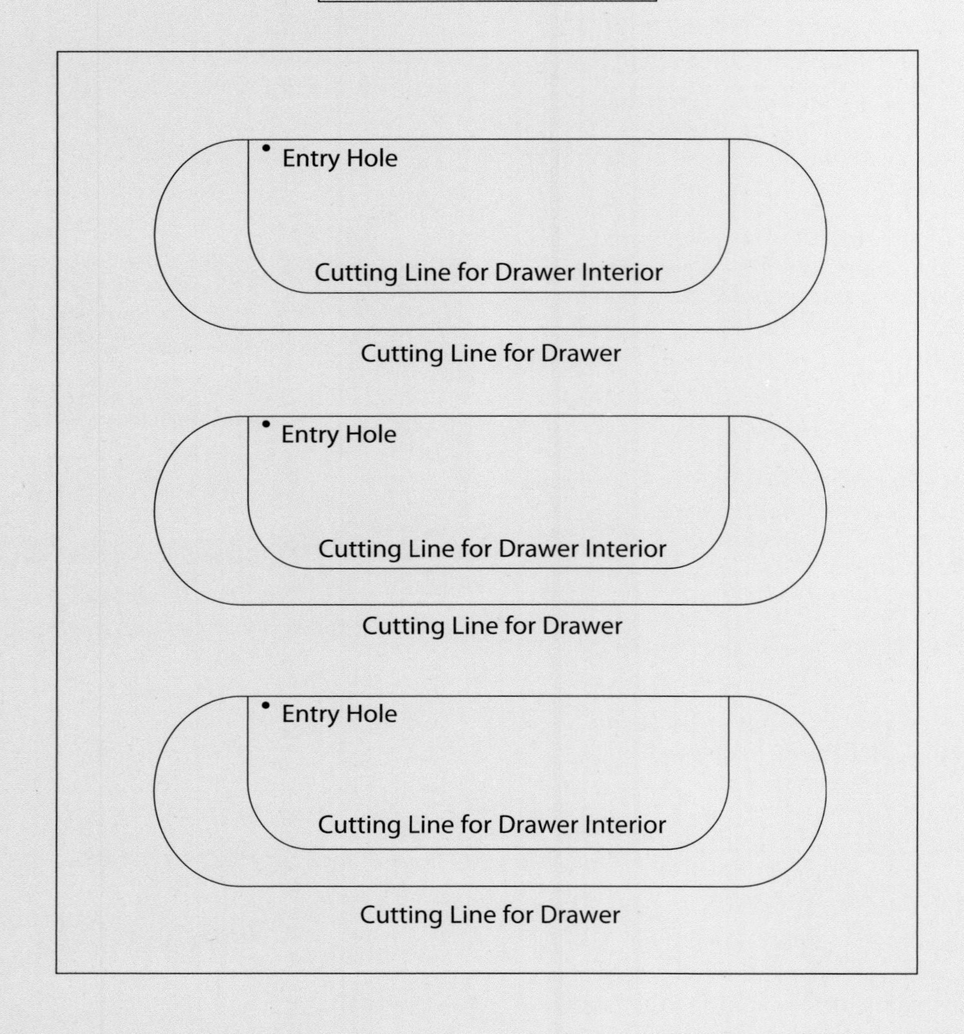

Bookcase Drawer Fronts Pattern
Copy at 100%

5" x 4½" (127 x 114mm)

Top Drawer

Drill

Drill

Middle Drawer

Drill

Drill

Bottom Drawer

Drill

Drill

Chapter 6

Pivot Lid Boxes

Boxes with lids that pivot are easy to make and lend themselves to infinite variations. The design is simple, yet elegance can be achieved through use of veneer or colorful, exotic woods. Even the most basic version, however, has charm, either by itself or as a container for a special gift.

Basic Pivot Lid Box: A Step-by-Step Guide

Difficulty Rating:

Although a pivot lid box is not difficult to make, the hidden lid mechanism adds an element of intrigue. This combination of simplicity and interest makes the box an ideal crafts fair item or gift. With the same pattern and instructions, you can make either a basic box or an elegant, veneered variation.

Instructions are provided for a thin-walled box with a brass rod pivot. Since thin walls require precision in drilling, and brass rod and epoxy may not be readily available, directions are provided in a sidebar for using hardwood dowel and glue, and for increasing the width of the walls to accommodate the larger diameter dowel.

Materials and Tools

Wood

- (1) 5½" x 5½" x ¾" (150mm x 150mm x 19mm) jotoba for box
- (2) 5½" x 5½" x ⅜" (150mm x 150mm x 10mm) white oak for box and lid

Materials

- Repositionable spray adhesive
- Glue
- Epoxy
- (1) ⅛" (3mm)-diameter brass rod, ¾" (19mm) long (actual size needed)
- Sandpaper for sanders of choice, assorted grits
- Sandpaper for hand sanding, assorted grits
- 0000 steel wool
- Shellac
- Clear spray lacquer

Tools

- #9 or #12 scroll saw blade
- #5 scroll saw blade for thinner wood
- ⅛" (3mm) brad point drill bit

  Note: Drill bits can vary from their marked size. If your ⅛" (3mm) bit is too small for the brass rod, use a 9⁄64" (3.3mm) bit instead.
- Awl
- Press or clamps for gluing
- Sanders of choice

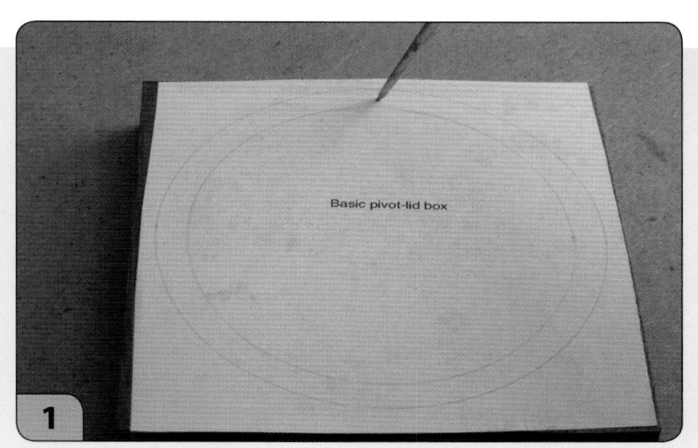

Marking the wood. Using repositionable adhesive, attach the box pattern to the piece of jotoba. Using an awl, mark the drilling point for the pivot hole where indicated on the pattern.

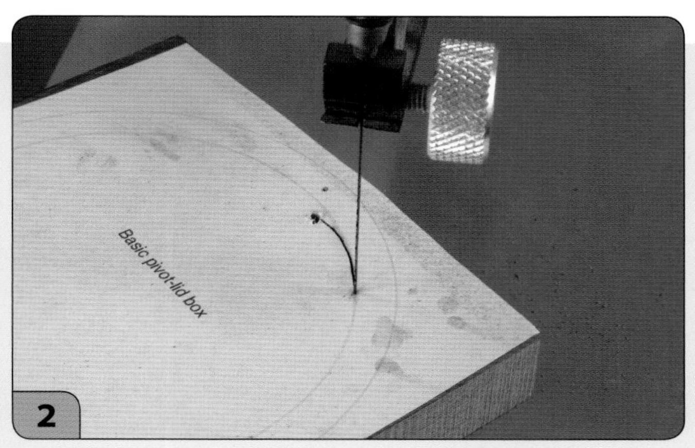

Cutting out the box interior. Drill an entry hole just inside the inner circle. Insert the saw blade, and cut along the inner circle.

Sanding the inside of the box. Remove the pattern and set it aside until Step 5. Sand the inside of the box until smooth, removing any fuzzies from the lower inside edge. A spindle sander makes quick work of removing blade and burn marks from the inside of the box.

Attaching the base. Glue one of the pieces of oak to the underside of the jotoba, keeping the grain running in the same direction. Clamp for 5 minutes. Remove the clamps to clean up any glue squeeze-out, then re-clamp until dry.

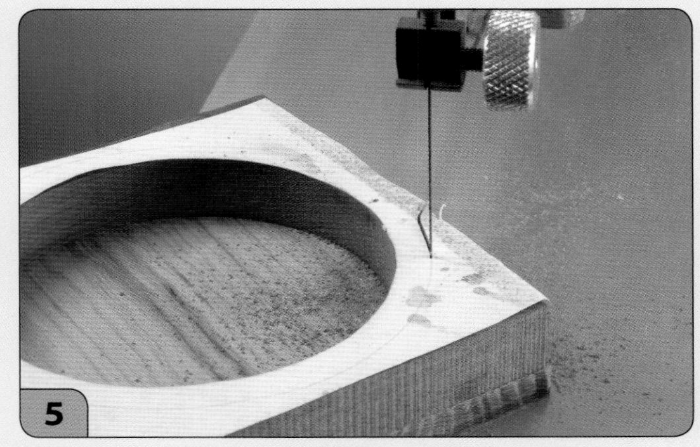

Cutting the outside of the box. Re-attach the box pattern, using the drilling point for alignment, and cut along the outer circle.

Sanding the outside of the box. Sand the outside of the box until smooth. A vertical belt sander is an ideal tool for this purpose.

Cutting out the lid. Attach the lid pattern to the remaining piece of oak, keeping the grain running in the same direction as on the box. Mark the drilling point with an awl. Cut along the outer line of the pattern.

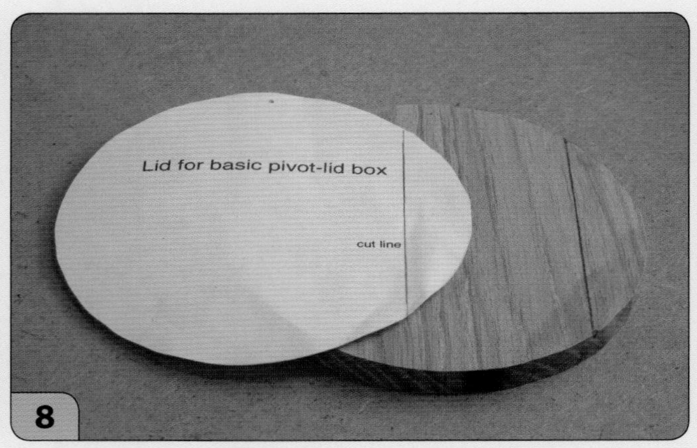

Marking the cut line for the lid stop. Mark the ends of the cut line on the lid edge. Remove the pattern and complete the line. Sand the sides of the lid to remove irregularities before making the bevel.

Making the bevel for the lid. Draw a line around the side of the lid, ⅛" (3mm) or slightly less from the upper face. Cut or sand a bevel between 30˚ and 45˚ on the upper edge of the lid, using the line as a guide. If you prefer, you can just round the upper edge.

Cutting the stop piece. Cut along the line that was drawn in Step 8 to make the stop piece for the lid. It will be glued on in Step 13.

Gluing in the pivot rod. Using the ⅛" (3mm) bit, drill a ¼" (6mm)-deep hole in the lid at the drilling mark. (If you used a 45˚ bevel on the lid, be careful not to drill deeper than ¼" [6mm] to avoid drilling through the top.) Drill a ½" (13mm)-deep hole in the box at the drilling mark. Using epoxy, glue the ¾" (19mm) piece of brass rod into the hole in the lid. Let it dry thoroughly.

Marking the location of the stop piece. Attach the lid to the box by inserting the brass rod into the hole and pressing down until the lid touches the box. Place the stop piece into position and mark its location.

Gluing the stop piece into place. Glue the stop piece into place and clamp. Let the glue dry for five minutes. Remove the clamp and clean up excess glue. Swing the lid closed to check the position of the stop piece. Swing it away, re-clamp the stop piece, and let the glue dry.

Completing the box. Hold the lid securely in the closed position and sand the sides of the box until they match perfectly. Soften the bevel on the lid and sand the box smooth. Apply several coats of shellac or clear lacquer to the box, rubbing between coats with 0000 steel wool, as needed.

Substituting Hardwood Dowel and Wood Glue

If you'd prefer to use hardwood dowel and wood glue, but are concerned that the ⅛" (3mm) dowel might shear, you can increase the wall width and dowel diameter slightly without sacrificing appearance. Here's how:

Decrease the diameter of the inner ring of the pattern to change the wall thickness to 7⁄16" (11mm) for a 3⁄16" (5mm) dowel. For a ¼" (6mm) dowel, you can use the 7⁄16" (11mm) width, or increase it to ½" inch (13mm). Adjust the location of the drill pivot hole so it is in the center of the re-drawn wall. Change the location of the pivot hole on the lid to match. Be sure to match the size of the drill bit to the size of the dowel.

Alternate Version

You can make a more elaborate version of the pivot lid box by using more exotic woods and adding veneer. The pattern and instructions are the same. Here are the changes:

1. For the box body, use 1" (25mm) thick maple burl.

2. For the lid, use ½" (13mm)-thick padauk, with maple veneer glued to the lower face.

3. For the base, use ⅛" (3mm)-thick padauk, with maple veneer glued to the upper face.

Laminating Wood

For success with your laminations, be generous with the glue and exert even pressure over the entire piece of wood. Here are three methods:

1 **If you don't have a press, use two boards and conventional clamps.**

2 **A shop-made press is easy to use, and exerts even pressure.**

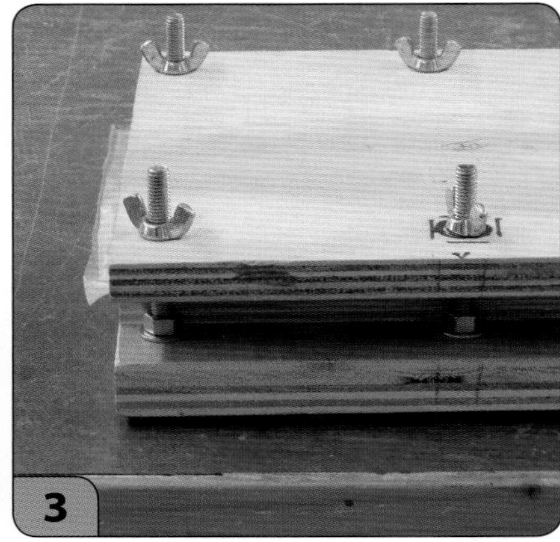

3 **A square press accommodates larger pieces of wood.** The height of the press depends on the length of the carriage bolts.

+
Drilling Mark for Pivot

Basic Pivot Lid Box Pattern

Copy at 100%

5" (127mm)-diameter circle, one ⅜" (10mm)-wide ring

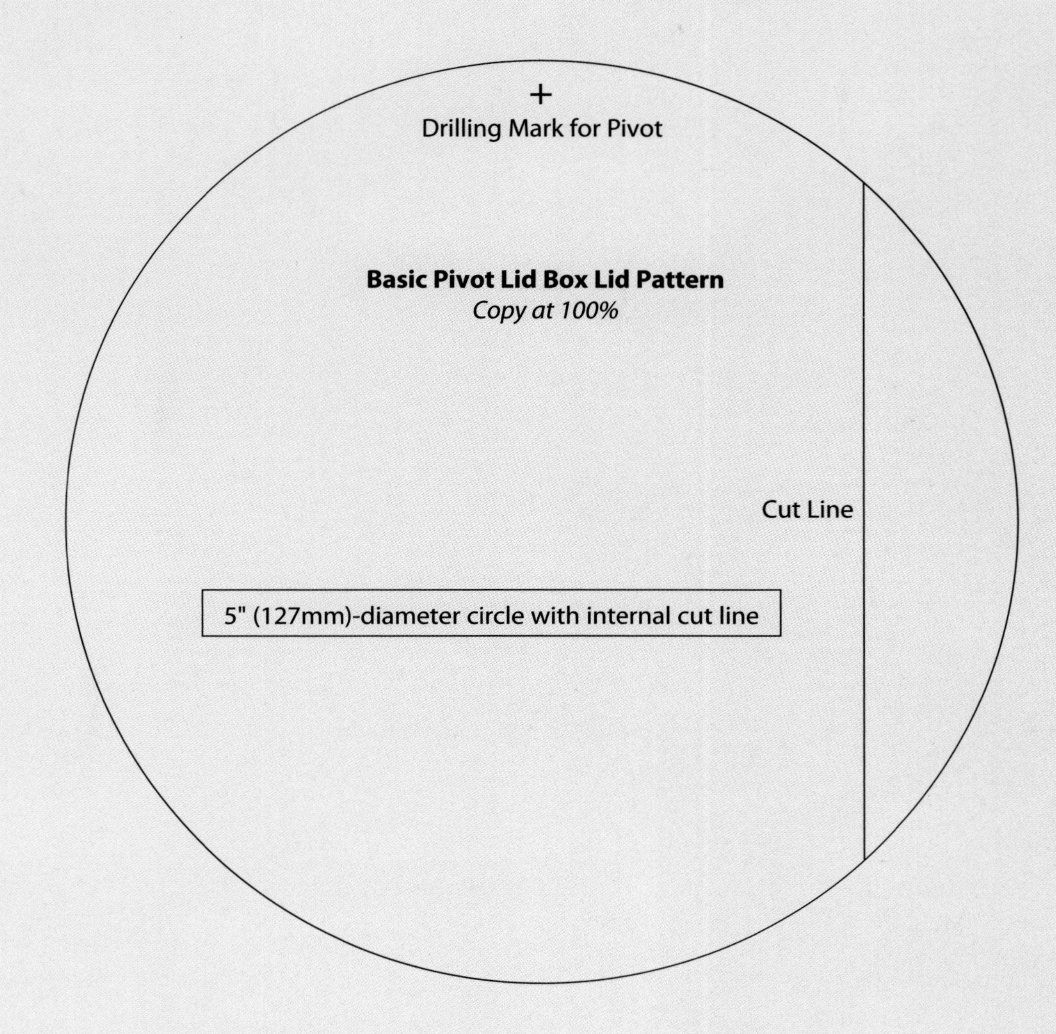
+
Drilling Mark for Pivot
Basic Pivot Lid Box Lid Pattern
Copy at 100%
Cut Line
5" (127mm)-diameter circle with internal cut line

Striped Pivot Lid Box

Difficulty Rating:

The colorful stripes of this pivot lid box disguise the opening, creating a new type of puzzle box. To ensure near invisibility between the stop piece and movable section, the lid is made in stages. The procedure is a little fidgety, but not difficult, and ensures a perfect match. You can vary the look by changing the color and thickness of the stripes.

Materials and Tools

Wood

- (1) 5¾" x 5¼" x 1¼" (145 x 135 x 32mm) walnut for box
- (2) 5¾" x 5¼" x ¼" (145 x 135 x 6mm) walnut for base and lid
- (3) 5¾" x 5¼" (145 x 135mm) maple veneer for base and lid
- (1) 5¼" x ¾" x 3⁄16" (135 x 19 x 5mm) bloodwood for lid
- (2) 5¼" x ¾" x 3⁄16" (135 x 19 x 5mm) yellowheart for lid
- (2) 5¼" x ¾" x 3⁄16" (135 x 19 x 5mm) maple for lid
- (2) 5¼" x ¾" x 3⁄16" (135 x 19 x 5mm) walnut for lid

Materials

- Repositionable spray adhesive
- Glue (Weldbond recommended)
- Epoxy
- (1) ⅛" (3mm) diameter brass rod, ¾" (19mm) long (actual size needed)
- Sandpaper for sanders of choice, assorted grits
- Sandpaper for hand sanding, assorted grits
- 0000 steel wool
- Shellac
- Clear spray lacquer

Tools

- #9 or #12 scroll saw blade for thick wood
- #3 scroll saw blade for thin wood
- ⅛" (3mm) brad point drill bit
- Awl
- Clamps
- Sanders of choice

1. To laminate the piece for the base, glue one piece of maple veneer to one of the ¼" (6mm)-thick pieces of walnut. Clamp and let dry.
2. To make the box body, follow Steps 1–6 of the Basic Pivot Lid Box, page 140, using the 1¼" (32mm)-thick piece of walnut for the box body, and the laminated piece, veneer side up, for the base.
3. To make the lid, glue the remaining pieces of maple veneer to each side of the remaining piece of ¼" (6mm)-thick walnut. Clamp together and dry thoroughly.
4. Sand a small bevel on the top edges of the long sides of the seven 5¼" (135mm)-long strips, leaving about ⅛" (3mm) flat on the sides. Soften the beveled edges.
5. Starting at the right side of the lid, glue the strips in the following order: Walnut, maple, yellowheart, bloodwood, yellowheart, maple. This leaves room at the left edge for the remaining walnut strip, which is glued on later. To get a good bond, rub each strip back and forth on the lid until the glue becomes tacky. Clamp and dry thoroughly.
6. Place the remaining walnut strip into position and center the pattern on the strips, using repositionable adhesive. Hold the loose strip in place and cut along the perimeter. Remove the loose strip. It will be glued on in Step 11.
7. Measuring carefully, transfer the mark on the pattern for the drilling point to the underside of lid. Mark this point with an awl.

4 **Beveling the sides of the strips.**

5 **Gluing the strips to the lid.**

6 **Marking the drilling point on the underside of the lid.**

Cutting the stop piece.

Positioning the stop piece.

Gluing the walnut strip to the lid.

8. With the striped side of the lid facing up, cut along the left edge of the maple strip to form the stop piece. It will be glued in place in Step 10.

9. Use the ⅛" (3mm) drill bit to drill a ¼" (6mm)-deep hole in the lid at the drilling mark. Use the same bit to drill a ½" (13mm)-deep hole in the box at the drilling mark. Using epoxy, glue the ¾" (19mm)-piece of brass rod into the hole in the lid. Let dry.

10. Attach the lid to the box by inserting the brass rod into the hole and pressing down until the lid touches the box. Place the stop piece into position and glue it into place.

11. Glue the remaining strip of walnut into place.

12. Hold the lid and bottom securely together and sand until they match perfectly. Sand a small bevel on the top edge of the lid. Soften the bevel and complete the shaping of the lid. Sand the entire box smooth. Finish with several coats of shellac or clear lacquer, rubbing between coats with 0000 steel wool, as needed.

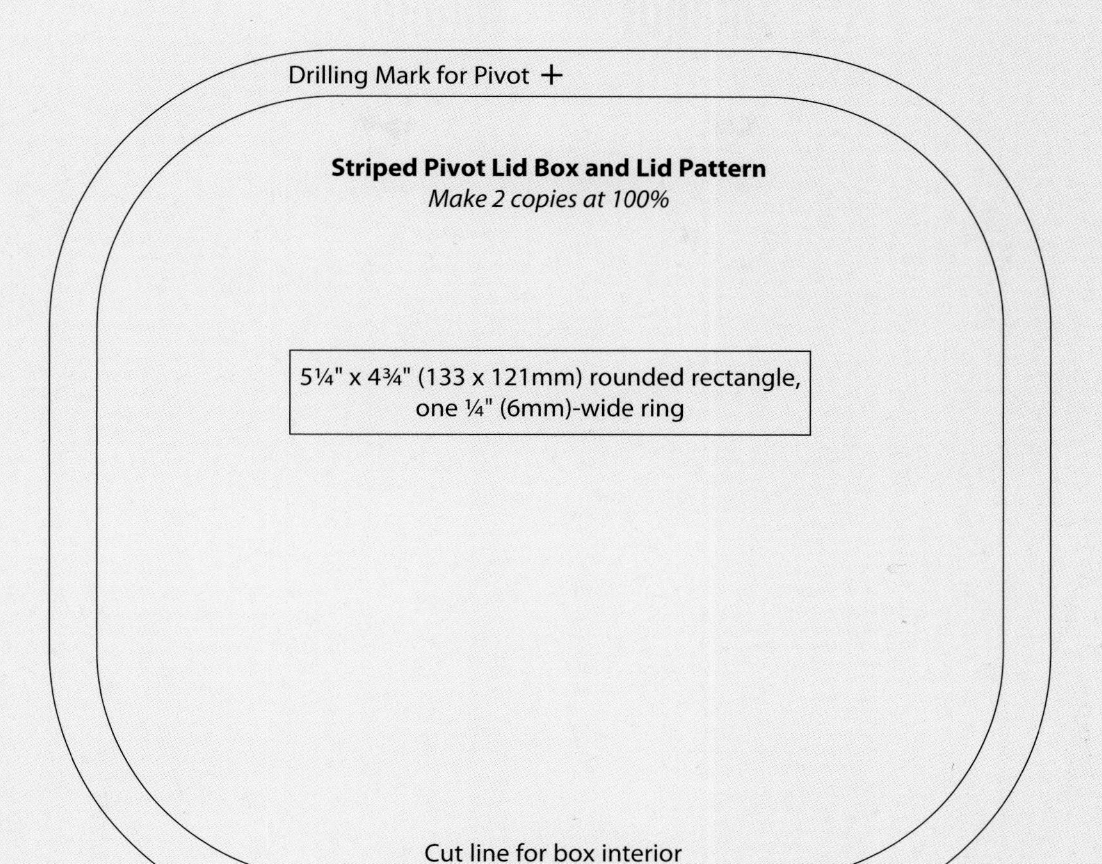
Drilling Mark for Pivot +
Striped Pivot Lid Box and Lid Pattern
Make 2 copies at 100%
5¼" x 4¾" (133 x 121mm) rounded rectangle,
one ¼" (6mm)-wide ring
Cut line for box interior

The Instabox

Difficulty Rating:

This quickly made little box uses a Forstner bit to create the box body in a single step, and a ¼" (6mm) dowel for the pivot. Instructions are given for a round box, but any shape that's easily sanded will be quick and easy to do. Choose your wood combinations carefully and you're sure to have an "instant" success.

Materials and Tools

Wood

- (1) 4" x 4" x 1⅛" (100 x 100 x 29mm) maple for box
- (1) 4" x 4" x ½" (100 x 100 x 13mm) canarywood for lid
- (1) ¼" (6mm) dowel, ¾" (19mm) long (actual size needed)

Materials

- Repositionable spray adhesive
- Glue (for dowel)
- Sandpaper for sanders of choice, assorted grits
- Sandpaper for hand sanding, assorted grits
- 0000 steel wool
- (1) 2⅜" (60mm) circle of adhesive-backed velvet (actual size needed)
- Shellac
- Clear spray lacquer

Tools

- #9 or #12 scroll saw blade for box
- #5 scroll saw blade for lid
- ¼" (6mm) brad-point drill bit
- 2⅜" (60mm) Forstner bit
- Awl
- Clamps to hold wood for drilling
- Sanders of choice

1. Attach a copy of the box pattern to the piece of maple. Mark the center and pivot holes with an awl. Remove the pattern and set aside until Step 4.
2. Using the Forstner bit, drill a hole about ¾" (19mm) deep at the center mark. Be sure to secure the wood so it cannot spin.
3. Sand the inside of the hole and soften the upper edge.
4. Re-attach the box pattern to the piece of maple, using the pivot hole mark to align the pattern. Cut out the perimeter of the box. Sand the outside smooth.
5. To make the lid and complete the box, follow Steps 7–14 of the Basic Pivot Lid Box, using the canarywood, ¼" (6mm) drill bit, ¼" (6mm)-diameter hardwood dowel, and wood glue.
6. Attach the circle of velvet to the bottom interior of the box.

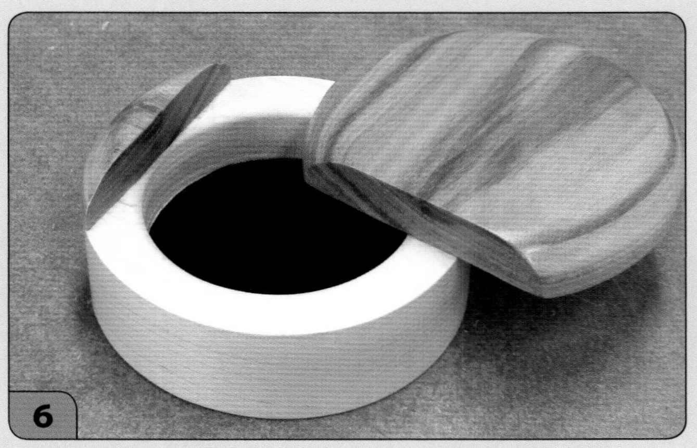

Attaching the velvet.

Instabox Box and Lid Pattern
Make 2 copies at 100%

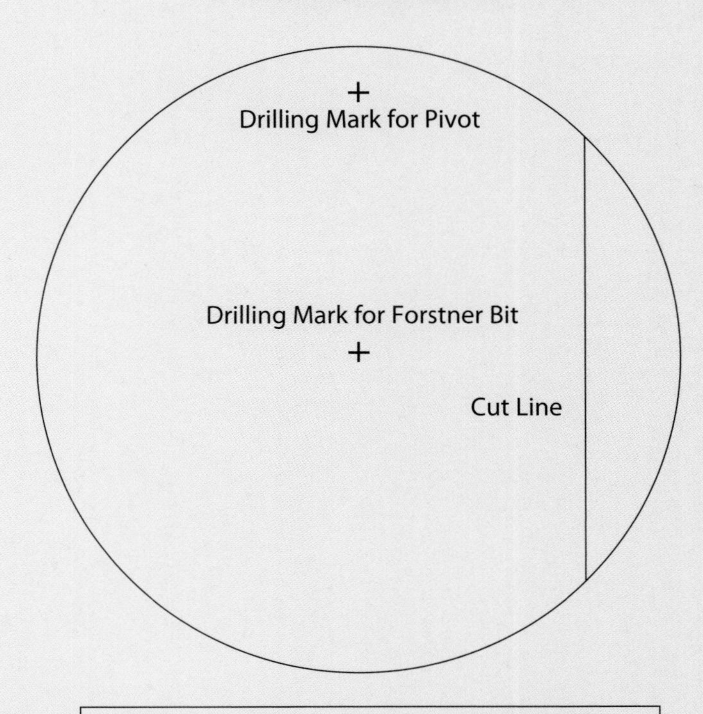

3⅜" (86mm)-diameter circle with internal cut line

Chapter 7

Artistic Boxes

Although artistic boxes are typically carved or made on a lathe, you can create projects of comparable interest and beauty with a scroll saw and sanders. In this chapter, you'll learn how to transform sets of rings—some angled and some straight—into boxes that can hold their own in any juried crafts fair.

Laminated Oval Box: A Step-by-Step Guide

Difficulty Rating:

Oval boxes are inherently graceful and elegant. This design, made of mahogany, features contrasting rings and a brightly colored handle. The rings, all cut from one laminated piece, serve several functions: they ease the transition between the halves of the box, set off the lid, and create an interesting base.

Materials and Tools

Wood

- (2) 8½" x 6½" x ⅞" (215 x 165 x 22mm) mahogany for box
- (1) 8½" x 6½" x ⅛" (215 x 165 x 3mm) padauk for rings
- (2) 8½" x 6½" (215 x 165mm) walnut veneer for rings
- (1) 5½" x 3½" x ¼" (140 x 90 x 6mm) walnut for lid liner
- (2) 2½" x 1½" x ⅛" (65 x 40 x 3mm) padauk for handle
- (1) 2½" x 1½" x ¼" (65 x 40 x 6mm) mahogany for handle

Materials

- Repositionable adhesive
- Glue (Weldbond recommended)
- Sleeves for inflatable round sander, assorted grits 80 to 320
- Discs for 2" (50mm) hook-and-loop pad sander, assorted grits 80 to 320
- Sandpaper for hand sanding, assorted grits
- 0000 steel wool
- InLace, color of choice
- Shellac
- Clear spray lacquer

Tools

- #9 scroll saw blade for thick wood
- #3 scroll saw blade for thin wood
- 1⁄16" (2mm) or #54 drill bit
- 18° shop-made angle guide (see page 18)
- 30° shop-made angle guide
- 40° shop-made angle guide
- Awl
- Ruler
- Multi-purpose press or clamps for gluing
- Inflatable round sander and pump
- 2" (50mm) hook-and-loop pad sander

Using ¾" (19mm)-Thick Wood

To make this box using wood that is ¾" (19mm) thick, use a 20° angle wherever 18° is specified. All other instructions remain the same.

Drawing the guidelines. Draw intersecting guidelines through the center of both pieces of mahogany. Decide which piece will be for the top ring set, and which will be for the bottom ring set. Mark the top of each blank.

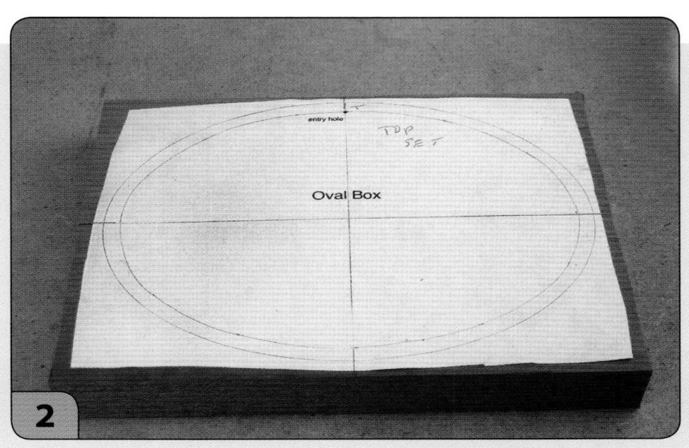

Attaching the pattern. Using repositionable adhesive, attach the box pattern to the blank for the top ring set. Align the lines on the pattern with the guidelines on the wood.

Cutting the perimeter of the top ring set. Tilt the saw table 18˚, left side down. Cut along the outer line of the pattern, cutting clockwise.

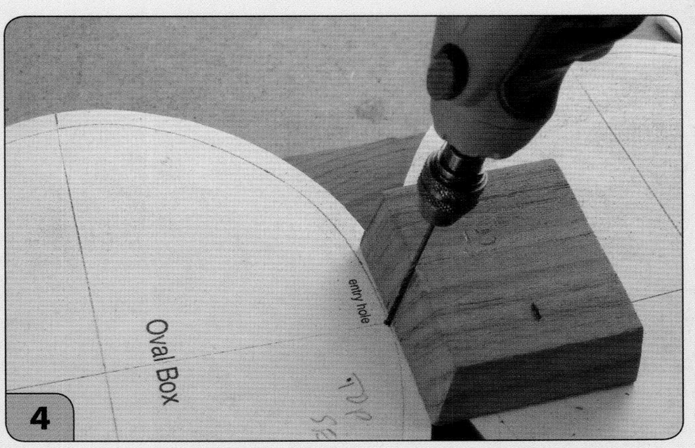

Drilling the entry hole for the first top ring. Use an awl to mark the entry hole where indicated on the pattern. Using an angle guide or drill press with a tilting table, drill an 18˚ entry hole. The hole must be angled toward the center of the blank.

Completing the first top ring. Tilt the saw table to 18˚, left side down. Insert the saw blade into the entry hole. Cut along the inner line at an 18˚ angle, cutting clockwise. Mark the top of the ring. This completes the first ring of the top section of the box. Remove the pattern.

Drawing the cutting line for the second top ring. Place the ring on the blank, aligning the tops, and trace the inside of the ring on the blank to form the cutting line for the second top ring.

Re-cutting the blank. Tilt the saw table to 30˚, left side down. Cut around the perimeter of the blank, using the top edge as a guide. Do not cut into the top edge. This cut helps to create a curved side for the box.

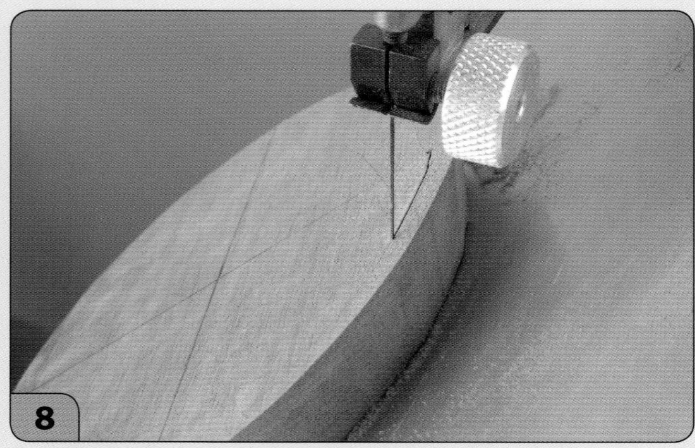

Completing the second top ring. Drill an entry hole at 40˚ on the line drawn in Step 6, facing the center. Tilt the saw table to 40˚, left side down. Insert the blade into the hole and cut clockwise. This is the second ring of the top. Save the remainder to form the lid in Step 25.

Cutting the bottom rings. Follow Steps 2–7 with the blank for the bottom ring set. To complete the second ring from this set, drill a 30˚ entry hole on the line drawn in Step 6. Tilt the saw table to 30˚, left side down. Insert the saw blade and cut clockwise.

Drawing the cutting line for the base. Place the second ring on the remainder of the blank, keeping the tops aligned. Trace the outer edge to form the cutting line for the base.

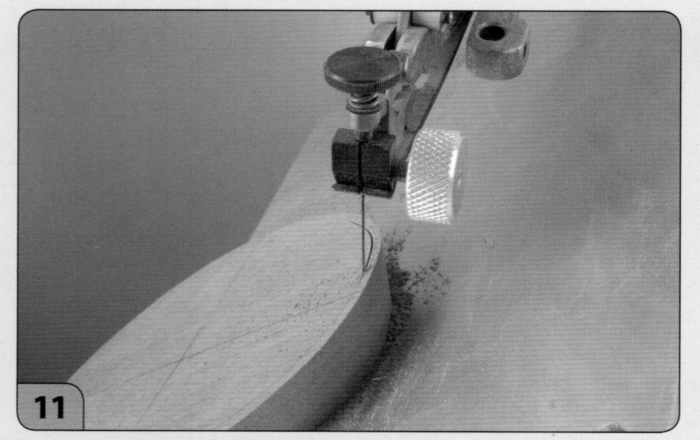

Completing the bottom ring set. Tilt the saw table to 40˚, left side down. Cut along the cutting line for the base, cutting clockwise. No entry hole is needed since the outer "ring" is discarded. The base will be glued on in Step 21.

Cutting the laminated center ring. Glue the big piece of padauk between the pieces of veneer. Clamp and let dry. Attach the box pattern and cut around the perimeter with the saw table level. Drill an entry hole just inside the inner line, insert blade, and cut along that line. The remaining wood will be used in Steps 16 and 23.

13

Gluing the first rings to the laminated ring. Glue the first rings from the top and bottom ring sets to each side of the laminated ring, using a press or conventional clamps. Let dry.

14

Sanding the inside of the rings. Using the inflatable round sander and a coarse sleeve, sand the inside of the glued-up rings until smooth.

15

Gluing on the second bottom ring. Glue the second ring from the bottom ring set to the first ring from that set. Clamp and let dry. Sand the inside face and the lower inside edge until smooth.

16

Cutting the lamination for the top. Place the second top ring, small face down, on the lamination. Trace the inner and outer edges. Tilt the saw table to 30°, left side down. Cut clockwise along the outer line. Drill a 40° entry hole on the inner line. Tilt the saw table to 40°, left side down. Cut clockwise along the inner line. Save remaining wood for Step 23.

17

Gluing the laminated ring to the second top ring. Glue the laminated ring to the second ring from the top set. Clamp the rings and let them dry. This is the completed second top ring. Sand the inside of the completed second top ring until smooth.

Sanding the box opening. Using the inflatable round sander, shape and smooth the smaller opening of the completed second top ring. This forms the opening of the box.

Gluing on the second top ring. Glue the second top ring to the first. Clamp and let dry. Sand the inner face where the rings are glued until smooth. Since access for sanding may be limited, lightly sand to match the rings before gluing.

Cutting the lid liner. Invert the box on the ¼" (6mm)-thick piece of walnut and trace the opening. Cut along this line with the saw table level to make the lid liner. Sand the piece until it is smooth. It will be glued on in Step 27.

Completing the gluing. Glue the base to the bottom of the box. Clamp for five minutes; remove the clamps and clean up any squeeze-out on the inside of the base. Re-clamp and let dry.

Sanding the outside of the box. Sand and shape the outside of the box with the hook-and-loop pad sander until you are satisfied with the shape and feel of the wood.

Cutting the laminated bottom piece. Place the box on the remainder of the lamination and trace the outline of the base. With the saw table level, cut along this line. Sand the edges smooth and glue this piece to the box bottom.

24

Thinning the wood for the lid. Sand the remainder of the blank from the top ring set evenly on its smaller face until the wood is about ½" (13mm) thick. This will give a better proportion for the lid. (You can also substitute a piece of ½" [13mm] mahogany that matches the box.)

25

Marking the lid. Place the thinned piece on its smaller face. Invert the box on this piece and trace the outline. Tilt the saw table to 45°, left side down. Cut clockwise along this outline to make the lid.

26

Shaping the lid. Shape the sides and edges of the lid to match the contours of the box. Keep the top of the lid flat for gluing on the handle.

27

Gluing on the lid liner. Check the fit of the lid liner cut in Step 20 and sand if needed. Place the lid liner on the underside of the lid. Invert the box onto the lid to position the liner properly. Mark its location. Glue the liner to the lid, clamp, and let dry.

28

Making the handle. Attach handle patterns to remaining mahogany and padauk. Cut outer line of all three pieces. Drill entry hole in one piece of padauk. Cut inner line, remove wood, and sand opening smooth. Glue up pieces as shown, clamp, and let dry. Sand smooth.

29

Completing the handle. Mix one tablespoon of InLace with 13–15 drops of hardener and fill the recess in the center of the handle. Let the resin dry thoroughly—overnight or longer—and sand smooth. Glue the handle to the center of the lid.

30. Apply a coat of shellac to seal the wood and reveal any glue spots. Sand the box until it is smooth and all glue spots have been removed. Apply several coats of clear lacquer, rubbing down after each coat with 0000 steel wool as needed.

Sanding Tips

1. Check wall thickness frequently as you sand to avoid sanding through the wood.

2. Use a flex shaft, if you have one, to increase access to the box interior with the inflatable round sander. If you are using a drill press, be careful not to damage the opening of the box with the chuck as you sand the inside of the box.

3. Use hand sanding for areas that you cannot access safely with mechanical sanders.

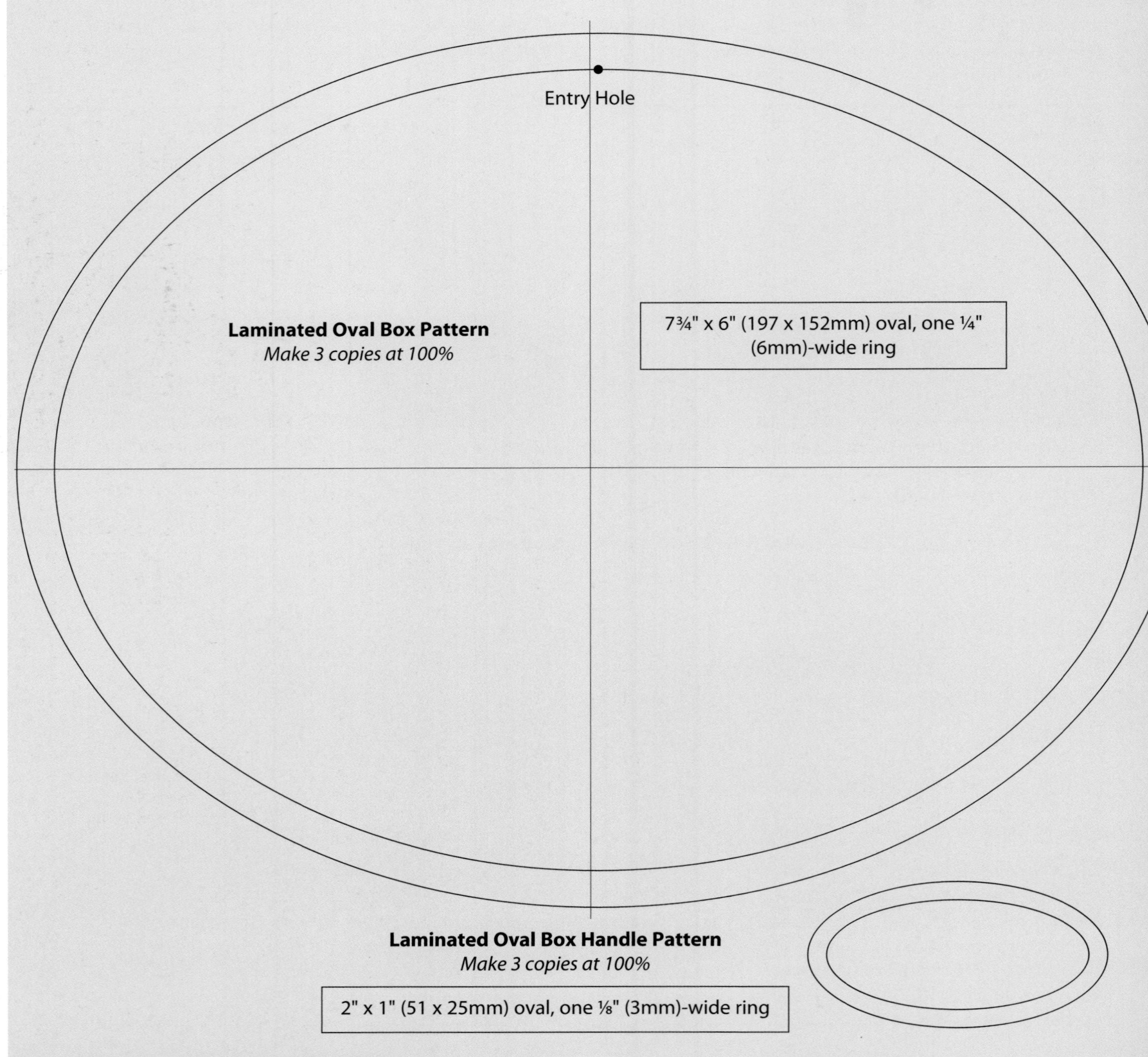

Laminated Oval Box Pattern
Make 3 copies at 100%

7¾" x 6" (197 x 152mm) oval, one ¼" (6mm)-wide ring

Laminated Oval Box Handle Pattern
Make 3 copies at 100%

2" x 1" (51 x 25mm) oval, one ⅛" (3mm)-wide ring

Multicolored Square Box

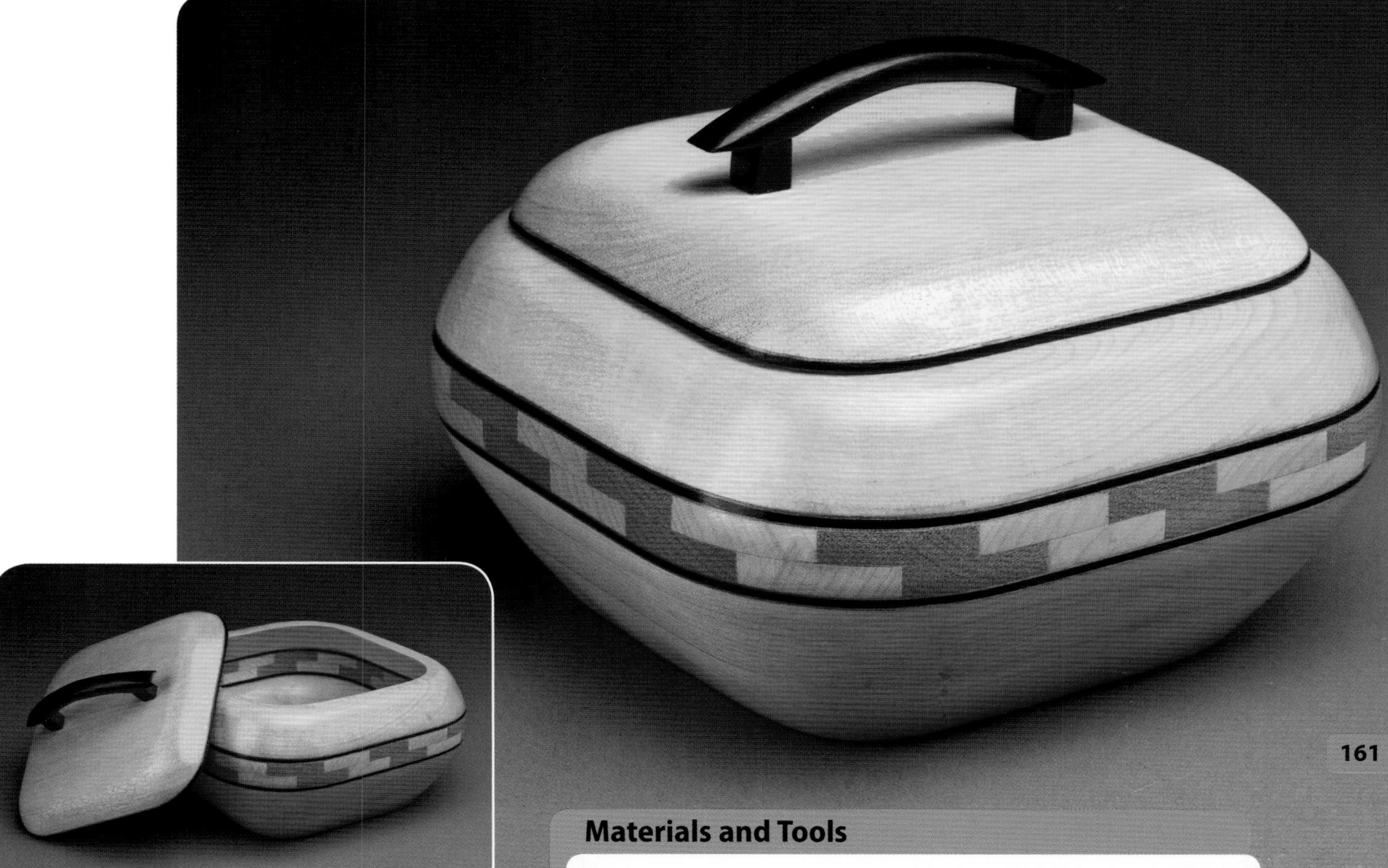

Difficulty Rating:

A small piece of ebony bought at a woodworking show was the inspiration for this boldly colored box. I maximized its impact by incorporating black dyed veneer—dramatic but far less costly—into a multicolored center ring, and saved the ebony for the handle. Making the ring is time consuming, but not difficult, and as an incentive, the piece left over can be used for the center ring of the appropriately-named Round Bonus Box on page 167.

Materials and Tools

Wood

- (2) 6½" x 6½" x ¾" (165 x 165 x 19mm) maple for box body
- (2) 8" x 4" x ¼" (205 x 100 x 6mm) yellowheart for center ring lamination
- (2) 8" x 4" x ¼" (205 x 100 x 6mm) maple for center ring lamination
- (2) 6½" x 6½" (165 x 165mm) pieces of black veneer for center ring lamination
- (4) 6½" x 6½" (165 x 165mm) pieces of cherry veneer for center ring lamination
- (1) 5½" x 5½" x ½" (140 x 140 x 13mm) yellowheart for lid
- (1) 5½" x 5½" (140 x 140mm) piece of black veneer for lid
- (2) 5½" x 5½" (140 x 140mm) piece of cherry veneer for lid
- (1) 5" x 5" x ⅛" (130 x 130 x 3mm) mahogany for lid liner
- (1) 3¾" x ¾" x ⅜" (95 x 19 x 10mm) ebony for handle

Materials

- Glue (Weldbond recommended)
- Repositionable adhesive
- Double-sided tape
- Sleeves for inflatable round sander, assorted grits 80 to 320
- Discs for 2" (50mm) hook-and-loop pad sander, assorted grits 80 to 320
- 0000 steel wool
- Sandpaper for hand sanding, assorted grits
- Shellac
- Clear spray lacquer

Tools

- #9 scroll saw blade for thick wood
- #5 scroll saw blade for thin wood
- 1⁄16" (2mm) or #54 drill bit
- 28° shop-made angle guide (see page 18)
- 35° shop-made angle guide
- Awl
- Ruler
- Craft or X-Acto knife for cutting veneer
- Inflatable round sander and pump
- 2" (50mm) hook-and-loop pad sander
- Press or clamps for gluing

Preparing the wood for the center ring.

Cutting the segments.

Gluing the semicircles.

Gluing the semicircles together.

1. Attach one piece of ¼" (6mm)-thick yellowheart and one piece of ¼" (6mm)-thick maple to each other with double-sided tape. Repeat with the other two pieces. Place the tape so the pieces will hold together after the circumference is cut. Cut the 20-segment pattern in half where indicated, and attach one half to each piece of taped wood with repositionable adhesive. Cut along each curved line to form two semicircles.

2. Cut along the lines to divide each piece into ten segments. Remove the pattern and number each piece. Separate the pieces and number each lower piece the same as its matching upper piece. Alternating colors, assemble the pieces in order to form four semicircles, sanding off the tips of the wedges as needed to obtain a close fit.

3. Glue the wedges of each semicircle together, keeping the circumference of the circle even. Use a flat edge to keep the pieces aligned. Clamp and let dry.

4. Glue each semicircle to its matching half to form two complete circles. Be sure the wedges for each circle are numbered consecutively. Clamp and let dry.

Alternate Version

If you spotted this beauty on the back cover, you were correct in looking for its specifics here. This smaller version of the Multicolored Square Box, with its very hard wood and tight inside curves, warrants a 6 icon rating—top level for both cutting and sanding. It's the Ultimate Challenge! If you want the colors of this variation but not the added difficulty, just use the appropriate wood and follow the sizes and instructions for the main box.

To make the Ultimate Challenge, you will need the following changes:

- Box is 5" (125mm) square, but ring width remains the same
- Center ring is mahogany and maple glue-up, laminated to oak, with walnut and maple veneer
- Lid is ½" (13mm) oak, with walnut and maple veneer
- Handle and box body are jotoba (Brazilian cherry)

5

Gluing the circles together.

6

Positioning the pattern.

5. Keeping the numbered sides up, make a mark on the outer edge of wedge number one for each circle. Erase all other marks on the circles and sand the surfaces smooth. Stack the two circles, matching the marks on the outer edge. Rotate the top circle half a segment and make a new mark on the edge so you can re-align them. Glue the two circles together in the rotated position, clamp with a press or conventional clamps, and let dry thoroughly.

6. Place a copy of the box pattern on the blank so the diagonal guidelines are centered in the segments at their endpoints. Extend the guidelines from the pattern to the wood. Attach the pattern to the laminated blank with repositionable adhesive, matching the guidelines. There should be about ¾" (19mm) between the straight sides of the pattern and the circumference of the blank.

7. With the saw table level, cut along the perimeter of the pattern to form the outside of the center ring. Remove the pattern and save it for Step 10.

8. Trace the perimeter of the laminated blank on each of the six pieces of veneer designated for the center ring. Trim the pieces of veneer to size with a craft knife, such as an X-Acto knife, allowing about ¼" (6mm) margin around each piece. Glue one piece of cherry veneer to each side of the blank and clamp. When the glue is dry, add a layer of black veneer to each side, clamp, and let dry. Add the last pieces of cherry veneer to each side. Clamp and let the piece dry thoroughly.

9. Trim or sand away the excess veneer until all the veneer layers are flush with the blank.

10. Attach the box pattern to the completed lamination. Drill an entry hole close to the inner line, as indicated on the pattern, and cut along the line to complete the ring. Set the ring aside until Step 17. The remainder of the blank can be used for the Round Bonus Box, page 167.

11. Using repositionable adhesive, attach one copy of the box pattern to each of the two pieces of ¾" (19mm)-thick maple. Mark the tops of the blanks. Mark one blank "top ring" and the other "bottom ring set."

12. To make the top ring, tilt the saw table to 28°, left side down. Cut along the perimeter of the blank for the top ring, cutting clockwise.

13. Using an awl, mark the entry hole on the inner cutting line at the point indicated on the pattern. Using an angle guide or drill press with a tilting table, drill an entry hole at 35° where indicated on the inner line. Drill the hole directly toward the center of the blank.

14. Tilt the saw table to 35°, left side down. Insert the saw blade and cut on the line, cutting clockwise. This completes the top ring. The remainder of the blank is not used for this project.

15. To make the bottom ring and base, tilt the saw table to 28°, left side down. Cut along the perimeter of the blank for the bottom ring set, cutting clockwise. Drill a 28° entry hole where indicated on the inner line. Insert the saw blade and cut clockwise, at a 28° angle, to complete the bottom ring. The remaining piece will become the base of the box.

16. Tilt the saw table to 40°, left side down. Using the upper edge as a guide, cut around the outside of the base piece, cutting clockwise, at a 40°angle. Do not cut into the upper edge. This is the base of the box.

17. Glue the laminated straight ring to the bottom ring. Clamp for five minutes, remove from clamps to clean up excess glue, re-clamp, and let dry.

Gluing Jig for Wedges

To make a gluing jig to keep the wedges aligned during glue-up, cut a piece of ½" (13mm)-thick plywood into an 8½" (216mm) square. Glue a hardwood strip measuring 8½" x 1½" x ¾" (216 x 38 x 19mm) to one end of the plywood. Clamp and let dry. Be sure to use wax paper to keep the wood from sticking to the jig.

18. Sand the inside of the glued-up rings until smooth and the inside edge of the bottom ring is nicely shaped.

19. Glue the top ring to the other side of the laminated ring in the same manner as in Step 17. Sand the inside of the glued-up rings until smooth. If access is difficult, sand until excess glue is removed and the inside looks neat.

20. Sand the inside edge of the top ring to enlarge it slightly and soften the edge. This forms the opening of the box.

Sanding the opening of the box.

21. Invert the glued-up rings on the ⅛" (3mm)-thick piece of mahogany. Trace around the box opening to draw the cutting line for the lid liner. Cut along this line to make the lid liner. Sand it smooth and set aside until Step 26.

22. Glue the base to the bottom ring. Clamp. Let dry 5 minutes, then remove from clamps to clean up any glue on the inside face of the base. Re-clamp and let dry.

23. Smooth and shape the outside of the box. Final sanding of the top ring will be done after the lid is completed.

24. Glue the remaining pieces of veneer to the ½" (13mm)-thick piece of yellowheart in the following order: yellowheart, cherry veneer, black veneer, cherry veneer. Clamp and let dry.

25. Attach the lid pattern to the veneer side of the laminated piece. Tilt the saw table to 35°, left side down. Cut clockwise along the cutting line. Sand the lid to smooth it and to contour the upper edge.

Completing the handle.

26. Check the fit of the lid liner cut in Step 21, and sand if needed. Place the liner on the underside of the lid. Invert the box on the lid to position the liner correctly. Mark its location. Glue the lid liner to the underside of the lid. Clamp and let dry.

27. Place the completed lid on the box and adjust the shaping of the lid and top ring by sanding, if needed.

28. Attach the handle pattern to the piece of ebony and cut out the piece.

29. Cut two additional pieces of ebony measuring ⅜" x 5⁄16" x 5⁄16" (19 x 8 x 8mm) from wood left over from the handle. Contour the pieces and glue them to the ends of the handle.

30. Center the handle on the lid and check to be sure that it sits flat. Sand the base of the handle as needed, then glue the handle into place. Apply a coat of shellac to the box and lid to seal the wood and reveal glue spots. Sand off glue spots and sand the entire box until it is smooth. Apply several coats of shellac or clear lacquer to the outside of the box and lid, rubbing down each coat with 0000 steel wool as needed.

Flattening the Ring

For a good glue joint, rings should meet with no spaces between them. Small spaces can often be removed by sanding the ring on a piece of sandpaper glued to a flat surface, such as a granite tile.

Multicolored Square Box and Lid Pattern
Make 4 copies at100%

6" (152mm) rounded square, one ⅜" (10mm)-wide ring
5" (127mm) rounded square

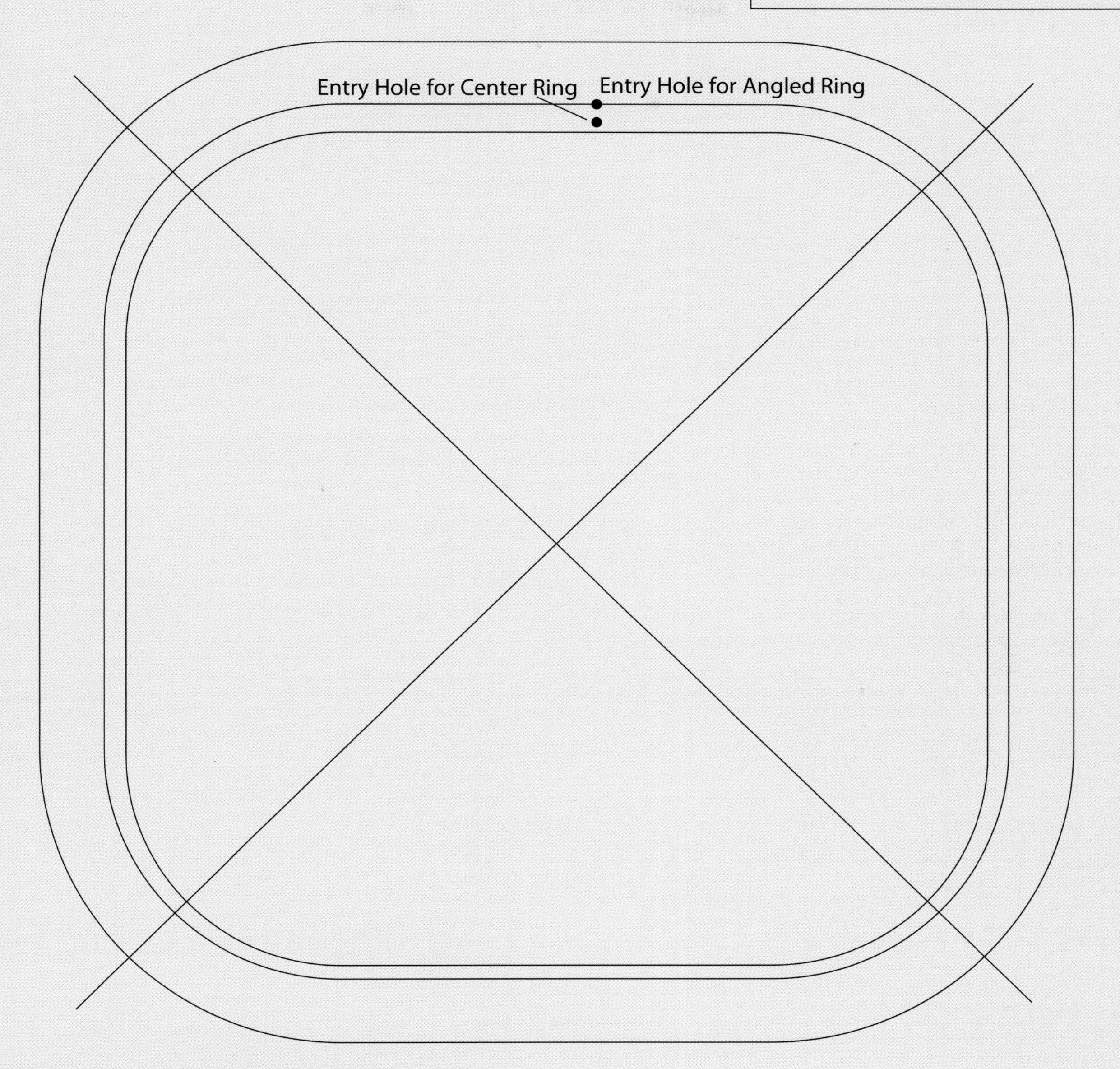

Note: The innermost ring is the lid pattern, which is a 5" (127mm) rounded square. One of the copies you make of this pattern will be to cut out the lid.

Multicolored Square Box Handle Pattern
Copy at 100%

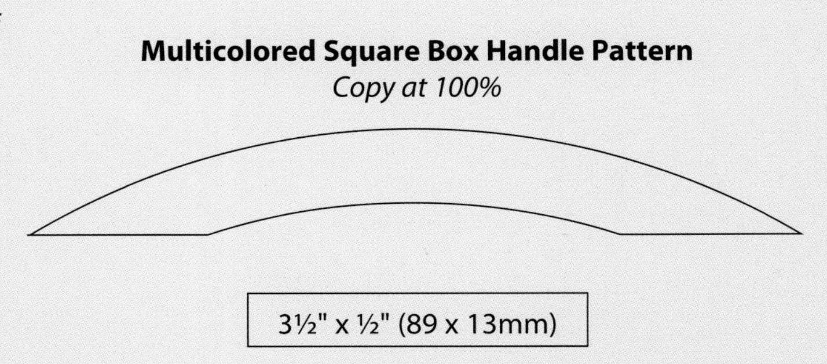

3½" x ½" (89 x 13mm)

Multicolored Square Box Lamination Pattern
Copy at 100%

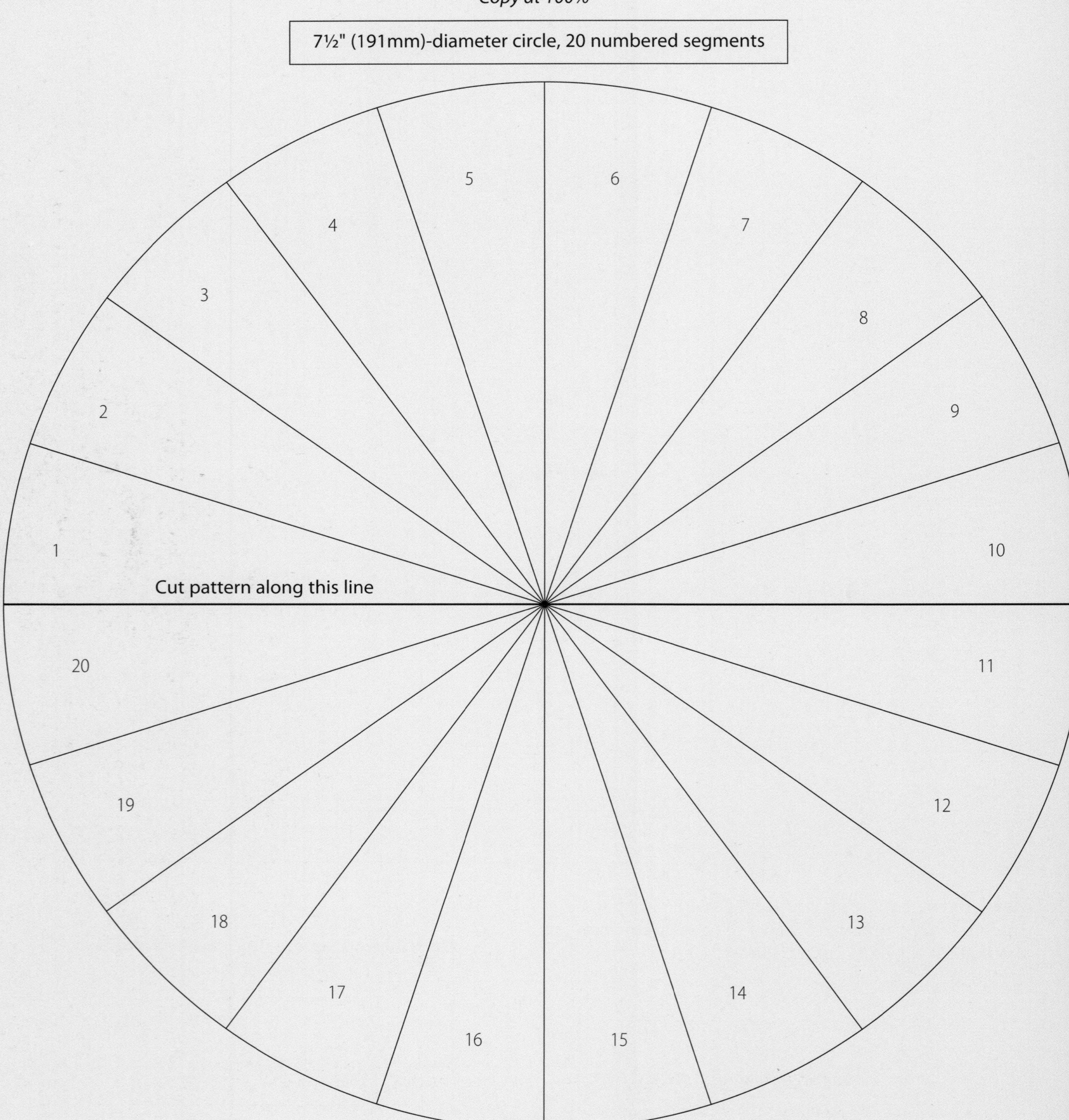

Round Bonus Box

Difficulty Rating:

The generous piece of laminated wood left over from the Multicolored Square Box (page 161) inspired the creation of a complementary project with the same color scheme. This small round box uses yellowheart as the primary wood, slightly different cutting angles, and a different lid design, but is otherwise constructed in the same manner as the Multicolored Square Box. The lid also used up the last of my precious ebony, but I think the results were worth it.

Materials and Tools

Wood

- (1) Laminated piece left over from the Multicolored Square Box (or see Steps 1–9, page 162) for box
- (2) 5½" x 5½" x ¾" (140 x 140 x 19mm) yellowheart for box
- (2) 4" x 7⁄16" (100 x 11mm) pieces of black veneer for lid
- (1) 4" x 7⁄16" x ½" (100 x 11 x 13mm) yellowheart for lid
- (2) 4" x 1½" x ⅜" (100 x 40 x 10mm) ebony for lid
- (2) 4" x 7⁄16" x ¼" (100 x 11 x 6mm) maple for lid
- 1) 4" x 4" x ⅛" (100 x 100 x 3mm) wood of choice for lid liner

Materials

- Repositionable adhesive
- Glue (Weldbond recommended)
- Sleeves for inflatable round sander, assorted grits 80 to 320
- Discs for 2" (50mm) hook-and-loop pad sander, assorted grits 80 to 320
- Sandpaper, assorted grits, for hand sanding
- 0000 steel wool
- Shellac
- Clear spray lacquer

Tools

- #9 scroll saw blade for thick wood
- #5 scroll saw blade for thin wood
- 1⁄16" (2mm) or #54 drill bit
- 40° shop-made angle guide (see page 18)
- 35° shop-made angle guide
- Craft or X-Acto knife for cutting veneer
- Awl
- Ruler
- Compass
- Inflatable round sander and pump
- 2" (50mm) hook-and-loop pad sander
- Press or clamps for gluing

1. Center the box pattern on the lamination. Attach with repositionable adhesive. With saw table level, cut along the outer circle. Drill an entry hole just inside the inner circle and cut along this circle to complete the ring. Set aside until you reach Step 17 of the Multicolored Square Box, referenced below.

2. Follow Steps 11–23 of the Multicolored Square Box making the following changes:

   Step 11. Use yellowheart instead of maple.

   Step 12. No changes.

   Step 13. Entry hole is drilled at 40°.

   Step 14. Inner ring is cut at 40°.

   Step 15. Perimeter is cut at 28°. Entry hole is drilled at 35° and inner ring is cut at 35°.

   Step 16–20. No changes.

   Step 21. Use wood of choice for liner. It will be glued on in Step 6.

   Step 22–23. No changes.

3. To make the lid, glue the remaining wood in the following order: ebony, maple, black veneer, yellowheart, black veneer, maple, ebony. The center stripe is slightly higher to facilitate sanding. Clamp and let dry. Sand smooth.

4. Use a compass to draw a circle on the lamination that is 3 15⁄16" (100mm) in diameter. Be sure the circle is centered. Cut out the circle with the saw table level.

5. Draw a line halfway up the side of the lid. Sand a 45° bevel to this line. Sand and shape the sides of the lid until a smooth curve is obtained.

6. Check the fit of the lid liner and sand to fit if needed. Place the liner on the underside of the lid. Invert the box to position the liner correctly. Glue the liner into place, clamp, and let dry.

7. Place the lid on the box and reshape the box or lid by sanding, as needed. Sand all surfaces smooth. Apply shellac to the box and lid to seal the wood and reveal glue spots. Sand off glue spots and sand the box smooth. Apply several coats of shellac or clear lacquer, rubbing down between coats with 0000 steel wool, as needed.

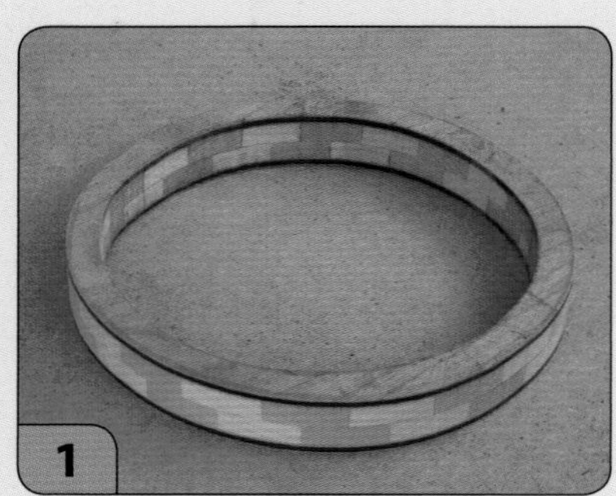

Cutting the center ring.

Beveling the lid.

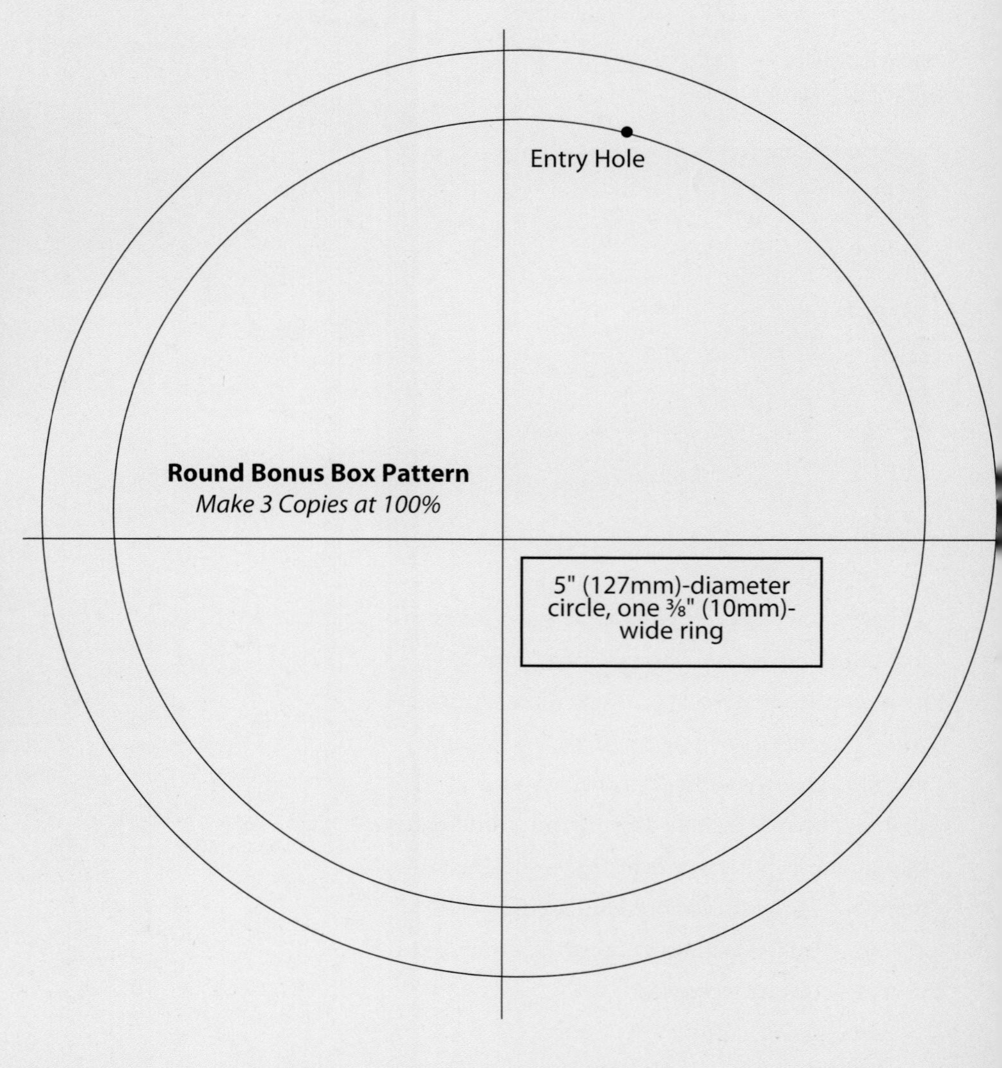

Five-Lobed Box

Difficulty Rating:

  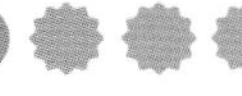

This curvaceous vessel, looking somewhat like a flattened pumpkin, is about as far from a conventional box as you can get. Although cut in the usual manner, its unusual proportions are the result of using wood only ½" (13mm) thick. The cutting is not especially difficult, but sanding the curves takes care and patience.

Padauk, an intensely colored wood, adds to the drama of this unusual box. Its sawdust, however, can be irritating, so be sure to wear protection and vacuum your work area frequently.

Materials and Tools

Wood

- (3) 8" x 8" x ½" (205 x 205 x 13mm) padauk, preferably from one 24" (610mm) board
- (1) 5" x 5" x ½" (130 x 130 x 13mm) canarywood for lid
- (1) 4" x 4" x ⅛" (100 x 100 x 3mm) walnut for lid liner
- (1) 2" x 1" x ¼" (50 x 25 x 6mm) padauk for handle

Materials

- Repositionable adhesive
- Glue (Weldbond recommended)
- Sanding sleeves for inflatable round sander, assorted grits, 80 to 320
- Sanding discs for 2" (50mm) hook-and-loop pad sander, assorted grits 60 to 320
- Sandpaper for hand sanding, assorted grits
- 0000 steel wool
- Shellac
- Clear spray lacquer

Tools

- #9 scroll saw blade for thick wood
- #5 scroll saw blades for thin wood
- 1⁄16" (2mm) or #54 drill bit
- Awl
- Ruler
- Compass
- 28° shop-made angle guide (see page 18)
- 35° shop-made angle guide
- Inflatable round sander and pump
- 2" (50mm) hook-and-loop pad sander
- Press or clamps for gluing

1. For each blank, draw two lines that intersect in the middle of the blank. Each line should be 4" (100mm) from the edge. These guidelines will serve as references for keeping the grain of the blanks oriented properly. Mark the top of each blank.

2. Attach one copy of the pattern to each of the blanks. Align the guidelines on the patterns with those on the wood. Label one blank "top ring set," another "middle ring," and the last, "bottom ring set."

3. Tilt the saw table to 28°, left side down. Starting with the blank for the top ring set, cut along the outer line of the pattern, cutting clockwise.

4. Mark the entry hole with an awl where indicated on the pattern. Using an angle guide or a drill press with a tilting table, drill a 28° entry hole facing the center of the blank.

5. Tilt the saw table to 28°, left side down. Insert the saw blade and cut clockwise along the inner line to complete the top ring. The remainder of this blank is the top piece of the box. Repeat Steps 3–5 with the blank for the bottom ring set to cut the bottom ring. The remainder of that blank is the base of the box.

6. With the saw table level, cut along the outer line of the pattern for the middle ring. Drill a straight entry hole where indicated on the pattern. Insert the blade and cut along the inner line to complete the ring. Save the center of this blank for another project.

Sanding the inside of the rings.

7. Stack the straight ring between the two angled rings, keeping the tops aligned, and check for spaces between them. Sand the surfaces as needed until no spaces remain. Glue the three rings together. Clamp with a press or conventional clamps and let dry.

8. Sand the inside of the three rings smooth. Be sure the inside edge of the bottom ring is nicely shaped, as it cannot be sanded after the base is glued on. Because of access difficulties, and to avoid sanding away too much wood from the gluing surfaces, you may need to complete the sanding by hand.

Matching Wood Grain

For the most attractive effect when using multiple sets of rings, cut them from one piece of wood, and keep the grain as continuous as possible.

9. To contour the top piece, tilt the saw table to 45°, left side down. Using the top edge as a guide, cut clockwise along the perimeter of the top piece. To contour the base, tilt the saw table to 40°, left side down, and follow the same procedure.

10. Glue the base to the underside of the bottom ring. Clamp and let dry for five minutes. Remove clamps and clean up any glue on the inside of the base. Re-clamp and let dry thoroughly.

11. Place the point of a compass at the intersection of the guidelines on the top piece and draw a 4" (100mm)-diameter circle.

12. Using an awl, mark an entry hole on the circle. Drill a 35° entry hole at that point, facing the center of the blank. Tilt the saw table to 35°, left side down, insert the saw blade, and cut clockwise around the circle. This piece, when inverted, is the top of the box, and the circle is the box opening.

13. Sand the box opening smooth. Round the underside of the lower edge of the opening.

14. Place the top piece, small face down, on the ⅛" (3mm) piece of walnut. Trace the box opening. With saw table level, cut along this line to form the lid liner. Set it aside until Step 19.

15. Glue the top piece to the box. Clamp and let dry.

16. Shape the outside of the box with the hook-and-loop pad sander. Use the inflatable round sander to smooth the indentations between lobes. Work from coarser to finer grits until the box is nicely shaped and smooth.

17. Shape the bottom of the box to soften and curve the lower edges.

18. To make the lid, use a compass to draw a 4¼" (110mm)-diameter circle on the ½" (13mm)-thick piece of canarywood. Tilt the saw table to 45°, left side down, and cut along the circle, cutting clockwise. Invert the piece so the smaller face is up. Sand to shape and soften the upper edge. Soften the lower edge slightly.

19. Place the liner cut in Step 14 on the underside of the lid. Invert the box on the lid to position the liner properly. Mark its location. Glue the liner to the lid, clamp, and let dry.

20. Attach the pattern for the handle to the ¼" (6mm) piece of padauk. Cut along the outline. Sand the edges to soften. Glue the handle to the center of the lid. Apply a coat of shellac to the box and lid to seal the wood and reveal glue spots. Sand away any glue spots, and sand the entire box smooth. Apply several coats of shellac or clear lacquer, rubbing down between coats with 0000 steel wool as needed.

Contouring the base and top pieces.

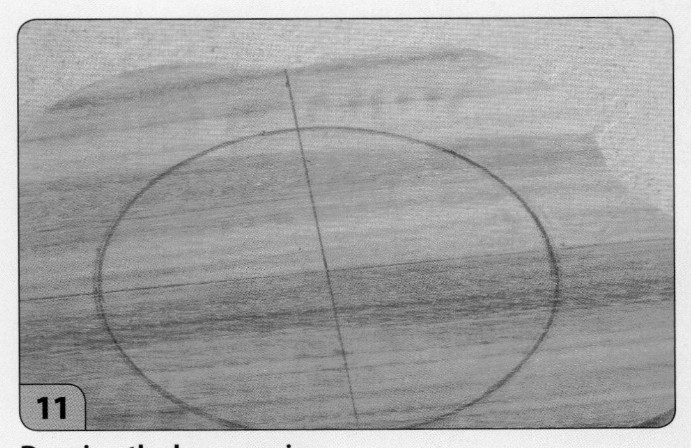

Drawing the box opening.

Shaping the outside of the box.

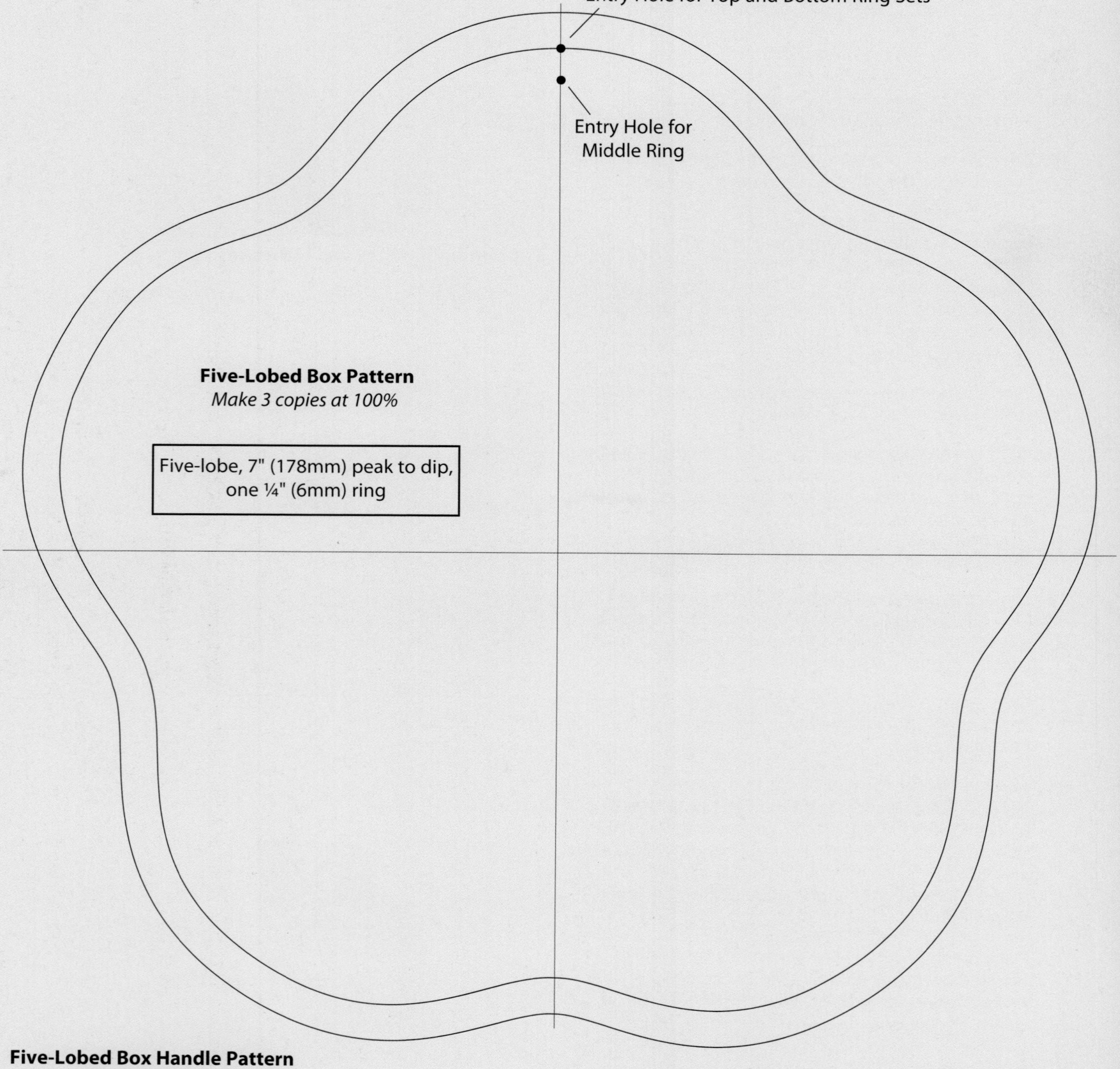

Entry Hole for Top and Bottom Ring Sets

Entry Hole for
Middle Ring

Five-Lobed Box Pattern
Make 3 copies at 100%

Five-lobe, 7" (178mm) peak to dip,
one ¼" (6mm) ring

Five-Lobed Box Handle Pattern
Copy at 100%

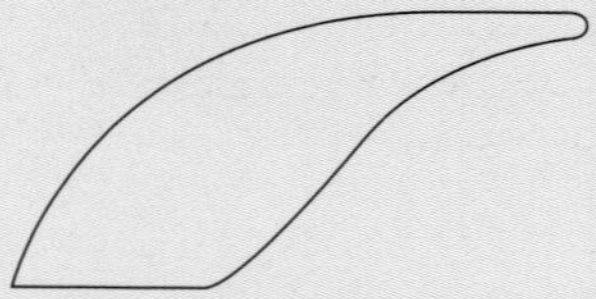

1½" x ¾" (38 x 19mm)

Multi-Purpose Press

A multi-purpose press, with optional spacers, is a good alternative to conventional clamps when even, downward pressure is needed, as when gluing up stacked rings or laminations. It is also invaluable for those projects where slippage is likely to occur.

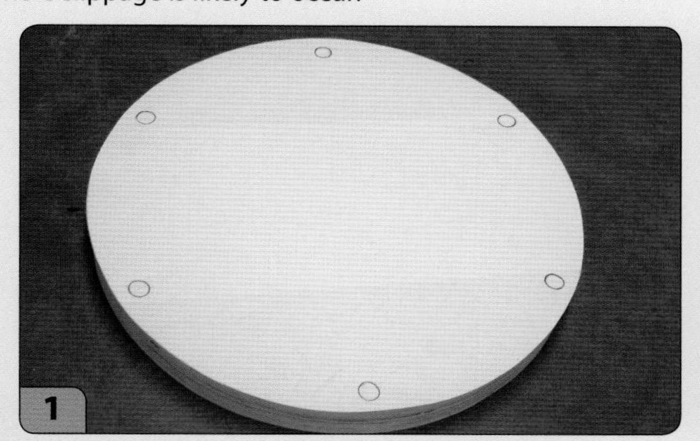

Cutting the plywood. Stack the plywood and attach the pieces to each other with double-sided tape. Center the pattern and cut out the perimeter with a scroll saw or band saw. Do not separate the circles.

Drilling the holes. Drill through both pieces of wood with a ⅜" (10mm) bit at the six places indicated on the pattern. Make an alignment mark on the edge of the pieces.

Completing the press. Separate the pieces. Push a carriage bolt through each hole on one of the pieces. This will be the base of your press. Place a washer and nut on top of the base and tighten the nuts evenly all around until the bolts are drawn in tightly. Enlarge the holes slightly on the second piece with a circular file or spindle sander until it fits easily over the bolts.

Using the press. To use the press, place a piece of wax paper on the base, place the piece to be glued on the wax paper, and place another piece of wax paper on top. Slide the top plate over the bolts. Tighten the wing nuts alternately until evenly tight. Do not over-tighten or you may force out too much glue.

Spacers are useful when gluing up a project that is not very high. They slide over the bolts after the top is in place, and allow you to tighten the press quickly. Use a hard wood that is at least 1" (25mm) thick, and as wide as the height you need.

Stand the wood on its side and mark six drilling holes spaced about 1½" (38mm) apart. Drill through the wood with a 7⁄16" (11mm) bit. Set the wood on its face and cut between the holes, forming six blocks. The spacers in the photo are about 1¼" x 1¼" x 2½" (32mm x 32mm x 64mm).

Materials and Tools

Materials

- (2) 10" (254mm) squares of ½" (13mm) plywood
- (6) ⅜" (10mm) x 6" (152mm) carriage bolts, non-galvanized
- (6) Nuts to fit the carriage bolts, non-galvanized
- (6) Washers to fit the carriage bolts, non-galvanized
- (6) Wing nuts to fit the carriage bolts, non-galvanized
- Double-sided tape
- 1¼" (32mm) x 2½" (64mm) x 9" (229mm) piece of hardwood for spacers (optional)

Tools

- ⅜" (10mm) (press) drill bit
- 7⁄16" (11mm) (spacers) drill bit
- Wrench to tighten nuts

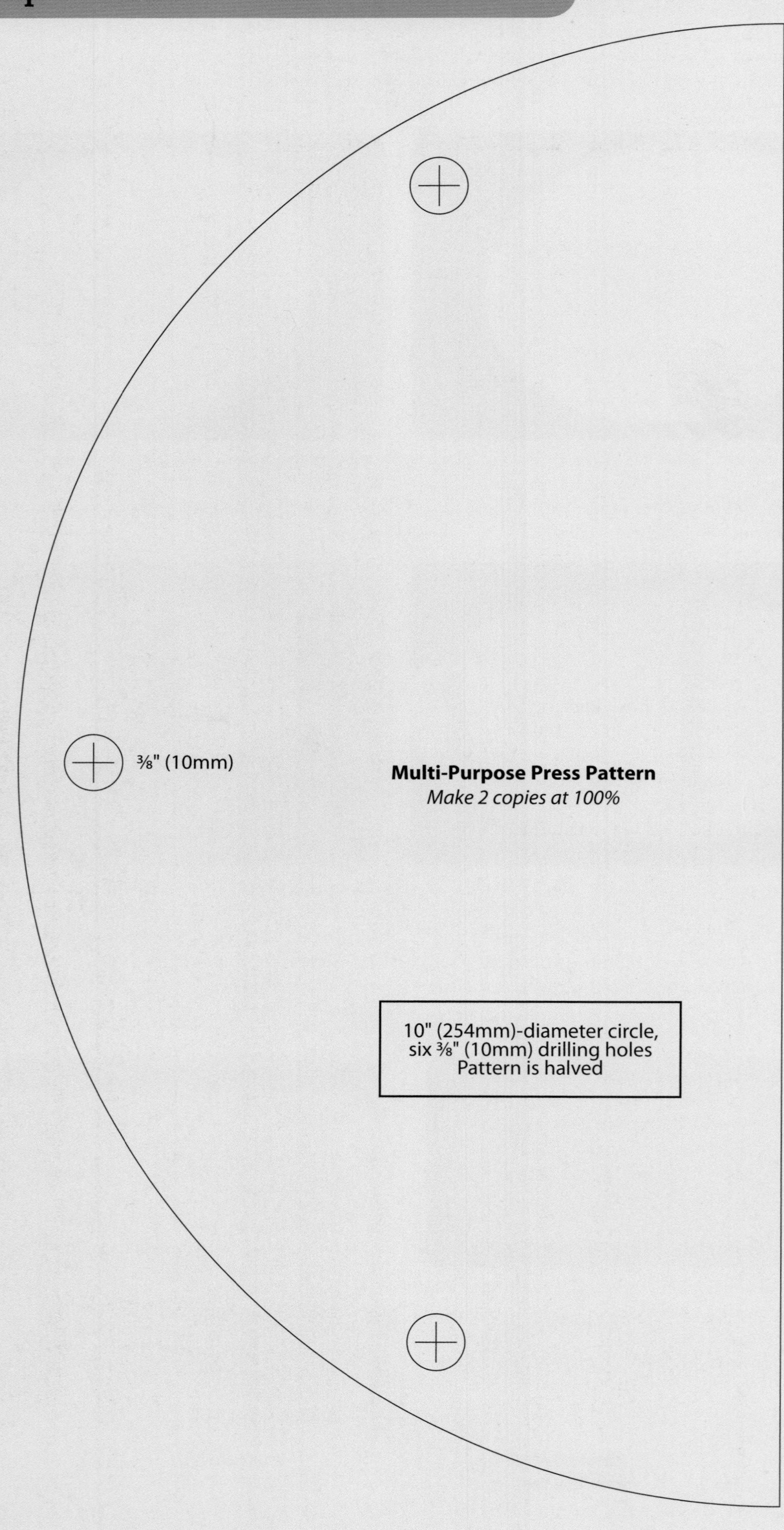

Multi-Purpose Press Pattern
Make 2 copies at 100%

Index

Acquisition and developmental editor: Kerri Landis

Copy editor: Paul Hambke

Cover and design: Lindsay Hess

Cover photographer: Scott Kriner

Layout designer: Ashley Millhouse

Proofreader: Lynda Jo Runkle